ASSESSING AND MANAGING RISK IN PSYCHOLOGICAL PRACTICE:

An Individualized Approach
SECOND EDITION

Samuel Knapp
Pennsylvania Psychological Association

Jeffrey N. Younggren
The Trust

Leon VandeCreek
Wright State University

Eric Harris
The Trust

Jana N. Martin
The Trust

www.apait.org

Published by:
The Trust
111 Rockville Pike, Suite 900
Rockville, MD 20850

Library of Congress Cataloging-in-Publication Data
Assessing and Managing Risk in Psychological Practice:
An Individualized Approach
SECOND EDITION

Includes bibliographical references and index.
ISBN-10: 0-9891221-0-7
ISBN-13: 978-0-9891221-0-8

CONTENTS

ACKNOWLEDGMENTS

We thank Dr. Bruce Bennett and the late Dr. Patricia Bricklin for their work and vision in developing the first edition of this book.

We thank Drs. Gerald Koocher and Julia Ramos-Grenier for their review of the Second Edition.

We thank the Professional Resource Press for allowing us to adapt tables from Rudd, M.D., & Joiner T. (1999). "Assessment of Suicidality in Outpatient Practice," in L. VandeCreek and T. Jackson (Eds.), *Innovations in Clinical Practice* (pp. 101–117), Sarasota, FL: Professional Resource Press.

We thank the Massachusetts Psychological Association for allowing us to adapt portions of the following articles:

Harris, E. (2003, Winter). Resolving some areas of continuing confusion. *MassPsych: The Journal of the Massachusetts Psychological Association, 47*, 18–22, 29.

Harris, E. (2004, Spring/Summer). Some (relatively) simple risk management strategies. *Mass Psych: The Journal of the Massachusetts Psychological Association, 48*, 27–28.

We thank the Pennsylvania Psychological Association for allowing us to adapt portions of the following articles:

Knapp, S. (2003, August). Could the Titanic disaster have been avoided? Or promoting patient welfare through a systems approach. *The Pennsylvania Psychologist, 63*, 4, 18, 36.

Knapp, S. (2004, November). Well-being and professional development among psychologists. *The Pennsylvania Psychologist, 64*, 13, 17.

Knapp, S., & Baturin, R. (2003, March). Child custody and custody-related evaluations and interventions: What every psychologist should know. *The Pennsylvania Psychologist, 63*, 3–5.

Knapp, S., & Gavazzi, J. (2012, April). Can checklists help reduce treatment failures? *The Pennsylvania Psychologist, 72*, 8–9.

Knapp, S., & Lemoncelli, J. (2005, October). Treating children in high-conflict families. *The Pennsylvania Psychologist, 65*, 4.

Knapp, S., Tepper, A., & Baturin, R. (2003, August). Practical considerations when responding to subpoenas and court orders. *The Pennsylvania Psychologist, 63*, 5, 16.

Mapes, B., & Knapp, S. (2005, December). Ethical and professional issues in assessing sexual offenders. *The Pennsylvania Psychologist, 65*, 3–4.

PREFACE TO THE SECOND EDITION

We have been pleased by the response to the first edition of *Assessing and Managing Risk in Professional Practice: An Individualized Approach.* The general reaction was that we succeeded in helping psychologists strive for professional excellence while reducing their risk of disciplinary actions. We did this by anchoring risk management on overarching ethical principles.

Enough has changed in the last six years to justify a second edition. More research has been done on factors related to quality services, such as the influence of relationships on patient outcomes, assessing and preventing suicidal behaviors, and understanding the influence of diversity on outcomes. In addition, we felt a need to give more attention to emerging and evolving areas of practice, such as telehealth, coaching, and forensic services. Finally, this edition references the new guidelines adopted by the American Psychological Association since the first edition was published.

Since the first edition, we have been saddened by the death of Dr. Patricia M. Bricklin, who was the project manager for that edition. Nonetheless, we have been faithful to her vision of risk management as an enterprise that, when done properly, builds on the strengths of practitioner psychologists and uplifts the quality of their services.

PREFACE

Practicing psychology is hard work. If you are the average psychologist, you are intelligent, hardworking, and committed to your profession. Yet you may find it difficult to do your best work in today's environment.

If you are the average psychologist who was licensed before 1990, you started your career in a practice environment in which managed care had minimal impact, and there was little risk of disciplinary action. You may not have had a separate ethics course in graduate school. Perhaps ethics was embedded in other courses or was something you were expected to pick up informally from your teachers and supervisors. You may have been shocked when you learned that one of your respected colleagues was accused of unethical behavior, was disciplined by a licensing board, or was removed from a managed care panel. You may have felt offended or anxious when you learned of the increase in legal risks when practicing psychology.

If you are the average psychologist who was licensed after 1990, you have practiced most of your career with managed care, may have had a separate graduate course in ethics, and have practiced in an environment in which legal risks are an acknowledged reality. You have not known the autonomy and freedom enjoyed in the days before managed care. Nonetheless, you share the same professional hassles and stressors as your older colleagues. Although we cannot make these hassles and stressors go away, we hope that the recommendations in this book will help make some of them more manageable.

STRIVE FOR EXCELLENCE, NOT PERFECTION

Strive for excellence, not perfection. You will make mistakes. You cannot help everyone. You will not know everything. You cannot go it alone. It is helpful to have a proper mix of confidence and humility.

You will make mistakes. In a litigious environment, psychologists may get the impression that they have to be perfect and cannot make any mistakes. That standard is unrealistic. You will make mistakes. Doing something that, in hindsight, was a mistake does not necessarily mean that you have been unethical or incompetent as long as you based your decision on generally acceptable clinical reasoning and knowledge. Our goal is to help you avoid making big mistakes, to minimize the frequency of smaller mistakes, and to help you to rectify the harm of whatever mistakes you made, if possible.

You cannot help everyone. But that does not mean that you cannot help a lot of people. It does not mean you are incompetent or insensitive if you turn away a patient who requires services beyond your expertise or who has needs that exceed your resources. In fact, it is prudent to select patients with deliberation.

You will not know everything. Your training and experience should have been broad enough to enable you to assist the large majority of your patients. Also, it would be ideal if you knew enough to assist colleagues who seek your consultation on problematic cases on which you have special expertise. However, it is important that you know the limitations of your skills or your *personal skill inventory*.

You cannot go it alone. You will have a much more difficult career and higher degree of risk if you try to go it alone. You will have no one around to tell you when you are about to make a mistake, when you are overestimating your competence in an area, when your skills are getting rusty, or when you have not kept up with advances in the field. Outliers risk becoming outlaws. (Remember, this book has several authors; none of us could have done as good a job if each of us had tried to write it alone.)

It helps to have a proper mix of confidence and humility. By accepting their limitations and working together, psychologists can pool their resources, benefit from their collective wisdom, upgrade the quality of their services, help more people, and limit their risks. Psychologists are part of a long tradition of healers, motivated by compassion, grounded in science, and enriched by their profession's heritage. Ideally, this book is one small step in furthering that heritage.

When Sternberg explained why smart people do foolish things, he noted that they often make mistakes because they fail to recognize the limits of their own knowledge or fail to consider the interests of other people. Although intelligence and knowledge are important, Sternberg argued for the importance of wisdom or "the use of one's intelligence and creativity toward a common good through balancing one's interests, other people's interests and infusing moral and ethical values" (Sternberg, 2003, p. 5).

OUR MODEL OF RISK MANAGEMENT

Our model for teaching risk management assumes that you have a general awareness of practice risks and key risk management principles. We reiterate those risks and strategies throughout this book, but we go beyond them. We value your skills, acumen, and professional commitment and encourage you to integrate your abilities, judgment, and dedication into your risk management strategies to improve the quality of patient care and reduce risks. We encourage you to think for yourself and to integrate the basic concepts of risk management into your overall system of patient management. Although the minimum standards of professional conduct come from external sources such as professional codes of ethics, laws and regulations, and the mechanisms provided by disciplinary bodies, the highest standards of professional conduct come from within.

As a result, it is not appropriate for you to consider this book a manual that presents a finite and absolute set of rules or gives clear direction in every situation that arises. Instead, in this book, we describe a process or general format to help you consider and evaluate the factors that should guide your decisions. Of course, this model appreciates that all psychologists must practice under a set of laws, regulations, and rules as determined by the American Psychological Association's "Ethical Principles of Psychologists and Code of Conduct" (the APA Ethics Code; APA 2010a) or state and federal laws and regulations. We review the most salient of these standards and laws in more detail in the chapters that follow.

USING BLOOM'S TAXONOMY TO DESCRIBE OUR MODEL

Our model can be viewed according to an educational taxonomy based on the work of Bloom (1956). Educators have used Bloom's taxonomy for many years to describe the process and goals of education. According to Bloom, educational experiences can progress through six levels (knowledge, comprehension, application, analysis, synthesis, and evaluation). Thus, information goes from a basic memorization of facts to more complex levels, culminating in the application, analysis, and evaluation of information.

We apply Bloom's taxonomy to risk management and describe how psychologists can progress from basic levels in which they memorize risk management principles and ethical standards to higher levels in which they judiciously apply and integrate ethically based risk management principles into their day-to-day clinical decision making. Older models of risk management emphasized the lower three levels of Bloom's taxonomy (knowledge, comprehension, and application). Our model emphasizes the higher three levels (analysis, synthesis, and evaluation).

We begin by reviewing the format of Bloom's taxonomy before applying it directly to risk management. According to Bloom's Level 1, *knowledge* is remembering previously learned material such as specific facts. It represents the lowest level of learning. At the knowledge level, learners primarily read, take notes during lectures, or otherwise memorize information. For example, in the knowledge level of risk management, psychology learners (students, workshop participants, consultees, or readers) should be able to repeat the definition of risk management. (Risk management requires calculating the probability of good or bad outcomes or consequences.)

In Level 2, *comprehension,* learners acquire the ability to grasp what the material means. It may mean translating material from one form to another or explaining or summarizing material. At the learning level, learners can demonstrate comprehension by explaining concepts to others. For example, at the comprehension level, learners can explain what risk management means.

Level 3, *application,* refers to the ability to use learned material in specific situations. The application level requires both knowledge and comprehension. At the application level, learners can apply the information to specific situations such as case vignettes, albeit at an elementary level.

Level 4, *analysis,* begins the level at which our risk management model builds on previous models. Analysis refers to the ability to break down material into its components so that learners can better understand its organization. Learning here requires an understanding of both the content and the structure or organization of information. For example, learners can apply, compare, or contrast the components of different risk management principles as they apply to specific cases.

Level 5, *synthesis,* refers to the ability to combine information to create meaningful structures. Learners can demonstrate synthetic ability when they are able to create a meaningful product or suggest helpful solutions to a problem. Whereas learners at the application level apply principles routinely and mechanically, learners at the synthesis level tailor strategies based on the application of overarching principles.

The last level, Level 6, *evaluation*, refers to the ability to judge the value of a given response. Learners demonstrate evaluative abilities by giving justifications or reasons for their decisions.

TAXONOMY OF RISK MANAGEMENT

Lower Levels

Knowledge: You have read the APA Ethics Code and are able to repeat and recognize many of the standards in the Code.

Comprehension: You can describe or summarize risk management to another psychologist (e.g., you are able to describe to another practitioner a potentially improper multiple relationship with a patient).

Application: In a given situation you can apply the relevant risk management principles (e.g., do not release confidential patient information without proper authorization).

Higher Levels

Analysis: You can separate risk management into general principles (such as informed consent, consultation, and documentation), compare and contrast their application, or categorize potential solutions.

Synthesis: You can incorporate risk management principles into your overall practice patterns. You can generalize them to novel situations and design or systematize risk management programs.

Evaluation: You can justify why you adopted certain risk management principles in your practice. You can compare different risk management strategies in specific situations and determine, evaluate, or infer their relative values.

ORGANIZATION OF THE BOOK

In Chapter 1 ("Calculations of Risk"), we explain the types of professional risks and the processes of licensing boards and other disciplinary bodies. Then, in Chapter 2 ("Key Elements of Risk Management"), we review the three major risk management strategies: informed consent, documentation, and consultation. In later chapters, we review specific areas of professional liability, including competence, boundary violations, breaches of confidentiality, forensic work, psychological assessment, treating patients who have suicidal or other life-endangering tendencies, termination and abandonment, business issues, and more.

A FINAL NOTE

Ultimately you must decide how much effort to put into implementing risk management principles into your professional practice. We have tried to explain these risk management principles clearly. Whenever we thought it would be helpful, we added charts, case illustrations, or summary points to assist your learning.

If you have suggestions about how we might improve this book or the quality of teaching risk management in general, please email us at riskmanagement@apait.org.

CHAPTER 1: CALCULATIONS OF RISK

It has been said that psychologists know more than they need to about how to do good in this world. That is, they tend to be *benefits oriented* and look for ways that they can help people. Although this is a commendable trait, it needs to be balanced with an appreciation that sometimes things do not go well, and sometimes things can go horribly wrong.

Although we wish to be positive about the practice of psychology, we acknowledge that bad events can and do occur. In this chapter, we describe one type of bad event (disciplinary actions from oversight bodies) that often occurs as a consequence of another type of bad event (patients being harmed or perceiving themselves to be harmed). It is an unfortunate reality that bad things happen to good psychologists. Highly competent psychologists may find themselves charged with ethical misconduct because they just happened to encounter the wrong patient under the wrong circumstances. However, by envisioning a worst-case scenario with a particular case, psychologists may be able to prevent themselves from experiencing that scenario. Fortunately, as we describe in more detail later, the acts that reduce the likelihood of disciplinary actions also decrease the likelihood that patients will be harmed and increase the likelihood that they will be helped.

In this chapter, we review the elements that contribute to risk. Of course, one of the major factors contributing to risk is the individual skills of psychologists, including the degree to which they can identify high-risk situations and follow the basic risk management strategies (informed consent, documentation, and consultation) that we describe in detail in Chapter 2 ("Key Elements of Risk Management").

Risk is the calculation of the probability of a good or bad outcome and positive or negative consequences. Some risks are so remote that it does not make sense to expend energy to avoid them. Other risks are so obvious or serious that psychologists should work hard to avoid them.

CLINICAL RISK

Clinical risk is determined by the interaction of the patient characteristics, the context of treatment, and individual psychologist factors. We review each of these factors in the sections that follow but give the greatest attention to individual psychologist factors.

Patient Risk Characteristics

Psychologists who are involved in assisting other psychologists in disciplinary proceedings have found certain characteristics overrepresented among patients who file complaints or lawsuits. High-risk patients include those who are diagnosed with serious personality disorders, have complex posttraumatic stress disorder or dissociative identity disorders, report recovered memories of abuse, have been abused as children, present a serious risk to harm themselves or others, are wealthy, or are involved in lawsuits or other legal disputes. Sometimes these lawsuits reflect a litigious personality or a problem-solving set of behaviors that focuses on aggressive confrontations. At other times, the stressors of a lawsuit may prompt patients to display behaviors commonly associated with borderline personality disorders. These high-risk characteristics are not mutually exclusive, of course, and a patient may have more than one of these qualities or characteristics.

Patients with serious personality disorders, such as borderline or narcissistic personality disorders, present special risks for psychologists. The specific diagnosis is less important than the presence of certain traits, such as a belief in one's entitlement to special treatment, a pattern of idealization and vilification of others, a pervasive inability to accept objective and constructive feedback, or the use of romantic seduction as a consistent strategy to express affection or closeness. Often these patients have difficulty forming healthy relationships with others, have weak social support networks, and lack insight.

Contextual Risk Factors

Context refers to the total circumstances under which patients are seen, including the setting of the service (e.g., a solo practice, small group, or institution) and the type of service provided (e.g., treatment or evaluative services). Institutional treatment settings may reduce risks insofar as the institution may have clinical and legal resources greater than those generally available in solo or small group practices. However, an institutional setting, such as a hospital, may also have greater legal exposure in that it has a greater degree of perceived control over the behavior of the patient and practitioner.

Context also includes the type of service being requested by the patient. Some services, such as evaluations with financial or relationship consequences or treatment in the context of a highly conflicted divorce, involve increased legal risks. Other contexts that present greater risks include services delivered when the potential of a clinically contraindicated multiple relationship exists.

Individual Psychologist Factors[1]

Psychologists can be more effective in calculating their risks if they accurately identify the individual factors that make up their *personal skill inventory* and accurately evaluate the value of the information they have in their *personal database*. Personal skill inventory refers to the knowledge, skills, past experiences, and emotional competencies of the psychologist. It is derived from their training, experiences, readings, study, consultation, and supervision. Personal database refers to the fund of information psychologists have about a particular diagnosis or area of professional practice. The personal skill inventory should include the routine use of risk management strategies (these are covered in more detail in Chapter 2, "Key Elements of Risk Management"). The personal database should include information about professional risks, including the characteristics of high-risk patients, contexts, and disciplinary consequences.

---

[1] Portions from "Well-Being and Professional Development Among Psychologists," by S. Knapp, 2004, November, *The Pennsylvania Psychologist, 64*, pp. 13, 17. Copyright 2004 by Pennsylvania Psychological Association. Adapted with permission of the Pennsylvania Psychological Association.

Psychologists can effectively use their personal skill inventory and personal database only if they understand them accurately. A continual danger is that psychologists' perceived personal skill inventory almost always will be greater than their actual skill inventory. Psychologists can reduce the gap between their perceived and actual skill inventories by ongoing contact and feedback with other mental health professionals. Psychologists who are professionally isolated risk developing significant gaps in their skill inventory and database without knowing it.

Having a strong social network (e.g., belonging to professional associations, participating in consultation groups) is one of the best systems of protection. The social network provides several benefits, including helping psychologists to identify gaps in their skill inventory because, among other things, it gives them access to important information about developments in the field of psychology and resources for consultation on specific difficult cases.

From an actuarial perspective, psychologists will have lower risks of disciplinary action if they are socially connected. For example, Knapp and VandeCreek (2012a) found that the likelihood of being disciplined by a state board of psychology was lower for psychologists who belonged to their state psychological association. Also, Kilmo, Daum, Brinker, McGruire, and Elliot (2000) found that orthopedic surgeons who belonged to their professional association had lower rates of malpractice, and Hickson and Entman (2008) found lower litigation risks among obstetricians who had a supportive work environment. The exact reasons for this relationship are not clear. Perhaps the more conscientious practitioners self-select into professional associations or strive to build teamwork and support within their workplace. The collegiality and social connectedness may also give them sources of information that improve their personal database and personal skill inventory.

This social connectedness can help reduce the pernicious impact of self-deception. A certain amount of self-deception is probably inevitable among all persons in all walks of life. For example, Epley and Dunning (2006) found that people often overestimate their virtuousness, such as how much they give to charity or how frequently they complete tasks on time. Health care providers are not immune from this self-deception. For example, D. A. Davis et al. (2006) found that a subset of physicians greatly overestimated their skill level on a variety of professional tasks, rating themselves above average when they were really well below average. In addition, Alexander, Humensky, Guerrero, Park and Loewenstein (2010) noted a tendency toward more defensiveness among physicians who scored higher on scales of narcissism. Younggren (2007) called this "professional narcissism" or an "overestimation of one's ability" (p. 515). Nonetheless, the quality of one's services increases as a result of productive self-reflection. Indeed, Wilkinson, Wade, and Knock (2009) considered self-reflection to be the key ingredient in professionalism.

Psychologists who appreciate the limits of their personal skill inventory recognize that they cannot help all patients. Depending on the situation or the nature of the patient's needs, some patients are better served by institutions or agencies that provide a wider range of resources, such as 24-hour immediate response coverage, a multidisciplinary team with more resources (such as case managers), ready availability of psychiatric coverage, options for day treatment programming, and easy access to inpatient services. These institutions or agencies may be able to provide more control over the patient, and for some patients, that degree of temporary control may be clinically indicated. At a time when many psychologists face a decrease in income as a result of managed care, it may be difficult to turn away patients even if they have problems that are on the fringe of psychologists' areas of competence. The decision to take such patients needs to involve consideration of the risk that the patients may not be getting the care they need and of the professional risks to the psychologist.

The personal skill inventory of psychologists is augmented when they have a strong *system of protection,* such as a consultation group, consultant, or other sources of high-quality feedback (we discuss consultation more fully in Chapter 2). Their personal skill inventory is diminished when external stressors distract their full attention from clinical tasks. For example, psychologists going through a painful and stressful divorce may find that their emotional energy for work is diminished, at least temporarily. Among other benefits, a strong social support network (either in personal life or professional life) can help psychologists emotionally during times of stress.

Often psychologists are required to balance risks or make difficult clinical decisions. Should they take that case that stretches the bounds of their expertise? Should they allow this patient to barter for services? Should they become more confrontational or directive with this patient? Ideally the decisions of the psychologists will be informed by an accurate assessment of their personal skill inventory and consultation (if necessary) and implemented with appropriate risk management strategies.

On the other hand, the careful decisions described here differ substantially from *shortcuts,* such as when psychologists stretch the bounds of their expertise without a full appreciation of the risks involved or become lax in their documentation or fail to get consultation because of time pressures. We do not claim to be faultless paragons of virtue. All of us have had times, as a result of external circumstances, when we failed to complete the day's notes, delayed returning a phone call, or postponed a professional obligation. It is inevitable that external pressures will force all psychologists to prioritize at some point. Psychologists who routinely take shortcuts, however, engender greater risks of disciplinary actions and may be delivering less than adequate professional services. Shortcuts are especially problematic during periods of increased personal or professional stress. According to the concept of *ego depletion,* one's risk of making mistakes or failing to adhere to usual precautions declines after intense mental or physical exertion (Baumeister & Tierney, 2011).

During stressful times, psychologists should increase their use of risk management strategies. The life of a psychologist can be stressful. Tamura's review (2012) found that the practice of psychology exposes psychologists to many adverse events, including the possibility of a patient suicide or a patient harming another person and being stalked or harassed, to name a few. These adverse events can seriously harm a psychologist's emotional functioning. Also, the practice of psychology includes chronic stressors such as the negative affect of patients (e.g., extreme sadness and descriptions of trauma), resistance (e.g., missed appointments and denial), serious pathology (e.g., psychopathology and compulsiveness), and passive-aggressive behaviors. Of course, these all occur in the context of the personal stressors experienced by everyone. As much as psychologists may want to separate their personal and private lives, it is impossible to do so completely. A bad day at home can spill over, even if minimally, to a less than optimal day at the office. Conversely, a bad day at the office can impact a psychologist's personal and private life, creating a potentially vicious circle of problems being transferred from home to office and office to home.

Personal and professional stressors increase during periods of life transitions, such as when moving or starting a new job. That is a time to be especially vigilant about potential risks or slips. Often personal life transitions may be anticipated, such as the decline in physical and mental skills as a result of aging, although many physical illnesses or injuries cannot be anticipated.

Although we believe that frank discussions about the stresses of professional life are important, the recognition of these stressors should not diminish psychologists' fascination with their profession. The life as a psychologist can be very rewarding. Patients do improve, and they frequently express great appreciation for the help they have received. The goal is to maximize the rewards and minimize the stressors. Certainly, cognitive and personal qualities are important, such as the ability to see humor in a difficult situation or to place setbacks in perspective. Coster and Schwebel (1997) found that well-being among psychologists was associated with high levels of self-awareness, self-monitoring, and strong social relationships (from peers, spouses, friends, and others). Optimistic perseverance is important as well. Dlugos and Friedlander (2001) found that passionately committed psychologists often approached obstacles in work as a challenge to be faced with persistence and creativity. Perhaps they experienced "flow" in their work. The passionately committed psychologists frequently solicited feedback on their work and sought diverse challenges or opportunities in their careers. These findings are not surprising because positive emotions are linked to more creativity, better health, and overall better performance (Fredrickson, 2009).

A strong personal life helps to counterbalance professional demands. Coster and Schwebel (1997) found that well-functioning psychologists often took time for their personal and family lives. Mahoney (1997) found that the self-care habits of psychologists included engaging in a hobby, reading for pleasure, taking pleasure trips, attending movies or artistic events, or participating in physical exercise. It is a pleasant paradox that those psychologists who are most able to distance themselves from work and immerse themselves in family, friends, or avocations are most able to return to work with curiosity, vigor, and optimism.

Life management skills do not come automatically. Psychologists can manage their lives best when they create a supportive environment to help deal with stressors and transitions. The first step might be to reflect on the Golden Rule ("Do unto others as you would have them do unto you."), which has been found in some form in all major world religions. In other words, if psychologists want to have a protective social network, it may be necessary to offer those same protections to others. Psychologists can display civic virtue by joining their local or state psychological association, serving on a committee, or volunteering to do some professional work—even if it is low profile or unglamorous at times. When psychologists see colleagues in need, they can offer to help them. They can offer to speak to a psychology class at the local university on a topic of interest to themselves and others.

DISCIPLINARY CONSEQUENCES

Practices of institutions that regulate the practice of psychology can be divided into the proactive (before-the-fact) controls and the reactive (after-the-fact) controls (Knapp & VandeCreek, 2012b). Proactive controls may reduce the likelihood of misconduct occurring and may increase the probability that psychologists will have the skills to benefit the public. For example, graduate programs help to ensure that their graduates have mastered the basic tools needed to be competent professionals. Licensing boards, through the licensing process, ensure that the graduates have had the required supervision and have mastered the body of knowledge unique to psychology. Professional associations and some professional liability insurance programs such as The Trust (1-800-477-1200) provide consultation services to psychologists.[2] Professional associations may also have peer assistance programs that indirectly prevent acts of misconduct by helping distressed psychologists who are at a high risk for unethical conduct. Of course, none of the proactive controls can prevent all misconduct.

Reactive controls respond after misconduct has occurred. For example, licensing boards accept complaints against licensees who have violated the licensing law or its regulations; ethics committees of professional associations accept complaints against their members who allegedly have violated their ethics code; and malpractice courts accept complaints when patients appear to have been harmed by negligence. Less frequently used miscellaneous controls such as lawsuits based on breach of contract or criminal conduct are also available. Criminal courts represent external controls to the extent that they enforce laws applicable to psychology, such as laws mandating the reporting of child abuse or prohibiting insurance fraud. Most states report disciplinary actions against health care practitioners to the National Practitioner Data Bank (www.npdb-hipdb.hrsa.gov), which was formed as a national data base for actions taken against health care professionals, including criminal and civil judgments (malpractice suits), licensing board disciplinary actions, and exclusions from Medicare and Medicaid.

---

[2] The Trust Advocate Program is intended to help individuals insured through The Trust Sponsored Professional Liability Program to avoid or reduce the risk of malpractice or disciplinary actions. The principal service is the availability of clinical and legal risk management consultation from experienced psychologists with significant expertise with legal issues and attorneys.

Licensing Boards

States, provinces, and territories establish licensing boards. Although their responsibilities vary somewhat from jurisdiction to jurisdiction, they are all established to protect the public, not to promote the welfare of psychologists. The license to practice a profession is a privilege established by the state; it is not a constitutional right (Bricklin, Bennett, & Carroll, 2003).

In most states, members of licensing boards generally include psychologists and one or more public members. The members of the board are volunteers or receive very little compensation. Some of the public members know the standards of the profession well; others do not. In other states, psychology is regulated by an omnibus board that also regulates other mental health professions. Problems can sometimes arise when nonpsychologists have decision-making authority over the activities of psychologists.

Although licensing boards' procedures vary considerably from jurisdiction to jurisdiction, the following are common features: When a complaint is received, an investigator reviews the case and determines if it warrants an investigation. In some jurisdictions the decision to prosecute is made without the input of a psychologist. Also, in some jurisdictions, the licensing board can prosecute for events beyond those identified in the original complaint. For example, the complainant may accuse the psychologist of a boundary violation. In the investigation, however, the psychologist may be exonerated of that charge but be charged with inadequate record keeping, which was only discovered during the investigation of the original charge.

The standard used by the licensing board is whether the licensing law, its regulations, or other laws were violated. It is not necessary to prove that a patient was harmed. Many licensing boards adopt the American Psychological Association's (APA's) "Ethical Principles of Psychologists and Code of Conduct" (hereinafter referred to as the APA Ethics Code; APA, 2010a) or some variation of it. Consequently, the Ethics Code takes on legal importance beyond its adoption by APA. Other licensing boards create their own ethics code or adopt the "ASPPB Code of Conduct" of the Association of State and Provincial Psychology Boards (ASPPB, 2005), the association of all of the psychology licensing boards in the United States and Canada. Because a licensing board action is an administrative rather than a criminal procedure, the respondent psychologist does not have the same due process rights, and evidence is not limited by the same standards of proof that exist in criminal cases. That is, the standards for the admission of evidence may be less stringent, hearsay evidence may be admissible, and the standard of proof may be lower.

Licensing boards may issue disciplinary notices or even suspend or revoke a license if the misconduct is serious enough. Indeed, a license may be suspended prior to the completion of an investigation if the allegations are serious enough to warrant such action. All disciplinary actions are reported to ASPPB, which compiles this information. Some licensing boards have the option of issuing educational letters that do not rise to the level of a disciplinary action.

Ethics Committees

APA and many state, provincial, and territorial psychological associations (SPTAs), have ethics committees. These associations have jurisdiction only over members of their associations, not over all licensees. However, most of the SPTAs' ethics committees perform educational functions only and do not discipline members. Similar to licensing boards, ethics committees only enforce a standard of conduct; they do not determine whether a patient has been harmed. Ethics committees can issue disciplinary notices or remove an individual from the association. Some ethics committees have the option of issuing educational letters to psychologists that do not rise to the level of a disciplinary action. Ethics committees may, under certain circumstances, report their findings to the state licensing board.

Malpractice

Malpractice is a type of civil liability law, sometimes referred to as a tort, under which parties allegedly injured in a professional relationship may seek monetary compensation for their damages. The four essential ingredients of a malpractice case all begin with the letter *d*. There must be a *duty* or obligation of the professional to the patient; there must be *damage* to the patient; the professional must have *deviated* from acceptable (or minimal) professional norms of conduct; and there must be a *direct* link between the damage to the patient and the behavior of the professional (Simon, 1992).

Psychologists have professional duties to the patients whom they are serving. When they act as supervisors, psychologists have duties to the patients seen by their supervisees because the supervisees have no legal authority to provide services, except as an extension of the psychologists. Psychologists do not have the same legal duties to collateral contacts (e.g., persons who enter the therapy room only to facilitate the treatment of a patient or patients of psychologists who have consulted with another psychologist). Of course psychologists should treat all persons, including collateral contacts, respectfully and orient them as to their role in providing services to the patient. In some states psychologists have duties to third parties who are readily identifiable victims of imminent danger by patients. In such situations, the duty is usually limited to warning or acting to protect that third party.

Malpractice actions are subject to a statute of limitations, which means that the lawsuit must be filed within a certain period of time. The exact length of the statute of limitations varies from state to state and sometimes by the nature of the alleged offense, but usually the periods of time are two or three years from the time of discovery. Some states allow the statute of limitations to be waived for minors (until they reach the age of majority) or for adults under the discovery rule, which means that the "clock" does not start to run until the patients know or should have known that they were damaged by the negligence of the professional. Some states use the standard of contributory negligence, which means a court could rule that the acts of the psychologist substantially contributed to the harm, but the patient also bore some responsibility, and the damages could be limited according to the relative portion of the harm caused by the actions of the psychologist.

Whenever psychologists have professional relationships with patients, they incur the duty to use a reasonable standard of care. Although courts may vary in their exact definition of this term, generally it refers to the knowledge and skill ordinarily possessed by members of the profession in good standing.

Reading malpractice cases may help psychologists to appreciate the applicable standard of care. However, these cases must be read carefully because fact patterns differ considerably among cases. Often case reports are based on suits against hospitals or other institutions that have a high degree of control over the patients. Such cases have limited application to outpatient treatment where psychologists have far less control over the actions of their patients.

Malpractice and Patient Factors

Among physicians, data show that not all negligent conduct results in a lawsuit, and not all lawsuits involve negligent conduct. The presence of a malpractice suit has a low correlation with the actual occurrence of an adverse event (Burstin, Johnson, Lipsitz, & Brennan, 1993). The likelihood of a suit depends greatly on factors other than the objective harm to the patient or the degree to which the physician deviated from reasonable standards of care. Even after controlling for the severity of the medical injury, poor patients are much less likely to sue for malpractice than wealthy patients (Burstin et al., 1993).

Relationship factors are highly important in whether physicians get sued for malpractice. Although data are not available on the correlation between relationship factors and malpractice for psychologists, the data from physicians may be instructive. Those primary care physicians who have fewer claims are more likely to use more orienting statements (explaining procedures to patients) and facilitating statements (statements that encourage patients to express their opinions or concerns; Levinson, Roter, Mullooly, Dull, & Frankel, 1997). When asked about their reasons for filing lawsuits, patients often reported that they felt that the physician had devalued their opinions, delivered information poorly, failed to understand their point of view, or tried to withhold information (Beckman, Markakis, Suchman, & Frankel, 1994; Levinson et al., 1997). Following their review of studies of communication styles and malpractice among primary care physicians, R. S. Beck, Daughtridge, and Sloane (2002) concluded that medical educators should continue to teach facilitative communication skills as a way to improve patient adherence to treatment and outcomes. Later, a review of the disciplinary data of physicians licensed in Quebec and Ontario found that rates of patient complaints were higher for physicians who scored low on patient communications in their national licensing examinations (Tamblyn, et al., 2007).

Of course, the practice of medicine is not identical to the practice of psychology. However, the findings suggest that psychologists can reduce their risk of a malpractice suit if they spend more time on informed consent (orienting statements), try to involve patients in decision making throughout the therapeutic process, and listen respectfully to their perspectives. These interpersonal skills should be part of the personal skills inventory of psychologists and may be especially important when dealing with high-risk patients. Consistent with this interpretation is the finding from a survey of psychiatrists showing that effective listening was their most important therapeutic tool, surpassing all other diagnostic and intervention skills ("Effective Listening Tops List," 2000).

Trends in Disciplinary Actions

Over the last 20 years certain trends have emerged in regard to disciplinary actions by regulatory bodies. Ethics committees are adjudicating fewer cases. APA, for example, has been disciplining fewer psychologists in recent years (in 2011, the APA Ethics Committee opened 13 matters against psychologists compared with 135 in 1995; APA, Ethics Committee, 1996, 2012). The reasons for this decrease are not entirely clear. It may be, in part, because many complaints are filed with both APA and licensing boards, and APA frequently requires the licensing boards to finish their adjudications before starting its own. In addition, certain criteria must be met for APA to open a case even after a licensing board has taken disciplinary action. Also, part of the decrease may be because APA now allows psychologists who have been charged with an ethics complaint to "resign under scrutiny" instead of having to go through adjudication by the APA Ethics Committee (although the names of such individuals are made public). Finally, many ethics committees of SPTAs have discontinued adjudications and now focus only on education.[3]

Although the incidence of malpractice for psychologists has been stable over the last 20 years, the risk of a licensing board complaint has increased during this same time period. Unfortunately, even a letter of reprimand, the lowest form of disciplinary action from a licensing board, can have serious consequences for psychologists. It may result in the removal of the psychologist from a managed care panel or the loss of hospital privileges. The economic consequences, let alone the emotional consequences, can be substantial. Some licensing boards have become aware of the career-altering implications of these types of actions and have modified their procedures allowing them to have an opportunity to correct and guide the practice of psychologists with an educational letter without seriously damaging their professional careers. In this, they have adopted a variety of "softer" administrative procedures that do not carry with them the professional stigma of letters of reprimand. However, these types of changes are not evident throughout the states.

Calculating the exact rate of disciplinary actions against psychologists is difficult for many reasons, including the fact that numbers taken from insurance pools are constantly changing; those who commit serious violations leave the provider pool, and new members join; people switch carriers; some practitioners retire from practice or change careers; and there are significant interrater reliability problems in claims reporting and tracking by insurance claims managers across carriers. Finally, sometimes the same action results in more than one disciplinary action. For example, the single act of failing to report suspected child abuse could result in a misdemeanor, a disciplinary action by a licensing board, and a malpractice suit.

---

[3] The authors wish to thank Dr. Stephen Behnke, Director of the APA Ethics Office, for his help with this chapter.

Because of the issues involved in reporting and tracking data, we cannot give a reliable estimate of the number of psychologists who are subject to disciplinary complaints each year. But, we know that risk varies on the basis of the nature of a practice. That is, those who do individual therapy have lower risk than psychologists who do child custody evaluations. In addition, practicing psychologists are far more likely to be confronted by a board action than they are to be sued.

Types of Complaints

Categorizing the complaints against psychologists is also difficult because the data are not collected in a standardized manner. For example, the Disciplinary Data System of ASPPB contains reports of individual licensing boards that until recently did not use a standard reporting system (Kirkland, Kirkland, & Reaves, 2004). In addition, the APA Ethics Committee does not categorize complaints the same way as does ASPPB. For example, an act of incompetent practice might be categorized by a licensing board as incompetent practice, but the APA Ethics Committee might classify it under an action arising out of a child custody case. Also, no uniform public reporting system or data set exists on criminal sanctions, institutional disciplinary actions, or other actions. In addition, some complaints involve violation of multiple standards but are coded under only one. Nonetheless, Van Horne (2004) estimated that 2% of licensed psychologists are subject to a licensing board complaint each year.

According to data from 2007 to 2012, the most common types of infractions addressed by the APA Ethics Committee were sexual relationships with adult patients, nonsexual boundary violations, insurance or fee problems, complaints arising out of child custody cases, and sexual relationships with minors (APA, Ethics Committee, 2007, 2008, 2009, 2010, 2011, 2012). According to data from 2005 to 2009, the most common reasons for disciplinary sanctions from licensing boards were, in order of frequency, unprofessional conduct, sexual misconduct, failure to maintain adequate or accurate records, negligence, conviction of a crime, nonsexual multiple relationships, inadequate supervision, substandard care, failure to complete mandated continuing education, and courtroom testimony without adequate foundation (DeMers & Schaffer, 2012).

Data from malpractice carriers are difficult to classify precisely because plaintiffs' attorneys often take a "shotgun" approach and file multiple complaints even though many of the allegations may eventually be dropped from the suit. Despite these and other problems in categorizing the data,[4] according to The Trust, the most common types of actions that led to malpractice complaints were, in order of frequency, ineffective treatment or failure to consult or refer, failure to diagnose or improper diagnosis, child custody disputes, sexual intimacy, harassment or misconduct, breach of confidentiality, suicide, and supervisory issues.

---

[4] In addition there is the ever-present interrater reliability problem when various insurance adjusters categorize malpractice complaints differently.

Despite the limitations of each of these individual data sets, certain common themes emerge. Sexual relationships, nonsexual multiple relationships, insurance and fee problems, participation in child custody cases, breaches of confidentiality, and ineffective practice are the major sources of complaints. Other common areas of concern are test misuse, inadequate supervision, patient suicide, and inadequate record keeping. In this book we focus much of the attention on these potential problem areas.

Emotional Consequences

Even for psychologists eventually found not guilty of an ethics violation, the very process of being investigated takes an emotional toll. In addition to the strain of the great expenditure of time and money, prosecuted psychologists often experience prolonged stress, social embarrassment, self-doubt, anxiety, and depression (Montgomery, Cupit, & Wimberly, 1999).

All of the authors have been involved in the disciplinary process at some level, either as board members; attorneys representing psychologists; expert witnesses; or consultants to psychologists being investigated, sued, or prosecuted. In those roles, we have seen the pain that such proceedings reveal and cause for both the plaintiffs and the defendants. Observing or participating in these proceedings has an unpleasant visceral quality that is hard to capture in words. We would not want to go through that process ourselves, and we do not want other psychologists to have to go through it either.

WHAT TO DO IF ACCUSED OF MISCONDUCT

Psychologists who receive notice that they are being sued or that a licensing board complaint has been filed against them should contact their professional liability insurance company immediately. Whether dealing with a malpractice suit or a complaint to a licensing board, they should not attempt to resolve the case themselves through negotiating with the person bringing the charges or anyone acting on behalf of that person, such as the patient's attorney. They must accept the fact that a patient has now taken a hostile action against them, and the matter has been turned over to other authorities that do not have the best interest of the psychologist as their focus. It is now an adversarial situation, and the tools of a psychologist are ill-suited to deal with this type of problem. Anything that psychologists say at this point can be used against them. They risk making self-incriminating statements if they discuss the situation with anyone but an attorney representing their interests. Psychologists should not alter or destroy records and should refer all communications from the plaintiff or the plaintiff's attorney to the attorney representing their interests.

Unfortunately, some well-meaning psychologists have responded to formal complaints by calling the patient and trying to talk out the problems. Throughout this book we emphasize the clinical and risk management importance of listening, communicating, and negotiating with patients. Certainly it is clinically appropriate to deal with expressions of discontent seriously and to repair breaches in the patient relationship. Certainly it is appropriate to apologize promptly for minor issues, such as being late for an appointment. When clinically appropriate, sometimes psychologists can show compassion and sensitivity by acknowledging an error in the application or timing of a specific technique. There has been considerable attention paid to recent research indicating that apologizing for mistakes can serve as an effective way of mitigating client anger and diminishing adversarial client actions. It also can help psychologists to resolve their own feelings about the rupture of the relationship.

After a complaint has been filed, however, the time for such communications with patients has ended. Naive psychologists may say things that could be used against them in future legal proceedings. For example, a psychologist may say to the person bringing the complaint, "I am sorry you feel this way," only to have the phrase repeated in court as an admission of guilt rather than as an apology.

It is important for the psychologists involved to be patient. Complaints can take years to resolve. Although it is only natural to want a quick resolution, the legal wheels turn very slowly.

CONSIDERING THE RISK MANAGEMENT FACTORS

Throughout this book we refer to several factors that influence risk. The following examples illustrate how psychologists might consider these factors. At the macro level, we can reiterate the basic principles of risk management. At the micro level, though, only psychologists can evaluate their personal skill inventory and their personal database and determine how to proceed.

These examples are composites based on many similar situations faced by psychologists. Of course, the factors are interactive by necessity (e.g., the intervention may reduce the severity of patient risk characteristics) and dynamic (e.g., a patient with whom a psychologist can work well at one point in time might be impossible to work with at another point in time). We also include potential disciplinary consequences in our discussion of the cases that follow.

CASE EXAMPLES WITH DISCUSSION

A psychologist was approached by the leaders of a religious denomination to evaluate an ordained minister who had a long pattern of disruptive behaviors including angry outbursts against parishioners for apparently innocuous behaviors that the minister interpreted as disrespectful. Efforts on the part of other ministers and lay leaders to encourage the minister to change were ineffective. Therefore, the denomination concluded that they had to intervene formally. They wanted a recommendation as to whether they could develop a rehabilitation program for the minister or, if necessary, whether they needed to remove her from ordination. What risk management factors should the psychologist consider in deciding whether to take the case? (1.1)[5]

---

[5] All of the examples are composites of cases and do not present information about an actual patient. Each example is followed by an identifying number in parentheses.

Patient risk factors. It was not possible for the psychologist to diagnose the client on the basis of the referral information, but there were suggestions of a possible personality disorder. The psychologist also considered the possibility that the client might be at a high risk to file a complaint especially if the psychologist's actions resulted in a change or loss of her job.

Context risk factors. The context was to make a recommendation to a third party that could have serious implications for the minister's career. The psychologist knew that this was a high-risk context. In addition, the psychologist knew that adversarial contexts such as this often bring out problematic behaviors on the part of the individuals being evaluated. In Chapter 8 ("Psychological Assessment and Testing"), we review the implications of third-party assessments in more detail.

Individual psychologist factors. The psychologist was very proficient in psychological testing and an excellent diagnostician, but she had never tested a member of the clergy suspected of impairment. Although she did not know the minister or any of the principals involved in the case personally, she was a member of the denomination and felt a responsibility to assist. Fortunately, this psychologist had done testing for third parties before and knew the basic informed consent, documentation, and risk management strategies that needed to be followed in such circumstances.

Disciplinary consequences. If the quality of the service fell below acceptable levels, there could be a malpractice suit or an allegation of misconduct before a licensing board or ethics committee. Even if the quality of service was acceptable, an angry patient could file complaints that the psychologist would need to address.

Outcome. The psychologist appropriately recognized that this professional obligation would entail substantial risks in that she had never before evaluated an individual for a religious domination. She sought consultation from a colleague who had done such work before she made a decision about taking this case. Eventually she took this case but retained the services of her colleague as a consultant to guide her through this process. From a business perspective, she understood that the cost of the consultant would substantially reduce her income for taking this case, but she anticipated that if she did a good job, it could lead to other referrals in the future.

We provide a second example.

An unmarried female psychologist treated a patient for an adjustment disorder and terminated after 4 weeks with a successful outcome. The patient was a well-educated woman who was adjusting to the death of her husband. There appeared to be no serious pathology. The patient reported no previous mental health treatment. Approximately one year after the last session the ex-patient met the psychologist at the local pet store, and they started a conversation. The ex-patient invited the psychologist to attend a barbecue at her house. Should the psychologist attend the barbecue and invite the possibility of a more extended social relationship? (1.2)

Patient risk factors. Although the psychologist only saw the patient for a few weeks, she did not appear to have any of the serious personality disorders that are associated with litigiousness. The patient appeared mentally healthy and reported no background of previous mental health treatment.

Context risk factors. The treatment had been brief and free of any complications. The bills had been paid promptly without complaint, and there appeared to be little likelihood that the patient would need further treatment. The psychologist had taken no actions during treatment to suggest or invite the possibility of a post-termination relationship.

Disciplinary consequences. The APA Ethics Code permits consecutive multiple relationships as long as they "would not reasonably be expected to cause impairment or risk exploitation or harm" (Standard 3.05a, Multiple Relationships). Consequently, the psychologist needs to consider the possibility of exploitation or harm to the ex-patient. Although this vignette does not imply the possibility of a sexual relationship, Standard 10.08 (Sexual Intimacies With Former Therapy Clients/Patients) of the Ethics Code has specific prohibitions against sexual relationships with former patients for at least 2 years after termination. Even then, the burden is on the psychologist to demonstrate that the former patient would not be harmed by the relationship based on the consideration of several factors enumerated in the Ethics Code.

Individual psychologist factors. The psychologist had been going through a difficult time because she recently moved to this town to take care of her aging mother who recently died. The psychologist had few friends in this new town and was anxious to establish a social network. She wondered if her interest in developing social relationships was blinding her to potential trouble spots.

Outcome. In this example, the patient and context factors suggest little clinical risk, but the psychologist factors may be suspect. Consequently, the psychologist politely informed her ex-patient that she had previously made plans that she might not be able to change (which was true), and that she would let her know later if she was able to attend. In the meantime, she sought consultation.

We provide one more brief example.

A psychologist was approached to provide therapy for children whose parents were undergoing a painful and contentious divorce. Although both parents agreed to the treatment, the psychologist wondered if she should take the case. (1.3)

Patient risk factors. There was no special indication that either of the parents had significant personality disorders. However, this psychologist knew that the stress of custody litigation could sometimes cause parents to exhibit behaviors suggestive of personality disorders.

Context risk factors. As we discuss in Chapter 4 ("Multiple Relationships and Boundaries"), whenever treatment is provided in the context of a conflicted divorce or custody case, there is the danger that one or more of the parents may perceive the psychologist, rightly or wrongly, as aligned with the other party. Parents in high-conflict divorces might not always present information accurately, may try to enlist the psychologist as an ally, or may be using the therapy to obtain information that can be used against the other parent in the upcoming custody fight. Allegations of child abuse are common in high-conflict divorces, although the frequency of founded cases is lower under these circumstances.

Disciplinary consequences. In high-conflict divorces involving custody disputes, it is not uncommon for parents to file complaints against therapists, custody evaluators, or other parties if they believe it will strengthen their cases.

Individual psychologist factors. The psychologist was a highly skilled child therapist and evaluator who had experience working with high-conflict families.

Outcome. The psychologist offered her service to the family under certain conditions. First, the court had to order the therapy (this was done to ensure that one parent would not use the threat of withdrawing consent as a means to influence the course of therapy in a countertherapeutic manner). Second, the parents had to agree that they would not request that the psychologist communicate to either of their attorneys or be otherwise involved in the custody dispute except for brief communications to any court-appointed custody evaluator. Third, payment had to be up-front for all sessions because the psychologist was aware that sometimes families use nonpayment as a means to try to influence the course and content of psychotherapy. Fourth, the psychologist had the parents sign a consent form that she reviewed with them in detail, including information on the reporting of suspected child abuse, the possibility that a specialized consultant might be involved if one or more of the children presented problems that appeared outside of her area of expertise, and other conditions relevant to this type of case. She documented the informed consent process in detail.

The psychologist appreciated the risks involved in this case but took steps to frame the context of treatment to increase the likelihood of therapeutic success. She also made ample use of the risk management strategies of informed consent, documentation, and consultation that we review in detail in Chapter 2 ("Key Elements of Risk Management").

A DETAILED CASE EXAMPLE WITH DISCUSSION

Our final example in this chapter is a detailed case faced by a psychologist. We expand on this particular case example throughout the book.

Dr. Doe has been providing therapy to a difficult 26-year-old patient from a wealthy background for the last 3 years. The insurance coverage has run out, and the patient is paying reduced fees. The treatment has had its ups and downs, some having to do with events in the life of the patient but others having to do with what is going on in the therapeutic relationship. The patient is making progress as measured by improvement in ability to manage her own life. The alliance seems solid overall. There has been less progress in the underlying dynamics, particularly regarding relationships. Under stress the patient tends to revert to dysfunctional thinking habits.

Then the patient misses sessions without adequate notice and bombards Dr. Doe with emails and telephone calls. She stops taking medications and falls behind in paying her bills. During these periods the risk of suicide gestures and attempts increases. About a year ago, in a similar situation, she made a suicide attempt of moderate lethality. There was a safety agreement in place at the time, and the patient did call Dr. Doe after she took the pills. Having been through this before, Dr. Doe is getting frustrated and having difficulty keeping those feelings out of the treatment.

Dr. Doe is feeling stress in his professional and personal life, including a reduction in income because of changes in managed care reimbursement. His child is ready to go to college, and he is uncertain how expenses will be paid. Dr.

Doe believes he should move toward termination with the patient, but he is afraid that this will be a major setback for the patient and may precipitate a suicide attempt. The patient has no real support network. She has strained relationships with her parents who still try to intrude in her life and are angry about the limits set on them. Dr. Doe believes that if the patient succeeds in committing suicide, the parents will blame him.

The patient's primary care physician prescribes her medication, but he has limited his relationship with the patient to strict 15-minute appointments. Dr. Doe has urged the patient to find a psychiatrist, but this is difficult because of the policies of the managed care company. Dr. Doe cares about the patient and identifies with the difficult struggles she faces in her life. If he could set and enforce adequate limits, the treatment might be productive, but any attempt to do so now will probably fail.

A new dialectical behavior therapy program has started in town, but the patient has avoided all suggestions about adjunctive involvement in the group. As long as Dr. Doe is available, the patient will never seriously consider this program. If he terminates, it is predictable that the patient will respond with hostility. He believes that there is a real risk of a serious suicide attempt.

> The patient knows the system well enough to avoid involuntary hospitalizations until she has made a gesture or attempt. Although Dr. Doe intends to offer adequate time to terminate, he is certain that the patient will not take advantage of the sessions and is likely to express her outrage through voicemails and emails. (1.4)

Now we consider this example while considering the risk management factors.

Patient risk factors. There are many, but we start with the obvious. Dr. Doe has diagnosed the patient as having a borderline personality disorder. The patient manifests a disturbed relationship with him and with others in her life. The patient has threatened to harm herself. The fact that her parents have financial resources increases the risk of a complaint or lawsuit.

Context risk factors. Dr. Doe is seeing the patient in a solo practice, and a primary care physician is monitoring the patient's medications. The patient is involved in no other mental health treatment activities. This is not the optimal setting of care. Ideally, she would have her medications prescribed and monitored by a psychiatrist or prescribing psychologist, and she would be treated as part of a larger system that has routine case consultation, 24-hour coverage, a day treatment program, or inpatient services if needed.

Disciplinary consequences. It is often a useful exercise to look at a worst-case scenario to identify the risks involved. If Dr. Doe terminates the patient and she harms herself through a suicide attempt or even is successful at committing suicide, he runs the risk of a malpractice suit, a licensing board complaint, an ethics complaint, or all three. If the patient has no family or relatives and no assets to pass along to heirs, these risks are minimized. Even if she does not harm herself, she still might be able to file a licensing board or ethics complaint. Perhaps she would argue that Dr. Doe violated the standards of the profession or the APA Ethics Code by his manner of terminating treatment. She might accuse him of abandonment. Even if Dr. Doe were eventually absolved of the charge of wrongful termination, the licensing board may find in the course of its investigation that he did not adequately document informed consent or committed some other violation unrelated to the initial complaint. As noted earlier, in some states, licensing boards have the option of amending their complaints to pursue the case against the psychologist.

Individual psychologist factors. These include Dr. Doe's emotional resources and the match between his knowledge, skills, experience, and strengths and the patient's needs. Psychologists will become better at making such matches if they have an accurate perception of their strengths and weaknesses.

Outcome. Of course, in this situation, Dr. Doe needs to ask himself what is in the best interest of the patient and what are his obligations to the patient. Even though she may be angry with him, it may be in her best interest for Dr. Doe to stop therapy. In fact, in some situations, continued therapy with such patients may be clinically contraindicated.

Dr. Doe also needs to protect himself, his practice, and his good name in the community. It does no one any good to be the object of a frivolous or unfounded complaint. Our goal is to describe how in this and other situations psychologists might reduce the risk of harm to both the patient and themselves.

In the subsequent chapters we review this case in more detail and provide other cases that present risks for psychologists. We also review ways that psychologists can reduce their risks through the application of informed consent, consultation, documentation, and other risk management principles. Knowledge of the laws and rules governing the practice of psychology is essential. However, we also emphasize the use of ethical principles as guides to promoting patient welfare.

SEVEN ESSENTIAL POINTS TO REMEMBER

1. Risk is a function of several factors, and the individual psychologist is the best judge as to whether a particular risk management action should be undertaken.

2. Being ethical means more than just obeying the APA Ethics Code.

3. The most common disciplinary actions against psychologists are in the areas of sexual boundary violations, nonsexual boundary violations, child custody, treatment and abandonment, supervision, and inadequate diagnosis.

4. Licensing board complaints are more frequent than malpractice suits or ethics committee complaints.

5. Psychologists who effectively manage their careers give sufficient attention to their emotional competence.

6. Effective career management includes embedding oneself into a supportive professional community such as the APA or a state, territorial, or local psychological association. The first step in that process may be to invest oneself in helping one's colleagues, community, or profession. Remember the Golden Rule.

7. Any purported risk management actions that appear to harm patients or degrade the quality of care need to be reconsidered.

CHAPTER 2: KEY ELEMENTS OF RISK MANAGEMENT

In this chapter we review the three key elements of risk management: informed consent, documentation, and consultation. It is important for psychologists to understand thoroughly what these concepts mean so that they can use them appropriately in real-life clinical situations. We have found that we can apply them best if we appreciate the moral principles on which they are based.

ETHICS AND RISK MANAGEMENT

As experienced psychologists know, being ethical is not necessarily the same as being legal (Bricklin, 2001). Handelsman, Knapp, and Gottlieb (2009) and Knapp and VandeCreek (2012b) have used the term *positive ethics* to refer to ethics as a way to promote patient welfare as opposed to the narrower view of ethics as a way to adhere to the literal letter of the law or to avoid disciplinary actions. Similarly, good risk management should involve more than just following the minimum legal requirements. Good risk management principles should help psychologists fulfill their highest ethical ideals.

The risk management principles that psychologists follow should be congruent with their general orientation toward their practice and, like other aspects of their practice, should be "consistent with your deepest values" (Pope & Vasquez, 2005, p. 3). Of course, we cannot deny the reality that disciplinary actions can occur in the practice of psychology. Risk management principles, however, should not be driven by often unrealistic fears but motivated by deeply held values, such as desiring to serve others and to have a rewarding career.

Ethical principles are relevant to the discussion of risk management for at least two reasons. First, good risk management principles are based on ethical principles; false or bad risk management principles contradict ethical principles. The best risk management principle is to provide good services that facilitate patient healing and growth and avoid unnecessary patient anger and resentment when the results are less than favorable. Second, ethical principles help guide behavior in situations in which laws or disciplinary codes do not give direction.

Psychologists are more effective in applying risk management strategies when they understand the moral principles on which they are based. Psychologists differ in their personal moral theories. They may base their moral behavior on virtue ethics, deontological ethics, feminism, or theories of moral behavior based on other traditions. However, many find that a principle-based frame of reference helps them to articulate their ethical values. Principle-based ethics, as applied to healthcare by Beauchamp and Childress (2009), was influential in framing the General (aspirational) Principles in the American Psychological Association's (APA's) "Ethical Principles of Psychologists and Code of Conduct" (hereinafter referred to as the APA Ethics Code; APA, 2010a). We make references to principle-based ethics as a foundation for risk management throughout this book but more for illustrative purposes.

According to principle-based ethics, individuals are generally obligated to follow certain overarching moral principles. Different principle-based ethicists may phrase or categorize these ethical principles differently. Beauchamp and Childress (2009) have identified beneficence (working to promote patient welfare), nonmaleficence (avoiding patient harm), justice, respect for patient autonomy, and professional–patient relationships as especially relevant for healthcare. Knapp and VandeCreek (2004) suggested general beneficence (obligations to society in general) as an additional principle, and the APA Ethics Code includes integrity as a separate principle.

Psychologists acting at the higher levels of Bloom's taxonomy (analysis, synthesis, and evaluation) can identify the relationship of these moral principles to their clinical actions. They can incorporate these principles into their clinical practices, apply them in novel situations, appreciate nuanced applications depending on the context, and use them to clarify why they chose one particular action over another

When practiced properly, risk management strategies should help psychologists better fulfill their professional roles and should promote good patient care. Any purported risk management principle that tells a psychologist to do something that appears to harm a patient or violates a moral principle needs to be reconsidered. False risk management principles are likely to occur at the lower levels of Bloom's taxonomy when psychologists fail to apply risk management principles or apply them inappropriately because they do not understand their overarching purpose. Or perhaps some psychologists gravitate toward simplistic and absolute rules as a way to reduce their (often unnecessary) anxiety. As Younggren (2011) has pointed out, psychologists "should not hide behind some minimalistic set of absolutes that do a disservice to their skills and deny them the right to think through ethical issues and arrive at the best decision for each individual that they see" (p. 10).

Table 2.A contains some false risk management principles that we have encountered in our presentations and consultations. These false principles contain absolute statements and appear to reflect a perception of a conflict between the interest of the psychologist and the welfare of the patient. For example, some psychologists perceive that they have increased their legal protection if they get a suicidal patient to sign a safety agreement. From a legal perspective though, these safety agreements are meaningless. From a clinical perspective, these safety agreements may be clinically contraindicated if they are forced on a patient (i.e., they may not respect the patient's autonomy) or if they inhibit the productive relationship needed for effective treatment (i.e., they do not promote beneficence).

In some situations, the application of risk management principles results in clear understanding of what to do (e.g., explain treatment and billing procedures to patients before therapy starts). In other situations, the risk management principles require the nuanced balancing of issues and strategies and an ethical decision-making process.

Table 2.A
False Risk Management Principles

1. Always get a suicidal patient to sign a safety contract.

2. Try not to keep records because they can be used against you if a complaint is filed.

3. Never keep detailed records when patients present a threat to harm themselves or others.

4. Informed consent obligations consist only of getting the signature of patients on an informed consent form.

5. Risk management is only concerned with protecting the psychologist from disciplinary actions.

6. Never self-disclose and never touch a patient.

7. When giving referrals always give patients three referrals, regardless of how appropriate they might be.

ETHICAL DECISION MAKING

Neither the laws nor the APA Ethics Code can provide an answer to every situation that a psychologist will experience. Knapp and VandeCreek (2012b) have identified four types of situations in which the disciplinary ethics standards do not give explicit direction. First, ethics standards in general, and specifically APA's, use qualifiers such as "reasonable" and "if appropriate," which indicate that psychologists have to use their discretion in applying that particular ethical principle. Second, the APA Ethics Code may be silent about how to act in an emerging area of practice. Third, the APA Ethics Code does not prescribe a specific course of action when institutional policies or laws conflict with the requirements of the Ethics Code or with each other. Instead the APA Ethics Code prescribes a general policy of asserting one's commitment to the Ethics Code while attempting to resolve the issues. It does not (nor could it) prescribe exactly how psychologists are to demonstrate this commitment or how to resolve the issue and what to do if the issue is irresolvable. Finally, the APA Ethics Code does not describe the supererogatory obligations of psychologists (self-imposed obligations to go beyond the minimum standards of the profession). In those situations psychologists need to look to moral or ethical principles or values to guide their behavior.

In most instances, treatment occurs without any conflict among these overarching ethical principles. However, at times these principles may conflict, and psychologists will have to weigh the moral principles and decide which one should be salient. For example, a psychologist cannot both respect the autonomy of a suicidal patient (and allow him or her to die) and promote beneficence (work for his or her well-being) at the same time. When psychologists trump one principle (respect for autonomy) with another (beneficence), as in this example, they should attempt to minimize harm to the offended ethical principle (respect for autonomy). For example, when deciding to place beneficence over respect for the autonomy of a suicidal patient, it is still desirable to give the patient as much control over treatment as possible, consistent with the goal of protecting his or her life. For example, the psychologist could invite the patient to assist in identifying how best to keep safe by removing the means of self-harm, by participating in changing the treatment plan, or in deciding how to alert significant others of the suicidal danger.

THREE KEY RISK MANAGEMENT STRATEGIES

It is important to understand the three risk management strategies (informed consent, documentation, and consultation) thoroughly to apply them appropriately in real-life clinical situations. These three key elements are especially important to use when the situation passes the "hair on the back of your neck test." As the potential for risk increases, the use of these strategies should increase.

Psychologists will apply these risk management principles better if they understand how they are linked to overarching ethical principles. Informed consent should not be a rote legal exercise completed during an intake session but an effort to promote patient autonomy by increasing patient participation in decision making. In addition, good informed consent procedures are linked to beneficence insofar as they have a secondary goal of improving patient adherence and investment in treatment. Tryon and Winograd (2011) reported that "better outcomes can be expected when patient and therapist agree on therapeutic goals and the processes to achieve these goals" (p. 50). Beahrs and Guthiel (2001) also argued that good informed consent procedures empower patients to gain information, ask questions, and use that knowledge to assist their recovery. Furthermore, informed consent procedures are linked to nonmaleficence insofar as they reduce the likelihood that misunderstandings of office policies or billing practices could harm the treatment relationship.

Documentation is related to the moral principles of beneficence and nonmaleficence. Documentation requirements are not just arbitrary rules created by oversight bodies but rules designed for several reasons, including the promotion of patient welfare. Good documentation demonstrates that the psychologist used a reasonable standard of care in conceptualizing and implementing treatment. Documentation also ensures better communication with current and future treating professionals. It is especially important for accurate communication with other staff members when working in an institution or agency.

Consultation helps ensure competence, which is related to the moral principles of beneficence and nonmaleficence. Consultation can be distinguished from supervision in that with consultation the psychologist is seeking suggestions but maintains full authority for the patient's care, whereas in supervision the supervisor carries the responsibility for the patient (see Chapter 10, "Other Areas of Concern for Psychologists: Consultant or Supervisor, Diversity Issues, Conflicts in Institutional Settings, Referrals, and Termination and Abandonment"). All psychologists should have lifelong competence-enhancing strategies that include, among other things, continuing education and a system for quality feedback. Although we assume that most psychologists have the basic skills in their personal skill inventory (and basic information in their personal database) to treat their patients, all psychologists will encounter unexpected or unique twists and turns in delivering services that require them to get professional consultations to ensure that a particular patient receives a reasonable level of care.

In summary, psychologists can use these risk management strategies to fulfill their highest aspirations as psychologists. The risk management strategies substantially reduce risks of disciplinary complaints and also improve the quality of patient care. The key elements of risk management can have a positive impact on the factors related to an increase in risk (i.e., patient characteristics, context, and individual psychologist characteristics). For example, informed consent will influence patient risk characteristics (to the extent that it reduces unrealistic expectations and the potential for misunderstandings about the nature of treatment) and the context of the treatment (by setting the parameters and expectations and procedures for treatment ahead of time). Documentation will strengthen the individual therapist factors by demonstrating care in developing and implementing the treatment plan. Consultation will strengthen the individual therapist factors by improving the personal skill inventory and personal database of the psychologist. Of course, the risk factors are interactive so that a strengthened personal skill inventory may influence patient risk characteristics, which influence context of treatment, and so on.

The use of these risk management strategies is especially important when taking therapeutic risks such as attempting a nontraditional treatment with a patient. Perhaps an intervention has an 80% chance of success and a 20% chance of harming the patient (and a 5% chance of resulting in a disciplinary complaint). In such situations it is especially important to increase usual risk management activities and to be scrupulous about the informed consent process, documentation, and consultation.

Informed Consent[1]

At the lower levels of Bloom's taxonomy, a psychologist would know what an informed consent form is and know to get it signed by a patient. At the higher levels, a psychologist would know the underlying principles behind informed consent (involving and empowering the patient into treatment), understand how that empowerment is related to the overall goals of therapy, and be able to justify the steps used to engage the patient into therapy.

Psychologists can incorporate procedures designed to empower patients throughout treatment, recognizing that empowering patients is an important tool in promoting patient autonomy and welfare. Using risk management strategies at the lower levels of Bloom's taxonomy (such as getting the informed consent form signed) is better than nothing, although the top psychologists work from the higher levels. Bloom's taxonomy with informed consent is shown in Table 2.B.

---

[1] In this chapter we focus on informed consent, documentation, and consultation as risk management strategies. More information on the Health Insurance Portability and Accountability Act of 1996 Privacy Rule and its implications for informed consent and documentation are provided in Chapter 6 ("Privacy, Confidentiality, and Privileged Communications").

Table 2.B
Bloom's Taxonomy of Informed Consent

Knowledge: You know that you are required to get informed consent.

Comprehension: You can describe to others the minimum requirements of informed consent.

Application: You can go through an informed consent process as it applies to most routine patients.

Analysis: You can identify the components of informed consent, such as the abilities to listen, communicate, and negotiate. You can also tailor the process to the unique context of treatment or the unique needs of the patient and in a manner that motivates and involves patients in the therapy process.

Synthesis: You can incorporate the informed consent process into your overall treatment relationship, which is geared to improving patient welfare and increasing patient autonomy.

Evaluation: In any particular case, you can explain why the particular informed consent process you used helped further the treatment goals.

Competency to Give Informed Consent

The APA Ethics Code requires psychologists to obtain informed consent from service recipients or their surrogates. Psychologists also give patients information relevant to the decision to participate, including informing them that participation is voluntary and that they have the right to ask questions (Standard 3.10, Informed Consent). When patients are not legally capable of giving informed consent, psychologists seek to obtain their assent, or general agreement with treatment.

Competency to make informed decisions is not an all-or-nothing matter but is probably better described as falling along a continuum. The informed consent process becomes problematic when the competence of the party to give informed consent is in question, such as when treating older adults with declining mental abilities, patients who are neurologically impaired, adults with intellectual disabilities, or those who are not fluent in the same language as the evaluator. Also, some patients may have the cognitive ability to understand the information under normal circumstances, but anxiety, pressure from family members or peers, or other psychological factors may interfere with their ability to process that information or to act on it independently. Consequently, at times it may be necessary to take additional steps or extra time to help patients understand their options.

Research on competence with persons with serious mental illnesses or intellectual disability shows that alternative or complementary modes of communication (such as audiovisual aides, conversations with friends and caregivers, and extra time to ask questions) can help them to evaluate their options to participate (Fisher, 2002). Although such individuals might not understand the general nature of therapy or assessment through the traditional discussion between psychologist and patient, they may reach a better understanding if the same information is given by friends or caregivers and they have time to ask additional questions.

Content of the Informed Consent Process

The minimum content of the informed consent process is established by governing authorities such as the APA Ethics Code, state laws, agency regulations, or the Health Insurance Portability and Accountability Act of 1996 Privacy Rule (hereinafter referred to as the Privacy Rule) and by research on the informational preferences of patients or prospective patients. We give more detailed information on the Privacy Rule in Chapter 6 ("Privacy, Confidentiality, and Privileged Communications"). However, for our purposes here, the salient question is, what would the average person want to know under the circumstances (use a "patient knows best" instead of a "doctor knows best" principle)? Patients enter therapy or other professional relationships with psychologists with implicit assumptions about what is or is not ethical and what should or should not occur. Although surveys show general congruence between the conceptions of what psychologists and prospective patients view as ethical, there are some differences that could impact the perception of what patients perceive to be unethical behavior.

In addition, when psychologists are working in forensic situations or when they are doing evaluations with external consequences to the client, it is especially important to attend to the unique informed consent issues associated with that work. More detail on informed consent when delivering forensic services can be found in the discussion that follows and in Chapter 7 ("Psychologists in the Courtroom"), and more detail on informed consent when doing evaluations with external consequences can be found in the discussion that follows and in Chapter 8 ("Psychological Assessment and Testing").

Ironically, as a result of today's statutes and regulations, psychologists may have to give patients such a large amount of written material that even some of the more sophisticated patients are unable to understand how it applies to them (Harris, 2003). Consequently, psychologists should not rely on the documentation alone to ensure that patients understand the important features of their services.

Special standards in the APA Ethics Code deal with informed consent for therapy, assessment, supervised services, and research. When conducting therapy, the Ethics Code requires psychologists to give patients information on the limits of confidentiality, the nature of therapy, and fees (Standard 10.01, Informed Consent to Therapy). When psychologists provide couples or family therapy, they inform parties ahead of time about their roles (Standard 10.02, Therapy Involving Couples or Families). If therapy involves couples, families, or social units, it is important to distinguish as soon as possible the patient from the collateral contacts and whether the interests of participants are in conflict (Standard 10.02, Therapy Involving Couples or Families). When psychologists provide group therapy, they describe the responsibilities and roles of parties ahead of time (Standard

10.03, Group Therapy). When psychologists provide court-ordered therapy, they inform recipients of the anticipated nature of services (Standard 3.10c, Informed Consent). When providing assessment services, psychologists inform patients about who will receive the report and pay the fee (Standard 9.03, Informed Consent in Assessments). Trainees must notify those they see of their supervised status and the name of the supervisor and contact information (Standard 10.01c, Informed Consent to Therapy).

State licensing boards may have additional informed consent requirements. Also, elements of informed consent are incorporated into HIPAA by way of the required Privacy Notice for covered entities (i.e., practitioners or agencies that transmit patient-protected health information electronically), which psychologists should give patients at the first session or as soon as feasible. We provide more information on the Privacy Rule in Chapter 6 ("Privacy, Confidentiality, and Privileged Communications"). However, we recommend that all psychologists act as if the Privacy Rule applies to them, even if they are not covered entities.

Braaten and Handelsman (1997) surveyed current patients, former patients, and nonpatients and found that they all valued information about the therapy process (e.g., what techniques will be used, what techniques are inappropriate in therapy, risks of therapy, alternatives available, and extent and limits of confidentiality), procedural issues (e.g., how to contact the therapist in an emergency, how appointments are scheduled, and how long appointments last); and billing issues (e.g., how much therapy will cost). In addition, it may also be prudent to discuss third-party reimbursement issues, policies concerning payment and collection of overdue debts, policies concerning cancellation of appointments (e.g., charging for canceled appointments), and access to records.

Pomerantz and Grice (2001) found that undergraduates were more accepting of multiple relationships than professionals but less accepting of mental health professionals who do things that make the patients uncomfortable, such as some methods of securing payment or selectively accepting patients. This suggests that some patients may conceptualize therapy "with little acknowledgment of the therapists' rights or desires, particularly as they involve the 'business' of therapy" (p. 746). Consequently, psychologists should be alert to the fact that some patients may be bothered by some of the usual business practices of psychologists.

We suggest that the informed consent document avoid emphasizing potential negative events if they are remote and unlikely. For example, it may not be necessary, unless required by law, to include in an informed consent form a discussion about negative events (such as the impropriety of sexual contact between psychologists and patients) in too much detail. Such an emphasis may, for example, give the patient the impression that the psychologist is preoccupied with sex or has impulses that are difficult to control.

In addition, psychologists may want to give more information to patients when providing specific treatment modalities. For example, when providing couples therapy, psychologists may give information concerning potential role conflicts and collateral contacts (Standard 10.02, Therapy Involving Couples or Families).

Psychologists also document informed consent (Standard 3.10d, Informed Consent). Often the patient's signature on an informed consent form fulfills this requirement. At the least, psychologists should document the informed consent procedure in their notes. The Trust has a sample patient agreement form that covers the minimum information that should be given at the start of therapy (readers can download the form at www.apait.org and modify as necessary). Written forms are best when they are easily readable and straightforward and use ordinary language. They should supplement, not replace, verbal communications. Next we discuss additional information that may be given or emphasized depending on the needs of particular patients.

Informed Consent as a Process

Traditionally, informed consent was viewed as a passive event that required giving patients information so that they could make an informed decision about whether to undergo treatment. The legal doctrine of informed consent derived from medical procedures such as surgery in which the patient was essentially a passive recipient of a procedure and one-time consent was sufficient. However, the process of psychotherapy differs substantially from surgery or other medical procedures. Although it is still necessary to give patients information, informed consent in psychotherapy is best viewed as an ongoing interactive process and not a one-time event. No one can predict the course of therapy or what new information or events may emerge over time. Consequently, the informational needs of patients will vary over the course of therapy.

We identified the belief that informed consent only consists of getting a patient's signature as a false risk management principle. Informed consent should not be a one-way street or a one-time event but an opportunity for the psychologist to learn more about the unique needs and perspectives of the patient. Here, as in other professional services, the ability to listen and show empathy ("the capacity to understand what another person is experiencing from within the other person's framework"; Bellet & Maloney, 1991, p. 1831) is important.

Certainly, one of the salient tasks is to get general agreement on the goals of therapy. It may or may not be helpful to share the specific diagnosis with the patient. However, it is important to have general agreement on the focus of treatment using lay language. Discussions of therapy goals should continue throughout the course of therapy. A meaningful discussion of goals should strengthen the therapeutic alliance. Patients' ownership and participation in treatment are enhanced when they understand treatment options and risks and agree on the goals and processes of treatment.

At times patients may not be able to make informed decisions immediately. The processes of preparing them for decision making may involve processes analogous to developing a scaffold or the titration process (in which bits of information are added and processed over time). If the patient responds poorly to the additional information, more time should be taken before the effort for full information is undertaken again.

A psychologist received a referral of a patient who had recently experienced a severe physical trauma. The patient's first words on entering therapy were that he only came in to get the doctor off his back and was never going to return. The psychologist knew that fear of talking about traumatic events is common among trauma victims. Consequently, she said that she respected the patient's choice and went on to describe how therapy would proceed if the patient were to decide to return, including the fact that in the treatment of trauma the patient retains complete control over whether, when, and how much to discuss the trauma. The patient left after 15 minutes without scheduling a follow-up appointment.

Later the patient rescheduled and asked more about specific treatments. The psychologist briefly described the processes of cognitive restructuring, relaxation, and adjunctive medications. In the first interview the anxiety of the patient rendered him incapable of receiving all the information that ordinarily would be given in the first session. However, the psychologist titrated the information by giving it over more than one session. (2.1)

The higher levels of informed consent (according to Bloom's taxonomy) tailor the process according to the overarching moral principles and the factors considered in calculating risk (e.g., patient characteristics, context, and psychologist characteristics). Psychologists acting at the higher levels of Bloom's taxonomy will convey an attitude that encourages genuine patient participation. Prescribing a process and implementing it are two different things. The manner of implementing the informed consent process can be as important as the content itself. The tone of voice, choice of words, and nonverbal communication should reflect a willingness to receive patients' questions, hear their concerns, and join with them as partners in treatment. Psychologists who view the informed consent process as an annoyance will find it harder to convey a participatory attitude.

Challenges to Informed Consent Recommendations

Some may argue that our emphasis on informed consent is misplaced because it requires spending an inordinate amount of time on remote issues that have little relevance to treatment. We view this matter differently. The informed consent process should focus on what the average person would want to know under the circumstances. This does not require spending valuable time on issues with no relevance to the patient. However, our experience has been that under some circumstances, such as when doing evaluations with external consequences or when treating children in the context of a high-conflict divorce, there is a very real potential for misunderstandings. Furthermore, the high emotional arousal of patients at the beginning of treatment may prevent them from attending closely when important issues are first raised by the psychologist.

Informed Consent and the Risk Factors

It may be helpful to view informed consent from the perspective of the factors related to risk as described in Chapter 1 (i.e., patient characteristics, context, and therapist characteristics).

Informed Consent and Patient Factors

In addition to the general information given to every patient, psychologists can give additional information based on unique circumstances. One of the salient characteristics is the diagnosis (or treatment needs) of the patient. For example, when treating patients with panic disorders, it may be desirable to describe some of the treatment options that could be effective. If the patient has already tried psychotherapy and has had a poor treatment response, the psychologist may be able to comment about the type of psychotherapy received and how it compares with other forms of treatment for this particular disorder.

Other factors that may be discussed include the apparent interpersonal qualities of the patient.

> A psychologist started treatment with a depressed patient with a comorbid dependent personality disorder. The psychologist wisely alerted the patient that he might feel frustrated at times because she would push him toward more independence than he might find comfortable. Also, the psychologist alerted him to the fact that his wish for approval might inhibit him from being honest with her about his satisfaction with treatment or the nature of his progress. (2.2)

At times it may be necessary to warn against iatrogenic problems with some patients.

> A psychologist had just started treating a patient with significant problems who announced after two sessions that she had elected to take a job out of state and would be moving in 6 weeks. The psychologist believed it would be clinically contraindicated to open up difficult issues, only to have therapy discontinue shortly thereafter. Prudently, he cautioned her about potential iatrogenic effects of continuing therapy only to have it interrupted in a few weeks. (2.3)

It may also be desirable to discuss the impact of therapy on significant others, especially in couples and family therapy.

A psychologist started treatment with a woman who desired to become more assertive in her marriage. However, the psychologist became concerned that an increase in her assertiveness could jeopardize her fragile marriage. Awareness of this possibility led the psychologist to discuss with his patient ways to mitigate those possible negative consequences, such as by including her husband in treatment. (2.4)

Another factor that may be relevant is the apparent need to include (or exclude) family members from treatment. This is especially important with adolescents and is discussed in detail in Chapter 5 ("Working With Couples, Families, and Children").

Informed Consent and Contextual Factors

The content of what is presented in informed consent forms or verbally depends, in part, on the context of the professional service. Some common contextual features include experimental or unconventional treatments, families in high-conflict situations, third-party assessments, and forensic services.

Psychologists should inform patients when they are recommending unconventional or experimental treatments, including information on treatment alternatives and the risks and benefits of the proposed treatment (Standard 10.01b, Informed Consent to Therapy).

When treating families in which there is high conflict, such as when there is a pending hearing concerning the custody of a child, it may be important to emphasize policies concerning court appearances, releasing information unrelated to treatment to third parties, payment for non-therapy-related services, and more. When assuming a hybrid role as a treating expert, it may be especially important to review the policy concerning payment for non-therapy services. If the court appoints a psychologist as a therapist, evaluator, family educator, or mediator, it may be important to emphasize the rules and limits concerning confidentiality. We discuss this in greater depth in Chapter 7 ("Psychologists in the Courtroom").

Third-party assessments can also influence the content of the informed consent information. These may occur in independent medical evaluations, fitness-for-duty evaluations, disability evaluations, recommendations to correctional facilities or law enforcement personnel, special education placements, organizational consultations, or for research projects or screenings for medical purposes (such as bariatric surgery). When conducting these evaluations, it is wise to document at the beginning of service the purpose of the evaluation, patient access to reports (if any), and limits of confidentiality. Psychologists should get the document signed before assessment begins. Even when informed consent is not legally required, it is advisable to give the patient or participant a copy of the informed consent document. We discuss third-party assessments in more detail in Chapter 8 ("Psychological Assessment and Testing").

Some psychologists use consumer-focused assessments, which involve patients in important decisions about assessments (Brenner, 2003). Although this is not usually done with third-party assessments, it is relevant in some circumstances.

When evaluating seminarians for candidacy into the ranks of the clergy, a psychologist routinely asked the seminarians "What do you want to get out of the process?" Most seminarians had not thought about the issues except to view the assessment as a hurdle they must jump or a potential obstacle to their career goal. However, the psychologist conducted the assessment over several weeks, instead of all at once. That way he got more than one sample of behavior, gave homework assignments, and allowed the candidates to reflect on what they could get out of the process. Although the evaluation did not consider the sincerity of the faith of the applicant, the psychologist often included questions about religious faith, personal calling, anticipated goals in the religious vocation, and more to break the ice and lower defenses. Giving feedback directly to both the applicant and the referral source allowed both to ask questions and clarify their understanding of the findings.

This technique helped the psychologist to fulfill his obligations to the third party (the denomination) and to the applicant as well. At times the candidates had problems so significant that they could not be recommended for candidacy. However, this participatory model helped them to reflect on their capabilities, limitations, and fitness for their religious vocation. (2.5)

Informed Consent and Individual Psychologist Factors

Psychologists may disagree about the extent to which they self-disclose private information to patients. Some self-disclosure, such as the nature of the training and expertise of the psychologist, would appear to be appropriate as part of any informed consent process.

A psychologist was contacted by an adult who wanted help in controlling his anger. Most of the problematic behaviors occurred at work, although he did mention some problems related to losing his temper with his children. The psychologist believed he could help the man with his work-related temper problems. He did note, however, that he did not have extensive experience in working with children. At the time it did not appear that the temper problems with the children were substantial (and most likely they were an overflow of problems related to work). However, the psychologist did note that if there turned out to be substantial child-rearing issues, he would refer the patient to a colleague more skilled with children. (2.6)

It would also be appropriate to disclose any potential conflicts of interest or potential multiple relationships.

A psychologist completed an intake on a patient who she learned was active in the state's Humane League. The psychologist had contact with the Humane League through occasional participation at the local chapter's annual banquet and other events. The participation of the psychologist was sufficient that it was conceivable that they might encounter each other, albeit briefly, at a state event. The psychologist discussed the possibility of brief contacts in those venues to give the patient the opportunity to assess her willingness to pursue therapy with the psychologist. (2.7)

Often potential patients who belong to traditionally marginalized groups (such as disabled persons, sexual minorities, cultural minorities) may actively seek a psychologist they know or know of through personal contacts (Zur, 2007). Often they decide to seek this psychologist because they fear that another psychotherapist will not sufficiently understand their perspectives or experiences. In these situations it is prudent to think through issues of self-disclosure to prospective patients carefully, including ways in which incidental encounters might be handled.

Informed Consent and the Detailed Case Example

What would be the optimal role of informed consent in the detailed case example introduced in Chapter 1? Some of the problems in the case are that the patient has missed appointments without adequate notice and then bombarded the psychologist with telephone calls and emails. She stopped taking medications against the advice of her physician, stopped paying bills, and refused a recommendation to participate in a special group designed for individuals with her types of problems.

An informed consent procedure will not ensure that these problems can be avoided. However, an effective informed consent policy that addresses these issues at the start of treatment and throughout therapy as necessary increases the likelihood that the problematic behaviors can be reduced and gives the psychologist greater leverage in enforcing rules of treatment. Furthermore, the informed consent process can be reviewed throughout treatment as these resistances or patient obstacles to treatment emerge.

In an effort to get patients to "buy into" therapy, some psychologists are overly lenient about enforcing basic rules regarding payment, between-sessions phone calls, or cooperation with medication recommendations. Later, when the patient begins to deteriorate or begins to demonstrate problematic behaviors, it becomes harder to enforce the rules. The best policy is to enforce the rules conscientiously. One psychologist, for example, adopts a *one-time* rule, which means he confronts the patient immediately about any rule that the patient breaks but allows the patient one mistake before raising the issue of termination. Later in this book we note that psychologists may (and often should) terminate patients who are noncompliant with treatment (see Chapter 10,

"Other Areas for Psychologists: Consultant or Supervisor, Diversity Issues, Conflicts in Institutional Settings, Referrals, and Termination and Abandonment," for more information on unwanted terminations). However, in the event of the need to terminate the patient against his or her wishes, psychologists will be able to reduce the negative consequences of that termination because they made the conditions of participation in treatment clear from the beginning.

If it comes to termination, the discussion should go beyond "you agreed to do this and now you have to follow through" and should focus on the clinical justification for the parameters set on treatment. Of course, the nature of some situations is sometimes best handled by avoiding a "tug of war" and deferring to the patient on whether to take medication or comply on some other issue. Nonetheless, a psychologist should never hesitate to give serious consideration to terminating a nonemergency patient who fails to comply with the essential elements of treatment. It is better to terminate a patient who is not in crisis early than to let the patient dictate clinically contraindicated restrictions on therapy that risk placing the psychologist in a role in which he or she is providing degraded treatment.

Documentation

At the lower levels of Bloom's taxonomy, psychologists know they are required to keep records, although they may not be particularly clear about why, except for the risk management benefits of doing so. At the higher levels of Bloom's taxonomy, experienced psychologists link record keeping to patient welfare, their overall management of patient care, and overarching ethical principles. Bloom's taxonomy applied to documentation is shown in Table 2.C.

Table 2.C
Bloom's Taxonomy of Documentation

Knowledge: You know that you have to document your services.

Comprehension: You can describe to others the ethical and legally mandated minimum documentation requirements.

Application: You can document the most routine psychotherapy sessions.

Analysis: You can identify the elements of good documentation (essential components of a treatment record), your thinking processes (the "math teacher" rule), and the purposes that the elements of good documentation fulfill.

Synthesis: You document carefully because, among other things, it reflects the careful thought processes required for quality care, communication with other treatment providers, evaluation of the progress of therapy, or other professional purposes.

Evaluation: In any given case you can provide clinical, ethical, and legal reasons why you documented the case in a particular manner.

Good records can provide the foundation for proper diagnosis and treatment. Good record keeping assists psychologists by refreshing their memories, justifying payment to third-party payers, creating a record to send to future or current health providers, protecting them in the event that there are allegations of misconduct, and meeting requirements for agency reviews or accreditation. In addition, some practitioners use records to gather data for archival research.

Documentation is directly linked to patient welfare insofar as it demonstrates how the psychologists analyzed the case and considered the advantages and disadvantages of different options. Documentation is indirectly linked to patient care as it shows compliance with institutional or legal requirements designed to ensure that the practice of the psychologist as a whole meets minimum standards of patient care. Documentation is also indirectly linked to patient care when archival research is used as a feedback mechanism or a source of data by which the overall quality of patient care in general is improved.

Documentation reflects competence and demonstrates that services were delivered in accordance with a reasonable standard of care. Although many definitions of competence are available, one useful one is "the habitual and judicious use of communication, knowledge, technical skills, clinical reasoning, emotions, values, and reflection in daily practice for the benefit of the individual and community being served" (Epstein & Hundert, 2002, p. 226). Although this definition was developed for use with physicians, it has application to the delivery of psychological services as well. That is, the documentation should reflect that the psychologist has knowledge relevant to the patient's presenting problem (i.e., cognitive knowledge and technical skills) and an adequate relationship with the patient and that the psychologist used clinical judgment in integrating that knowledge, skill, and relationship in the delivery of services.

Documentation has unique risk management usefulness as well. From a legal perspective, the general rule is "if it isn't written down, it didn't happen." In a disciplinary action, courts will generally assume that events occurred the way the records described them. If the record states that a patient was asked about suicidal ideation and denied it, it is assumed that this is what happened. The complainant would have a very high (and almost impossible) burden to overturn what was written in the psychotherapy record. In some cases, psychologists who have delivered an adequate level of care have been found negligent or forced to settle out of court because documentation did not sufficiently reflect that adequate standard of care. Poor or incomplete documentation can get psychologists into trouble even if they did a good job. On the other hand, many potential malpractice cases or disciplinary cases are never pursued because the quality of documentation reflected an adequate level of care.

The minimum standards for documentation can be found in the APA Ethics Code in Standards 6.01 (Documentation of Professional and Scientific Work and Maintenance of Records) and 6.02 (Maintenance, Dissemination, and Disposal of Confidential Records of Professional and Scientific Work). More commentary can be found in APA's "Record Keeping Guidelines" (APA, 2007), in state laws and state board of psychology regulations, and from Medicare or other insurers. There have been detailed discussions concerning the impact of the Privacy Rule on documentation and the relative merits of keeping psychotherapy notes separate from the rest of the patient's record. We discuss those issues in more detail in Chapter 6 ("Privacy, Confidentiality, and Privileged Communications").

What should be included in records depends on the relevant agency, state, or federal requirements. Typically they should include an evaluation summary, treatment goals, and session notes that demonstrate the thinking process of the professional in making treatment decisions. A relevant metaphor is that of the math teacher who gives credit to the student for following the proper steps in solving the problem as well as the eventual answer. The students would get credit for correct procedures for working with the problem even if they did not get the answer completely correct. Likewise, records of consultations with other professionals and other documents (such as patient productions or notes from other treatment providers) that influence treatment decisions will support the practitioner's actions in dealing with a complaint.

Technology has changed the way that many psychologists create or store records. The Security Rule (the federal law governing storage and retention of confidential health care information, which is discussed in detail in Chapter 6, "Privacy, Confidentiality and Privileged Communications") is *technology neutral* in that it does not have a fixed list of protections that all health care providers must use when storing or sending information electronically. Nonetheless, prudent psychologists will take a number of precautions to protect their data, such as the use of passwords, firewalls, encryption, backup systems, or training employees (Baker & Bufka, 2011).

Many psychologists store records on a computer or even in a cloud (*cloud* is the term for the electronic storage of data in distant locations by computer). We know of dozens of companies that provide cloud storage of data. It is impossible to evaluate all of them and designate some as safe and others as unsafe given that the number of companies is always expanding and that their standards of practice can always change. However, psychologists can look at general security features of companies to help them decide whether to use them. Psychologists need to ask themselves, among other questions, whether the company uses encryption to transmit data, requires password protection, identifies who has access to the stored records, and has a backup system.

In addition, the Health Information Technology for Economic and Clinical Health (HITECH) Act of 2009 has given incentives and penalties for healthcare systems to adopt electronic medical records systems. Although psychologists are not mandated by this law to keep records electronically, many psychologists work within healthcare systems that do use electronic records. Many details of electronic medical records have yet to be finalized. However, one of the major issues will be how to balance the need for sharing data with the need to protect sensitive health care information, such as mental health information.

Some psychologists communicate with their patients by email. For clinical and risk management purposes we urge psychologists to think through their policy of emailing patients carefully and ensure that they can point to a clinical justification for the use of email. This issue is discussed in more detail in Chapter 3 ("Competence").

However, here we are focusing only on storage of emails. We do not believe that it is necessary for psychologists to keep every email, such as routine emails about scheduling. However, it is prudent to keep a copy of clinically relevant materials, either by moving the email into an electronic folder or printing it as a hard copy. In addition to providing a more comprehensive record of treatment, retaining emails can have practical benefits as well. In one situation a client apparently cut and pasted the contents of an email to mislead his spouse concerning the recommendations of the psychologist. Fortunately, this psychologist had kept a hard copy of his emails and could use them to address the misrepresentation. Of course, psychologists providing forensic services should keep a copy of all communications, including all emails no matter how trivial they appear at the time.

Psychologists can use many different formats for keeping records. Most psychologists probably developed their recordkeeping habits from their first practicum or internship placements. Nonetheless, here are some recommendations about records.

Good records are comprehensive. That is, they include identifying information, a diagnosis (or presenting problem), a treatment plan, and sufficient information to establish the diagnosis (or understand the presenting problem) and to justify the treatment plan. The documentation should demonstrate to a knowledgeable observer that appropriate and competent services were delivered. When treating long-term patients, psychologists may find it important to periodically document the symptoms that justify continuing treatment and how the treatment is directed to address those on-going concerns.

Psychologists should always document consent (APA Ethics Code, Standard 3.10d, Informed Consent). Often this can be done by securing the patient's signature, indicating that he or she received a copy of the informed consent or therapeutic agreement. Psychologists who do not use such forms need to document in their records that their discussions with the patient fulfilled the informed consent requirements.

Whenever possible, records should be written objectively. That is, psychologists could describe problem behaviors (such as the circumstances under which they occur, frequency, point of onset and degree of disruption), including their impact (such as the impact on home, work, physical health, and relationships with others). As much as possible, the goals and objectives should be measurable and achievable (such as to reduce the frequency of panic attacks or increase the ability to leave home without having a panic attack). Psychologists should avoid more abstract goals, such as to increase awareness of the inner self, healing the inner child, or where there is id, there ego shall be.

Psychologists should create records with the expectation that the patient will someday read them (be prudent in phrasing and descriptions). Although psychologists own the paper on which the records are created, they do not have complete control over their disposition. The patient or a third party may someday read them and control who else may see them.

Psychologists should indicate the sources and reliability of information. For example, writing "husband alcoholic" is less desirable than writing "the patient reports that her husband is an alcoholic." Writing "patient is a time bomb" is less desirable than writing "patient reports he feels like a time bomb."

Records should be substantive, and the content should be related to the overall treatment goals. The quality of the documentation should increase as the degree of risk to the patient increases. As much as possible, the records should show the connection between the presenting problems and the treatment strategies. That does not mean that psychologists cannot change their opinions about a patient, alter their diagnoses, or change the treatment plan. However, psychologists should document why they made those alterations.

Finally, records should be retrievable, which means that if they are handwritten, they should be legible. Psychologists should also store them securely. The exact nature of the security precautions may vary according to the location of the office of the psychologist (high-crime or low-crime area), the overall security of the building, and other factors.

Challenges to Documentation Recommendations

Some psychologists may argue that our conception of documentation is flawed, that such extensive documentation takes too much time and produces little benefit to themselves or their patients. They would rather spend this time on other professional tasks. Furthermore, they may argue that our conception of documentation as improving patient welfare is exaggerated and that little thought or reflection needs to go into creating the patient's record.

Other psychologists may go further and say that aside from the time factor, keeping records in the manner we suggest actually degrades the quality of treatment. They may, for example, reference a statement from the American Psychoanalytic Association "Psychoanalysts refrain from documenting psychoanalytic treatment session by session. We believe that documenting the content of psychoanalysis seriously alters that treatment process and conflicts with fundamental clinical psychoanalytic skills" (1995, p. 1).

We believe that we are being realistic about the need for comprehensive records. Not every psychotherapy note has to be exhaustive, although any individual psychotherapy note should be comprehensible in the context of other adjacent notes. Concise notes are fine as long as they cover essential information. Many psychologists use abbreviations, shorthand notations, or symbols that create no problems as long as the psychologist can translate them easily. Sentence fragments are acceptable as long as others can discern the general meaning.

Also, we concede that we know many psychologists who have kept poor (or sometimes no) records for years without obvious negative consequences. That being said, we reiterate our belief in the importance of good records. Although we respect the conscientious intent of our psychoanalytic colleagues, we urge psychologists to recognize that the failure to comply with the minimum standards of psychology could result in a disciplinary action if the work of these psychologists were ever to come under scrutiny. We urge psychologists to make any decision to violate a standard or law carefully and to try to find a middle ground whereby they can fulfill their therapeutic ideals and at the same time adhere to the standards of the profession.

Furthermore, we have seen the negative consequences when no notes were kept or when they were poorly kept. We are aware of psychologists who have lost substantial insurance payments when a subsequent audit revealed no notes or inadequate notes. We know psychologists who have been disciplined because the quality of their records did not substantiate the quality of care delivered. We are aware of psychologists who confused cases because they could not recall specifics of the case and their own documentation was not adequate to give them useful information. In one case the practitioner was unable to read her own notes.

Bad things can happen to good psychologists. Our considered judgment is that psychologists and their patients are better off when good records are kept.

Documentation and Patient Factors

Experienced psychologists can appreciate the link between documentation and risk factors. Documentation should include information about the patient and should increase as the presence of high-risk patient characteristics increases. For example, a psychologist conducted the first interview with a highly emotional patient who told dramatic stories of past abuse, failed treatments, and suicidal ideation and gestures. Such information may suggest that this is a patient who may present the therapist with significant risk management problems. There is a greater likelihood that treatment will be ineffective (or iatrogenic); a complaint will be lodged; and the behavior of the psychologist will come under scrutiny, first by the patient and later by outside groups. Consequently, greater vigilance should be taken in showing the relevant facts about the patient and how they were integrated into the treatment plan.

Documentation and Contextual Factors

Documentation should include information on the context of treatment, such as whether the patient was being seen under duress, the expectations of the patient for treatment, and other factors. Some aspects of the context are assumed (practitioners in solo practice need not document that they are in solo practice). Other contextual factors should not be assumed, such as the presence of a cotreating psychopharmacologist or the involvement of other family members as collaterals in treatment.

> A psychologist referred a patient to the hospital in an emergency. He communicated his concerns over the phone to the physician in the emergency room, summarized salient concerns in a letter that was faxed to the attending physician, and followed up the fax by mailing the letter to the hospital the same day. (2.8)

Documentation and Individual Psychologist Factors

Documentation has its clearest impact on the individual psychologist factors. That is, it demonstrates clear thinking on the part of the treating psychologist. Many psychologists find that their conceptualization of cases changes as they begin to create thoughtful notes or as they review notes from previous sessions. Also, documentation can be considered part of the context of treatment when treating a patient in an institutional setting where cooperation among treating professionals is important.

> A psychologist was treating an intellectually disabled man who was displaying highly disruptive behavior in his employment in the sheltered workshop. The psychologist used a multiple baseline design to document the problem behaviors and the effect of the interventions. These data were useful in helping the facility determine that sufficient progress was being made so that they would continue the man's employment. (2.9)

At times, psychologists have found it helpful to involve a patient in the documentation process in an effort to help the patient understand the patterns that were occurring. The most obvious examples of this occur when psychologists ask patients to record behaviors or complete homework assignments. However, other psychologists have involved patients in their note-taking as a way to give feedback to patients on the psychologist's perceptions of the problems being faced or the defenses or strategies being used.

Documentation and the Detailed Case Example

As noted previously, documentation serves many purposes, including promoting the quality of patient care and providing protection to the psychologist in the event of an allegation of improper conduct.

Documentation becomes especially important with high-risk patients such as the one presented in Chapter 1. There is a possibility that Dr. Doe's treatment relationship will be disrupted and the treatment ended (either by Dr. Doe or the patient) with ill feelings. There is also a possibility that Dr. Doe's patient will make, or may actually succeed in, a suicide attempt. As noted previously, all records should describe the treatment goals and processes. In this case, the details of Dr. Doe's documentation should be increased to describe, among other things, an analysis of the risk of suicide and efforts to reduce that risk. In these situations Dr. Doe must balance the short-term risks of a suicide attempt with the long-term potential for therapeutic gain. Although a short-term hospitalization may reduce the risk of suicide, it might be clinically contraindicated. Dr. Doe's note-taking should take the form of the math teacher who was as interested in the process of thinking through the problem as in obtaining the correct answer. The advantages and disadvantages of treatment options should be candidly discussed along with the reasons why a particular action was chosen.

One of the shortcomings found in many records is that they do not always include the actions that the psychologist did not take. For example, although it is appropriate to describe why the intensity of outpatient treatment was increased, it may also be appropriate to describe why the patient was not hospitalized, relatives were not notified, or a referral for medication management was not made. It is as important to describe what was not done as what was done and why, especially if at a later date there is likelihood that what the psychologist did not do may be the basis of a complaint or lawsuit.

Consultation

At the lower levels of Bloom's taxonomy, psychologists view consultation as necessary when they feel a general "SOS" motivated by a fear of being overwhelmed by incompetence and danger to the patient. At the higher levels of Bloom's taxonomy, psychologists will be better able to specify the need for consultation more clearly and precisely. The type of consultation sought will vary according to the patient characteristics, context of treatment, and individual psychologist factors. Bloom's taxonomy of consultation is shown in Table 2.D.

Table 2.D
Bloom's Taxonomy of Consultation

Knowledge: You understand the need to get consultation for high-risk patients or when involved in high-risk situations.

Comprehension: You can describe to others what a consultation is and how to go about getting it.

Application: You know when a case-specific consultation would be recommended, from whom to get it, and how to present the case.

Analysis: You can identify the different types of consultations and whether they focus on the clinical features of the patient, the context of treatment, the items in your skill inventory, or more than one factor related to risk.

Synthesis: You view consultation as one part of the "system of protections" by which you better understand the patient; the context of treatment; the legal consequences of your behavior; or personal cognitive, emotional, or behavioral reactions that impact patient care.

Evaluation: In any particular case you can defend how consultation helped you promote patient welfare and avoided harm to both the patient and yourself.

As noted in Chapter 1, even experienced psychologists have a gap between their perceived and actual skill level. (Remember: Perceived psychologist factors are usually greater than actual psychologist factors.) Psychologists are only human, and like others, they risk overestimating their competence. These overestimates can be reduced if they receive high-quality feedback.

As stated earlier, consultation differs from supervision. In consultation the psychologist retains the independent ability to make decisions about a patient. In supervision the supervisor actually directs the treatment of an individual (e.g., an unlicensed trainee) who lacks the legal authority to act independently. Sometimes psychologists use these terms incorrectly and refer to peer consultation groups as peer supervision groups. These are important distinctions, however, because they are differentiated in law.

Consultation, like documentation, helps psychologists ensure that they are delivering services in accordance with a reasonable standard of care. To reach and maintain that goal of delivering services with a reasonable standard of care, psychologists need to embed themselves in a protective network that gives them high-quality feedback concerning their performance. The most obvious way to ensure that quality of feedback is to develop a working relationship with their patients who feel free to tell their psychologists how they are progressing toward their goals. Other sources of quality feedback include those with whom the psychologists share their offices or those whom they seek out for consultation.

Some consultations are done within an ongoing group; others are case specific. Ongoing consultation may occur in a peer consultation group or in a support group, such as Balint groups (Salinsky, 2009). We discuss peer consultation, support groups, and Balint groups in more detail in Chapter 3 ("Competence").

Often psychologists learn through incidental encounters with other psychologists. This may occur through attending continuing education programs, participating in journal clubs, supervising practicum students or interns, making professional presentations, being an adjunct or visiting faculty member, serving on the committee of the local or state psychological association, or volunteering on the board of a local mental health organization.

In addition to participating in these lifelong systems of protections, it may be necessary to get case-specific assistance on a particular patient through consultation. In case-specific consultation a psychologist seeks consultation according to the type of patient problem presented, whether it involves consequential (legal), clinical, or personal factors. We recommend that psychologists regularly seek consultation with high-risk patients even if it appears that they have the situation under control. Other situations in which consultation should be sought include when there is a therapeutic impasse, when there are reasons to perceive an increase in legal risks, when there is danger to self or others, or when the psychologist has strong reactions (either positive or negative) toward a patient. In those situations it is important that psychologists shore up their personal database and get feedback on the relevance or effectiveness of their personal skill inventory.

Consultants can help psychologists when nonrational factors begin to influence their case conceptualization or thinking patterns. All people are prone to using mental shortcuts, or heuristics, such as anchoring (having one's decisions influenced by an arbitrary starting point), the availability heuristic (allowing the ease with which an example comes to mind to influence one's perception that an event is likely to occur), or the confirmation bias (selectively looking for facts that support a predetermined conclusion (Rogerson, Gottlieb, Handelsman, Knapp, & Younggren, 2011). The problem is that these thinking errors can sometimes lead one astray and cause one to reach inaccurate conclusions. Consultants can sometimes help psychologists identify these errors though probing questions

Knapp and Gavazzi (2012) suggested that many psychologists should adopt a lower threshold for seeking consultation.[2] They noted the study by Stewart and Chambless (2008) that found that psychologists averaged a median 12 sessions before they began to reconsider a case by seeking a referral or consultation. However, Knapp and Gavazzi recommended that if patients fail to improve by the fourth session in the absence of obvious reasons or fail to develop a productive therapeutic relationship, it may be prudent to revisit the patient goals, the therapeutic method, and the treatment relationship. Of course, some patients fail to improve by the fourth session for reasons that are obvious and do not require a reconsideration of treatment. For example, a patient may have just been laid off from work, thus exacerbating a preexisting depression. Or a psychologist may need several sessions to develop a good working relationship with a distrustful teenager. In these situations, the reasons for the lack of progress or the lack of a good relationship are clear and do not trigger the four-session rule. However, if there is no progress or no good working relationship by the fourth session, we recommend a candid discussion with the patient about the perception of the relationship or the extent to which treatment goals are being met, a reconsideration of the case, or a consultation. Collecting systematic data on patient progress may supplement perceptions in identifying those patients who are failing to progress adequately (Lambert & Shimokawa, 2011).

In addition to the obvious patient benefit aspects, consultation can also be viewed as an important element of personal self-care. Feelings of stress can be diminished when psychologists have the opportunity to discuss their deepest professional fears and uncertainties with competent and trusted professionals.

A psychologist became director of a large mental health center, and he noticed that the staff often sought impromptu discussions with each other in the hallways and in a manner that threatened to violate patient privacy. Of course, he cautioned against that practice, but he also realized that the staff did not have regularly scheduled opportunities to discuss cases. The impromptu hallway consultations were the only opportunity the staff had to get feedback on cases. Consequently, the psychologist initiated supervision and peer consultation groups. (2.10)

[2] Portions from "Do checklists have a role in psychological practice" by S. Knapp and J. Gavazzi, 2012a, *The Pennsylvania Psychologist*, 72, pp. 8–9. Copyright 2012 by the Pennsylvania Psychological Association. Adapted with permission of the Pennsylvania Psychological Association.

The type and source of consultation may vary according to patient needs and the psychologist's dilemma. Consultation may be obtained from a practitioner who is also treating the patient, such as a psychiatrist who is prescribing medication for the patient. At other times, it may be desirable to have the consultant evaluate the patient directly, for example, to screen for neuropsychological disorders, to refer to a physician who will screen for the potential of a coexisting physical problem that may contribute to the patient's problems, or to refer to another mental health practitioner for a second opinion on the patient and services delivered.

Novice practitioners sometimes toss out a general cry for help. More experienced practitioners will clarify the "ask" or the nature of their request when they get a consultation. That does not mean that they will only accept responses related to their questions, but they help the consultant by describing the case and framing the issues as clearly and precisely as possible.

Not all consultations are created equal. Effective consultants are critical, honest, and skilled. Do not seek self-validation from "the choir" or close friends or those who have reasons not to be critical (e.g., a spouse, supervisee, or person with less training and experience). Also, consultations are effective if there is complete honesty about the situation, including information about transference or countertransference problems or therapeutic errors. Selective presentation of facts will lead to less than optimal advice, reminiscent of the computer adage "garbage in, garbage out."

Often it is helpful to receive consultation from a clinician with a different theoretical orientation to reduce the likelihood that ideological factors are blocking awareness of other sources of explanation. For example, it may benefit a cognitive behaviorally trained psychologist, at times, to seek consultation from a psychologist with a psychodynamic orientation. Often it is desirable to seek consultation from a psychiatrist or prescribing psychologist to determine if psychopharmacological options need to be considered.

At times it may be desirable to have the consultation in writing, especially if it involved a face-to-face interview with the patient. Many more specific consultations can be done verbally, although even in those circumstances it may be desirable to repeat back to the consultant the general nature of the recommendations and to record them accordingly.

General requests for information on electronic mailing lists need to be done judiciously. It may be quite appropriate to learn the titles of specific journal articles or books on a topic or the names of particular psychologists who have expertise in an area. However, detailed requests for comments on a particular case are problematic. It is hard to give enough detail to make the consultation meaningful, and the consultant on the electronic mailing list would not have access to therapy notes and other documentation. Furthermore, a psychologist risks violating patient privacy by giving that amount of detail.

Challenges to Consultation Recommendations

Some might argue that we are too quick to recommend consultation and that we fail to appreciate its costs to the practitioner in terms of the time spent seeking consultation with a colleague (and time spent giving consultation to a colleague in the event there is a reciprocal agreement). At other times, there are direct financial costs in paying for a consultation.

This point highlights the fact that risk management is not only a clinical and a practice management decision. That is, it may take time and cost money to get consultations. The same point could be made for the time put into informed consent and documentation. Of course, each psychologist will have to decide how much time to invest in each of these risk management strategies. Those psychologists who keep the number of high-risk patients in their practice low; have good risk management habits; know the APA Ethics Code, relevant state and federal laws, and the latest update on their applications; and are well trained will have less need to invest extra time and emotional energy on burdensome patient management issues that appear out of control.

Consultation and Risk Factors

Consultations can be specific for the dimension of the risk factors and can include requests for information on the patient's characteristics (e.g., Is this patient's behavior influenced by his or her physical condition?), context of treatment (e.g., Are there special circumstances dealing with high-conflict families that I am missing here?), or the individual psychologist factors (e.g., Am I overestimating my competence to deal with these types of patients?).

Some examples of how consultation was used effectively are provided next.

A psychologist was treating a patient who, during the course of treatment, was diagnosed with fibromyalgia. He requested information from the electronic mailing list of his state psychological association concerning books or articles about this disorder. (2.11)

A psychologist was asked to treat a Korean woman. Although he had little experience or knowledge of Korean culture, no other psychologist in his city did either. Consequently, he accepted the patient but consulted with a Korean American psychologist concerning unique cultural factors that might influence conceptualization of patient needs and implementation of the treatment goals. (2.12)

A psychologist accepted a child in therapy. During the course of therapy, the parents decided to divorce and became involved in a bitter child custody dispute in which, among other things, allegations of parent alienation syndrome were made. The intensity of the anger of the parents shocked the psychologist and she sought consultation from an expert concerning the unique factors to consider when treating families with allegations of parent alienation syndrome. (2.13)

An academician received a request for a consultation from a former student/family therapist who recently went through a difficult divorce. While treating a couple for marital therapy, this former student developed a very strong negative reaction to the husband. The former student wondered if her reaction was influenced by her own recent divorce. She spoke to the psychologist/teacher about the intensity of her feelings that alarmed her. After speaking with her former teacher she transferred the couple and sought therapy for herself. (2.14)

Fortunately, this therapist had sufficient insight to seek input from a trusted professional. At other times psychologists have allowed their personal skill inventory to become obsolete over time or to be filled with their personal but often faulty perspectives on life, which may have been influenced by their own continuing personal difficulties. For example, some psychologists are not aware of the latest research in therapeutic or assessment techniques. This obsolescence is more likely to occur among psychologists who are "outliers" or who do not participate in continuing education activities (except to the minimum required by a licensing board), who do not participate in professional association activities, or who otherwise isolate themselves.

When preparing to receive consultations, some psychologists engage in a comprehensive treatment review to help them formulate areas of concern to discuss with the consultant.

One such system is the MOST CARE model suggested by Clayton and Bongar (1994; Medical/medication needs; Overall management of the case; Specific concerns; Therapeutic alliance; Crisis intervention plans in case of an emergency; Alternative, adjunctive, or additional treatments; Risk/benefit analysis; Ethical or legal considerations). Other competent psychologists use other formats such as the BASIC ID (Lazarus, 1989) or the PAINT system (Ginsburg, Albano, Findling, Kratochvil, & Walkup, 2005) that is used for adolescents. (The PAINT acronym refers to Presenting problem; Antecedents and consequences; Identification of goals, strengths, and weaknesses; Noting the context; and Treatment data).

Consultation and the Detailed Case Example

In the high-risk case presented in Chapter 1, consultation becomes very important. Ongoing consultation and social support are necessary to handle the frustration that this patient will likely generate. On a personal level Dr. Doe might be overwhelmed with anger and then guilt because of the anger. An ongoing support system can help to reduce those feelings, normalize them, and allow Dr. Doe to use those feelings to better understand the clinical dynamics of the patient.

In addition, the techniques for handling the case suggest the need for a consultant with detailed information and knowledge about dialectical behavior therapy or another treatment for borderline personality disorder. Consultation is especially important whenever patients show life-endangering qualities. The general rule is never treat life-endangering patients alone. Always consult with others.

Synergy of the Risk Management Strategies

The three risk management strategies that we have described have a synergistic effect; they are not isolated or disembodied techniques. They are designed to promote patient welfare, avoid harm, and help psychologists better fulfill their obligations to patients. For example, documentation should indicate that informed consent was obtained, that consultation was sought, or that consultation may be obtained on how to maximize patient investment in the treatment process.

We have already described how informed consent can promote patient autonomy. Typically, psychologists do not think of documentation or consultation as ways to promote patient autonomy. Nonetheless, in some circumstances they can be. For example, patients may be involved in the content of the documentation as an exercise in helping both parties articulate the problems or progress in treatment. This is not typically done, but psychologists may be more creative in these kinds of strategies if they remember that documentations (or consultations or informed consent) can be substantive acts that further patient welfare.

RISK MANAGEMENT AND DEFENSIVE PRACTICE

Defensive medicine refers to "a deviation from sound medical practice that is induced primarily by a threat of liability" (Studdert et al., 2005, p. 2609). It can include *assurance behaviors,* such as supplying additional services of marginal or no value. As applied to psychology, it can apply to obtaining consultations for a case in which the psychologists only want to say they got a consultation; they really do not expect the patient to benefit from the consultation. It can also consist of *avoidance behaviors,* such as refusing to treat certain patients only because they have a higher risk of filing an allegation of misconduct.

Assurance Behaviors

Some readers may claim that the risk management strategies that we are suggesting are an assurance form of defensive medicine that drives up health care costs and provides little or no benefit to patients. They may claim that the documentation and consultation recommendations contribute little or nothing to patient welfare. Some may even argue that they degrade services because they divert attention and resources away from patient care and may disrupt relationships with patients.

Depending on the circumstances, the risk management strategies we review may or may not improve the quality of treatment. If these strategies are used only to provide a sense of personal safety, they are unlikely to increase the quality of health care and may increase costs. We defer to the clinical judgment of psychologists as to when or how to apply the risk management recommendations. They are in the best position to determine how much time they need to spend on documentation or consultation for any particular patient. They will be more likely to make a good decision if they are informed by an accurate self-perception and their services are delivered in the context of a system of safety with redundant checks on their behavior.

Furthermore, if these risk management strategies are applied pro forma only for defensive purposes and divorced from any overarching philosophy of patient care, we agree they would risk becoming clinically meaningless or unhelpful defensive medicine exercises. However, we urge psychologists to consider the risk management strategies from the standpoint of Bloom's taxonomy. Informed consent, documentation, and consultation, if done at the higher levels of Bloom's taxonomy, are integrated into and improve overall patient care. At the lower levels, these risk management strategies may save psychologists from complaints and lawsuits but may add little to the management of the case. Remember that caring for patients not only means a feeling of concern but also diligence ("conscientiousness, self-scrutiny, and a concern for excellence"; Peteet, 2004, p. 53) in meeting patient needs.

Avoidance Behaviors

Critics may also claim that our recommendation to show discretion in treating high-risk patients represents avoidance behavior that results in denial of care to vulnerable patients. Often these patients are from historically disadvantaged groups that have had a high rate of victimization. Instead of reaching out to help these individuals, it could be argued that our risk management recommendations tend to discourage psychologists from treating them by encouraging psychologists to refer them to community agencies that are traditionally underfunded and often staffed with uncredentialed mental health providers.

We are not urging avoidance of all high-risk patients. Indeed, the moral principle of distributive justice (the fair distribution of health care resources; Beauchamp & Childress, 2009) would suggest that special efforts should be made to treat those needing treatment, those whom other health care providers might avoid. However, the moral principle of distributive justice needs to be balanced with the moral principles of beneficence (promoting welfare of others) and nonmaleficence (avoiding harming others).

Consequently, we are saying that psychologists should make an informed decision to treat such patients and to recognize that sometimes, despite their best intentions, their treatment may not help and may, in fact, harm them. Good intentions are not enough; they need to be informed good intentions. Even informed good intentions can lead to angry patients who look for ways to retaliate.

In addition to personal responses to individual patients, we ask each psychologist to consider the public policy issues that are involved. We agree that public mental health services are underfunded. Psychologists can play an important role especially in a volunteer capacity in promoting better patient access to quality psychological services.

SEVEN ESSENTIAL POINTS TO REMEMBER

1. The purposes of informed consent are to (a) maximize patient participation in the treatment process, (b) avoid creating a sense of betrayal, (c) explain office policies, and (d) explain billing and payment policies ahead of time.

2. Informed consent, which is a process, not a one-time event, is especially important when conducting evaluations with consequences.

3. It is difficult to overestimate the importance of good documentation.

4. Good records should explain what was done and the reasoning behind those decisions. In high-risk situations, good records should also explain what was not done and why not.

5. When in doubt, get high-quality consultation that focuses on the areas of clinical knowledge, disciplinary consequences, or a strong personal skill inventory.

6. Psychologists can often get better consultations from persons who are objective, not beholden to them, willing to be critical of what has been done, or who view things from a different perspective and value patient welfare above all.

7. Psychologists will be better able to apply the risk management recommendations if they fully understand what informed consent, documentation, and consultation mean.

CHAPTER 3: COMPETENCE

Competence means the ability to perform according to the standards of the profession. Pope and Brown (1996) described competence as involving three factors: knowledge, emotional competence, and technical skills (which could include technological competence for those who use technology in the delivery of psychological services). We would add a fourth factor, cultural competence, which involves specialized knowledge, technical skills, and attitudes about diverse groups.

Generally, psychologists' graduate programs and supervised experiences will have helped them acquire the necessary knowledge and technical skills, and their mastery of the content for the psychology licensing examination will have furthered their goal of becoming knowledgeable. Typically, psychologists' areas of competent practice are derived from the content of their graduate programs, practica, internships, and other supervised experiences, subject to some kind of external control. After becoming licensed and with some experience, most psychologists feel comfortable stating that they are competent in certain areas of practice, such as in the treatment and assessment of adults, health psychology, neuropsychology, or another domain of practice. It may be helpful to consider competence from the standpoint of Bloom's taxonomy (see Table 3.A).

Table 3.A
Bloom's Taxonomy of Competence

Knowledge: You can identify the mutually agreed-upon goals (based on the patient's diagnosis or presenting problems) and the professional services (such as interventions) that should be used.

Understanding: You can describe or define the goals of treatment or assessment and describe the interventions used.

Application: You can implement an intervention appropriate to the treatment goals with a patient in the context of a professional relationship.

Analysis: You can identify the components and sequence of the interventions that you implemented, the elements of your professional relationships, and their relationship to specific agreed-upon treatment or assessment goals given your individual factors, including emotional resources, time resources, and skill inventory appropriate for this patient in this context.

Synthesis: You can integrate the components of your intervention or assessment within the context of an overall professional relationship given your individual psychologist factors, including emotional resources, time resources, and skill inventory appropriate for this patient in this context.

Evaluation: You can justify the assessment and intervention strategies you used, how they were related to the patient's problems and goals, and how they were appropriate considering the totality of your individual psychologist factors and their appropriateness for this patient in this context.

Furthermore, some psychologists are specialists in that they have acquired more expertise in a certain domain of practice through supervision, course work, or postdoctoral training. Some psychologists indicate their area of specialty by earning a diploma from the American Board of Professional Psychology or a certificate from the College of Professional Psychology. Specialists often spend a large portion of their time working in their area of specialty.

At first appearance it looks like competence is identical to the individual psychologist factors (personal data set and personal skill inventory) described in Chapter 1 ("Calculations of Risk"). However, competence is not a fixed entity but varies according to the unique needs of the patients, context of services, and the life circumstances of the psychologist. For example, psychologists with a very strong personal skill inventory will be able to work well with a wide range of patients. However, even those psychologists may encounter challenging patients or find themselves in situations beyond their range of effectiveness, thus increasing their risk of practicing incompetently. On the other hand, psychologists with a more limited personal skill inventory may be aware of their limitations and consequently select patients or situations carefully and ensure that their skills will be applied where the likelihood of success is high.

> When the spouse of a highly respected psychologist became disabled, the entire burden of family income fell on him, including the burden of paying for his children's college expenses. He began to work longer hours and accept patients whom he ordinarily would have referred elsewhere. He accepted a high-conflict family, and because he lacked the time to respond quickly to the many phone calls, he became alienated from one of the parents. A complaint before the licensing board followed.
>
> Although the complaint was not founded and he was exonerated by the licensing board, it nonetheless represented a treatment failure and a burden for the psychologist to defend himself before a licensing board. Although the psychologist might have been competent to deal with this family when his life was less hectic, he was not competent to deal with them when his professional resources were more taxed. (3.1)

Awareness of the extent of one's competence is one of the factors in a psychologist's individual skill inventory. The care with which psychologists make decisions about the application of their skills depends on how accurately they judge their abilities and resources. Those psychologists who consistently overestimate their abilities or resources will find themselves in situations in which they are less likely to perform competently.

Fortunately, most patients have fairly routine problems. Nonetheless, psychologists need to be cautious when dealing with high-risk patients, such as those who are involved in litigation, present a threat of harming themselves or others, or have a serious personality disorder. When psychologists are asked to provide services outside of their zone of competence, they should refer that patient to another provider for evaluation or treatment or at least consult with a more experienced colleague. Psychologists should know when to pass up the opportunity to treat certain patients. Some patients have complex needs and are best treated in an institution where a team approach is available that includes coordinating services during psychologists' absences and emergencies, 24-hour coverage, availability of psychiatric and medical care, and access to hospital or day treatment programs if needed. Psychologists with solo practices who see such patients will need more skills or more resources to help them. That is not to say that psychologists should refer all of their patients with serious personality disorders or other serious disorders. Nonetheless, if they do accept them as patients, they need to appreciate the emotional and time demands that they will make. Many psychologists restrict themselves to only one or two such patients at any given time.

> A psychologist agreed to accept a patient with a serious personality disorder and chronic suicidal ideation for therapy. The psychologist was proficient in the treatment of such disorders, had received advanced training, and had a strong network of supportive professionals. The next day she received a referral of another patient with a similar symptom presentation. She declined this referral, recognizing that her ability to respond to the needs of this patient (and indeed her entire caseload) might be compromised by the presence of one more highly disturbed patient in her caseload.
>
> The psychologist recognized the limits of her individual psychologist factors. She had the self-awareness to understand that she could not help everyone. She avoided "runaway compassion," or the belief that she has to help everyone. She also understood that the legal right to treat does not mean a legal mandate to treat. (3.2)

It is common for one parent in a high-conflict family to want a psychologist to assess or treat the child and the other parent to object. Even if the psychologist is legally allowed to assess or treat that child, at times the family conflicts make the very act of providing services iatrogenic. Sometimes it is best not to assess or treat. Psychologists need to weigh these situations carefully and consider whether their ability to help the child will outweigh the harm caused by the added tension of providing services to a family that is partially opposed to these efforts.

There are few substitutes for honest self-reflection. Psychologists should think about their strengths and where they want to concentrate their efforts ahead of time. They should solicit and consider quality feedback (from patients and peers) on their strengths and weaknesses as they relate to their desired areas of practice.

EMOTIONAL COMPETENCE

The American Psychological Association's (APA's) "Ethical Principles of Psychologists and Code of Conduct" (hereinafter referred to as the APA Ethics Code;

APA, 2010a) requires psychologists to be alert to early signs of personal problems that may prevent them from fulfilling their professional obligations. Sometimes unresolved personal problems can lead psychologists to act impulsively or to be insensitive to the needs of their patients. If psychologists neglect their self-care, they may be more prone to disrespect their patients, denigrate the importance of their work, feel an array of dysphoric emotions, or make more clinical mistakes (Pope & Vasquez, 2005).

Compassion fatigue is especially likely to occur when psychologists treat patients who have had severe traumas or who otherwise have great personal needs. Psychologists may need to distance themselves from their patients' problems to be effective. They may need to limit the number of needy, seriously disturbed, or taxing patients with whom they work. Psychologists' individual factors may be adequate to take one patient with a serious personality disorder, but by doing so they limit their flexibility in taking on a second such patient.

When they become aware of personal problems (e.g., fatigue, burnout, depression, or substance abuse) that could significantly impair the quality of their work, psychologists note that the APA Ethics Code requires that they address such problems and in the meantime limit, suspend, or terminate work-related duties. Psychologists are especially likely to make errors when they are undergoing personal crises or stresses. Paradoxically, people are more likely to engage in denial when they are emotionally compromised, thus making it more difficult for them to identify their vulnerable state.

> A psychologist had a friend from graduate school who had just gone through a divorce. He contacted his psychologist friend, and they had lunch together. It was a way for the psychologist to express his concern for his friend and to offer assistance or nurturance if it was needed. (3.3)

Of course, the goal should not be just to avoid impairment but to maximize physical and emotional health. Psychologists need to be aware of their physical and mental needs. They benefit when they take routine care of their basic physical needs such as diet, exercise, and medical care and make certain that they feel adequately refreshed in the morning. Psychologists should show equal concern for their mental health by taking time to nurture their support systems and enjoy their friends and family members.

Ideally, psychologists will be continually moving toward greater self-awareness through self-reflection. Of course, self-awareness can often come through supervision or personal therapy. However, it may also come through keeping a diary of important clinical experiences, group consultation, or Balint groups (see the website of the American Balint Society, www.americanbalintsociety.org), which is a structured format for health professionals to reflect on the emotional reactions generated from their work.

Unfortunately, some psychologists are unable to meet the minimum standards of their profession as a result of physical or mental disabilities. Fortunately, many licensing boards or state psychological associations have developed colleague assistance programs. The nature and procedures for these programs varies from state to state, but typically they provide a means for impaired psychologists to receive treatment and offer the option that they can continue in or return to professional service (APA, 2006).

COMPETENCE WITH DIVERSE POPULATIONS

As the American population becomes more diverse, all psychologists will be more likely to encounter patients from diverse cultural, ethnic, or religious backgrounds. Ideally, all persons who request mental health services should be able to receive them from someone who respects and tries to understand their culture.

Griner and Smith (2006) found that psychotherapists improved their outcomes when they adapted their interventions to account for cultural factors. Psychologists will be more effective when they recognize that patients from diverse backgrounds can express their distress and react to psychological treatment in unique ways. Similarly, psychologists need to account for unique diversity variables when conducting assessments. They should be aware of the unique needs or perspectives of patients who are from diverse religious backgrounds, are members of sexual minorities, or have physical and mental disabilities, and they should strive to learn from such patients about how their special cultural expressions may influence their mental health services. Psychologists should invite diverse patients to share their perspectives and collaborate with them in understanding their needs and appreciating how their cultural background interacts with their socioeconomic status, educational level, sexual orientation, and personal history to form their unique identity (Brown, 2009). Psychologists are encouraged to follow the APA "Guidelines on Multicultural Education, Training, Research, Practice, and Organizational Change for Psychologists" (APA, 2003) and "Guidelines for Psychological Practice With Lesbian, Gay, and Bisexual Clients" (APA, 2012c).

Fortunately, information on how to respond more effectively to individuals from cultural or linguistic minorities is emerging (see also Hays, 2009; Stuart, 2004). Also, a body of literature is emerging on the unique clinical concerns of patients with same-sex attraction. Psychologists will be more effective if they know this literature (see, e.g., APA, Task Force on Appropriate Therapeutic Responses to Sexual Orientation, 2009; Lasser & Gottlieb, 2004; Lyons, Bieschke, Dendy, Worthington, & Georgemiller, 2010; Pachankis & Goldfried, 2004; Schneider, Brown, & Glassgold, 2002).

The Ethics Code allows limited exceptions to competence that can be made in emergencies or when working with closely related problems in underserved geographic areas (Standard 2.02, Providing Services in Emergencies).

In emergencies, when psychologists provide services to individuals for whom other mental health services are not available and for which psychologists have not obtained the necessary training, psychologists may provide such services in order to ensure that services are not denied. The services are discontinued as soon as the emergency has ended or appropriate services are available.

Nonetheless, psychologists who continue to deliver services under these circumstances should acquire competence through study and supervision or consultation.

MAINTAINING COMPETENCE

How do psychologists ensure that they are maintaining their competence (keeping up with the knowledge base of the field, ensuring adequate technical skills, and maintaining emotional competence)? Knapp and Keller (2004) found that psychologists rated interaction with colleagues as the source that did the most to develop their professional skills. Other sources were continuing education (CE) workshops, newsletters, professional and scientific conventions, and journal articles. Of course, these global ratings failed to give specifics concerning the type of colleague interactions, CE programs, or other sources and how they related to the development or maintenance of any particular skill. Nonetheless, the ratings suggest that professional development is likely to be enhanced by participation in activities that increase one's connections with peers, such as through peer consultation groups, electronic mailing lists, or attendance at professional meetings.

Moreover, the value of CE should not be minimized. Most psychologists reported that they learned something relevant to their professional practices through CE programs and were able to translate that learning into their professional practices (Neimeyer, Taylor, & Philip, 2010). Also, in their detailed review, Marinopoulos et al. (2007) reported that CE did improve the effectiveness of physicians. When looking at those studies with adequate methodology, Marinopoulos et al. concluded that more than two thirds of the CE activities improved knowledge, and many resulted in long-term improvements in behavior as measured by improved skills or patient outcomes. The most effective programs included case presentations or participant interaction, case discussions, and opportunities to practice skills learned (Mansouri & Lockyer, 2007).

The failure to maintain one's competence has been called *practitioner decay*, although that might not be the best term to describe this phenomenon. It is true that some psychologists may have been competent at one time, but their knowledge base has become obsolete over time. However, it is also possible that some were not entirely competent from the beginning. Choudhry, Fletcher, and Soumerai (2005) found that the quality of performance of physicians was inversely related to their years of practicing. Also, Handelsman (1997) found that Colorado psychologists who had been licensed more than 15 years were more likely than the average licensee to have an ethics charge levied against them. Cullari (2009) found a similar trend among psychologists in Pennsylvania.

The reasons for this vulnerability to lapse into substandard quality of service delivery are not known. Perhaps over time psychologists overestimate their competence. They can compensate for this tendency by receiving high-quality feedback. It is important for psychologists to embed themselves in a *system of protection*.

REDUNDANT SYSTEMS OF PROTECTION[1]

The literature on medical errors may be relevant here. According to the Institute of Medicine (Kohn, Corrigan, & Donaldson, 2000), between 44,000 and 98,000 hospital patients die each year because of preventable medical errors. These errors included such mistakes as administering an incorrect medication (either the wrong medication was given to the patient; the patient was given a medication that was known to cause an allergic reaction in that individual; the incorrect dose of a medication was given; or the patient was given medications in combination when it should have been known that the interaction of these medications would have an adverse effect). Other errors included laboratories that mixed up the results from patients, surgeons who operated on the wrong patient, and more.

These medical errors were frequently caused by the breakdown of communication among staff members. For example, a physician might not read the nurse's notation in the patient's chart; a pharmacist might not read the physician's prescription accurately (perhaps the pharmacist was in a hurry or perhaps he or she misread the physician's scrawl); or a physician who had a history of scolding nurses who questioned his or her orders or who asked questions about patient care might intimidate other health care personnel from presenting useful information relevant to patient outcomes.

In the ideal system, the likelihood of an error is reduced when health care personnel check on each other. For example, if physicians order an unusual prescription of medication, pharmacists or nurses should feel free to double-check with them.

These system wide problems occur primarily in institutional settings. The interventions include medical procedures in which patients are essentially passive participants and which, of necessity, involve many health care professionals. These situations directly apply to psychologists working in hospitals or large agencies.

On the surface these findings do not appear applicable to outpatient practices. However, further thought suggests otherwise. Even those psychologists who work in a solo practice should not consider themselves as working alone with patients. First, the patient should be part of the treatment team and should feel free or encouraged to help direct his or her treatment by identifying goals, giving feedback on what works and what does not work, and more. Second, psychologists should, when appropriate, involve family members or significant others in the treatment process, perhaps as collateral contacts, if they, in consultation with the patient, believe that such contacts would be necessary to ensure the adequate treatment. Third, psychologists should be part of an ongoing consultation group that will give feedback on their general skill level, needs of particular cases, and ongoing professional development in assessment and treatment.

---

[1] From "Could the Titanic Disaster Have Been Avoided? Or Promoting Patient Welfare Through a Systems Approach," by S. Knapp, 2003, August, *The Pennsylvania Psychologist, 63*, pp. 4, 18, 36. Copyright 2003 by the Pennsylvania Psychological Association. Adapted with permission of the Pennsylvania Psychological Association.

Finally, psychologists are strongly encouraged to create a redundant system of protection when possible. For example, one psychologist made a point of randomly double-checking his scoring whenever he administered a standardized psychometric test. Another psychologist routinely gave patients with a risk of suicide a brief screening instrument of suicidal ideation to supplement the interviews he had with them. Sometimes the screening instrument picked up suicidal ideation that was not detected in the interview.

It is also possible to view the three essential components of risk management as a method of increasing redundant systems of protection. For example, obtaining informed consent should involve patients in the decision-making process and ensure that they feel comfortable raising issues relevant to the progress and success of therapy. Also, documentation ideally should be a time to reflect on the intervention and determine the extent to which goals are being met. Finally, consultation, which is especially important when working with high-risk patients or when working in high-risk contexts, could be considered another form of redundant protection insofar as the consultant gives feedback on the quality of treatment provided.

CONSCIENTIOUS CONTINUING EDUCATION

All psychologists want to continue to grow and improve as they progress through their careers. They can do that through "reflective practice, ongoing learning, critical thinking, and self-care" (Elman, Illfelder-Kaye, & Robiner, 2005, p. 373). However, even among the best practitioners, a gap will usually exist between the best known intervention and how they commonly practice. The top practitioners and researchers may have cutting-edge knowledge of what works best with a particular disorder, but there is a gap of at least a year before that knowledge gets published, a longer gap before the most well-read practitioners read and incorporate the findings into their practices, and a still longer gap before the practices become generally incorporated by the average practitioner. To the extent that a new procedure requires specialized training and supervision, the time period will be further extended.

Psychologists sometimes say that there is so much to learn, and they have limited time to invest in CE. We recommend that psychologists focus on those situations, patients, or problems that they are most likely to encounter in their practices. Rather than focus on low-risk or low-probability events, it is better for them to invest their time on the high-risk or high-probability situations.

For example, every psychologist can expect to encounter patients with a high risk for suicide or who are perpetrators or victims of domestic violence, and competence in the evaluation and treatment of such patients is essential. The likelihood, however, of encountering a duty-to-protect situation in which a patient threatens an identifiable third party (other than in domestic abuse situations) is far lower. Consequently, it would be more prudent for the average psychologist to take proportionally more CE courses in suicidology or domestic violence than in situations that have lower risk or a lower probability of occurring.

MOVING INTO NEW AREAS OF PRACTICE

Periodically psychologists may wish to branch out and practice in areas of psychology in which they did not receive education, training, or supervision in their graduate programs. Although psychologists may have acquired general skills that apply to that new area of practice, they may need additional study, training, consultation, or supervised experience to become competent. The general rule is that professionals should seek consultation, guidance, or some kind of external review of their competence before stepping outside their areas of competence. The reason for this is that psychologists must acknowledge their own vulnerability to error and misinterpretation. When they overestimate their skill level and areas of competence, they become especially vulnerable to allegations of incompetence should something go wrong. Consultation with other professionals is a useful way to gain feedback on skills.

Psychologists can acquire a specialty credential from well-respected organizations such as the American College of Professional Psychology, the American Board of Professional Psychology, or similar organizations. Such credentials are typically based on a work product demonstrating professional achievement. As a word of caution, however, it may not be worthwhile to acquire credentials from "vanity boards" that "grandparent" a large number of practitioners in exchange for a fee but have low competency standards.

Of course, a special credential does not exist for all areas of specialty or subspecialty. Consequently, psychologists sometimes will need to create their own system of feedback. Belar et al. (2001) described a self-assessment program designed to help psychologists determine the competencies they need before expanding into clinical health psychology. The methodology they used is applicable for psychologists who are considering moving into other new areas of practice, too. Some of the questions Belar et al. encouraged psychologists to ask are whether they have the necessary basic scientific knowledge (biological, cognitive behavioral, social, and developmental bases of behavior and their interactions), basic knowledge of interventions, technical skills in implementing the interventions, and knowledge of the unique features of the professional context (policy, ethical, legal, and other professional issues concerning the service).

Our description of competence according to Bloom's taxonomy may be relevant here as well. Ideally, when psychologists expand into a new area of treatment or assessment they will be performing at the higher levels within the taxonomic system before they practice independently. That is, they will be able to analyze, synthesize, and evaluate the patient, context, and skill factors needed for effective professional service.

EMERGING AREAS OF PRACTICE

Emerging areas of practice for psychologists include health psychology, personal coaching, psychopharmacology, or psychotherapy via telecommunication devices. The APA Ethics Code provides very general guidelines for moving into new areas of practice, stating that psychologists should "undertake relevant education, training, supervised experience, consultation, or study" (Standard 2.01c, Boundaries of Competence).

Today, psychologists have expanded opportunities to move into new areas of practice, such as electronic media, which could include face-to-face video therapy, other forms of digital therapy, or telephone therapy. Others are moving into personal coaching for which well-developed standards of practice have not yet been established. It is not feasible to go back to school to get a doctorate in coaching, in part because no such specialized academic programs exist. Nonetheless, psychologists may need some in-depth training and supervision in the new area of practice. They need to engage a psychologist consultant with expertise in the area they are moving into for a year or two so that they can be assured that their lack of knowledge or technical skill does not harm clients.

Telepsychology

More psychologists are providing services through telecommunication devices whether it is by email, face-to-face video therapy, telephone, or other distance services. We acknowledge some advantages of telehealth services, yet present some caveats in the paragraphs that follow. Proponents of telehealth note that this means of providing services makes it possible to reach more people who could not otherwise get therapy because they live in rural areas with little access to health care professionals; have physical disabilities that make traveling difficult; or need a specialist and none practices in their geographical area. Furthermore, some patients may prefer or benefit from a written mode of communication, such as email, because they feel they can be more honest than they could in face-to-face communications, and psychologists have more time to think about and phrase their responses carefully, including the option of referring to the exact words that the patient used. In addition, email may be more convenient for patients in that it may allow more flexibility in scheduling. Finally, there is evidence that it can be effective. Although the outcome research on distant therapy is just beginning, Brenes, Ingram, and Danhauer (2011) reviewed data comparing telephone with traditional face-to-face therapy for a variety of conditions and found them compatible in terms of outcomes. In addition, technology is being used effectively as an adjunct to treatment. For example, Aguilera and Muñoz (2011) used automatic text messages to patients undergoing cognitive behavior therapy. The texts asked them about their mood, positive thoughts, pleasant activities, and more. The patients were to respond to the inquiries as soon as feasible. Gulec et al. (2011) used an Internet-based intervention for the maintenance of women recovering from anorexia. The program involved education and peer support, and a chat group (monitored by a professional). Luxton, McCann, Bush, Mishkind, and Reger (2011) described many applications for smartphones, including those that track mood and alcohol use, give information on specific problem areas, and teach relaxation exercises or other applications. Wade, Oberjohn, Conaway, Osinska, and Bangert (2011) reported on parent coaching using Skype for families with children with brain injuries. It involved 10 to 14 sessions of structured parental coaching. Outcomes were slightly better than for traditional face–to–face coaching.

Nonetheless, as we noted previously, psychologists will want to consider several problems and cautions associated with telehealth. Before using telehealth psychologists need to ask a series of questions such as whether they can verify the age and identity of the client (could the person be a minor posing as an adult); if informed consent has been given, including knowledge of limits of confidentiality and any limits of third-party reimbursement (although Medicare and the medical assistance programs in some states will pay for distant therapy under limited circumstances, most commercial insurance companies do not); and whether the modality is appropriate for the concerns of the client.

Although the outcomes for distant therapy are promising, psychologists cannot assume that all of the positive outcomes for in-person therapy necessarily generalize to telepsychology. In addition, psychotherapy via telecommunication modalities may be contraindicated for some patients, such as those with serious personality disorders or serious mental illnesses (Rummell & Joyce, 2010). Harris and Younggren (2011) noted that "it would be prudent to assume that patients who present high risks in more traditional contexts may not be good candidates for remote treatment" (p. 417). Psychologists can better judge the helpfulness of a distant modality service with patients they know well (Harris & Younggren, 2011). Some patients with complex issues are better off being treated in a location where the psychologist has access to emergency or support services. Psychologists do not want to be in a situation in which a patient needs an immediate psychiatric hospitalization, and they do not know any local psychiatrists, any of the local hospitals that accept psychiatric patients, or even the laws governing psychiatric admissions in that state. Ethical practice would dictate that if psychologists practice using telecommunication modalities, it is incumbent on them to know how to access local emergency resources if needed.

We noted previously some ways that professionals have used email to help patients. However, psychologists should be able to articulate a clear professional rationale for emailing patients. For example, we know of one complaint before a state licensing board in which the emails between a psychologist and her patient were used, among other evidence, to show that her relationship with the patient had been transformed from a professional to a social relationship. More information on email and professional boundaries can be found in Chapter 4 ("Multiple Relationships and Boundaries"). As we go to press, APA is working on guidelines for the practice of telepsychology, which may become an indispensable resource.

Psychologists also need to ensure that they and their patients understand the confidentiality limits of whatever electronic media they use. For example, if a psychologist emails patients, it may be prudent to review with them the security the patients have on their own computer. The psychologist may ask, for example, if the patients have a firewall and a passcode and whether other people in their home have access to the computer.

Of course, psychologists may use standardized patient background or intake forms or brief screening instruments online, as long as they are interpreted with their limitations in mind. However, they should not use formal psychological tests online. Psychologists would not know if the person took the assessment under conditions that approximated those of in-person administration or if the patient asked a friend or family member to respond. Consequently, the norms that apply for in-person psychological assessments should not be used to evaluate assessments completed through distant means. Test publishers also expect psychologists to exercise reasonable control over the copyrighted materials.

Finally, the issue of compliance with state laws is complicated. To our knowledge, no psychologist has been disciplined by a licensing board for practicing psychology without a license when providing distant services to a patient who lives in a state where the psychologist does not have a license. Nonetheless, informal opinions from many members of licensing boards suggest that they believe that those boards do have the right to prosecute such psychologists. On the other hand, a legal review of criminal and civil cases, unrelated to licensing board issues, shows a trend toward allowing interstate practice through distant means (Harris & Younggren, 2011). Until the legal issues are settled psychologists are encouraged to consult and be prepared to provide a rationale when providing such services.

Psychologists are better able to provide distant services if they take several steps to ensure the usefulness of their services. First, they need to know how to use telecommunication technologies, including knowledge of emoticons and abbreviations. They need to have reasonable privacy protections and a back-up plan for handling failures in technology. For example, psychologists could have a phone number for the patient (and the patient should have the psychologist's phone number) in the event that a computer crashes.

Psychologists are advised to have a detailed informed consent form that identifies potential risks from telepsychology, applicable confidentiality laws, release of information procedures, how electronic patient communications will be stored, and when or how often the psychologist will respond to messages. Psychologists should also ensure that they comply with the laws of the state in which the patient is located. Compliance means not only the idiosyncratic laws governing telepsychology (Baker & Bufka, 2011) but also the laws regarding reporting suspected child abuse, involuntary psychiatric hospitalizations, responses to subpoenas, duty-to-warn or duty-to-protect laws, and any unique conditions that an individual state places on telecommunications.

Coaching and Performance-Focused Interventions

Coaching refers to "behavioral science based interventions to individuals who are seeking to improve their lives or their performance" (Harris, n.d.-a, p. 1). In this role, some psychologists help business executives function more effectively in their jobs (executive coaching); athletes perform better (sport psychology); or help artists, such as dancers or musicians, improve the quality of their performances.

There is some debate as to whether coaching constitutes a set of skills entirely separate from professional psychology and whether psychologists who engage in coaching are really engaging in psychological practice. Some argue that a psychologist who practices coaching is not practicing psychology any more than a psychologist who sells cars. In addition, members of other professions provide coaching services, some without any license. Although we know of no licensing board cases that deal with this issue directly, the general assumption is that psychology licensing boards will assume jurisdiction if the focus and the content of the intervention is psychological in nature. Consequently, it is possible (but by no means inevitable) that a psychologist could convince a licensing board that his or her work on team building for a local company was not the practice of psychology. But it is less likely that such an argument could be made if the psychologist was coaching a candidate for bariatric surgery on lifestyle changes using inventories or interventions that are sometimes used with patients with mental or physical illnesses (Harris, n.d.-a).

Psychopharmacology

Psychologists involved in health care need to understand basic psychopharmacology appropriate to the populations that they serve (APA, 2011b). They need to know enough about the proper use of psychotropic medications to discuss those treatment options with patients. Many disorders, such as depression or anxiety disorders, can be treated with either medication or psychotherapy, although the research indicates that a combination of both may work best. Also, a 2001 study found that about 50% of patients in psychotherapy are on psychotropic medications at some point in their treatment (Borkovec, Echemendia, Ragusea, & Ruiz, 2001) and that figure has probably increased in more recent years. Psychologists will be in a position to monitor patients' responses to medication, and if necessary, communicate their observations to the treating psychopharmacologist. Some of the questions to ask include, Are you feeling better since you started taking the medication? Are you taking the medication as prescribed? Are you experiencing any side effects? It may be helpful to inform the patient what side effects are common with the prescribed medication. When ascertaining whether patients are taking their medication, it is important to ask patients how often they are taking a drug and what the dosage is. For patients who are unable to recall such facts, it may be indicated to query further to ensure that they are taking medications as prescribed (APA, 2011b).

Many medication errors occur because of the lack of communication between health care personnel. Psychologists who are coordinating treatment with prescribing professionals should be careful to inform them of any significant changes in patient behavior or other relevant information, such as lack of adherence to medications or use of self-prescribed herbal remedies.

Because most psychologists are not, at this time, authorized to prescribe medications, they should be careful about making medication suggestions to physicians or other prescribing professionals. Nonetheless, many physicians will ask psychologists for their opinions concerning the appropriate medications to prescribe. Decisions about what psychologists can or cannot say depends to a large extent on the interpretations of the scope of practice by the licensing boards, but most agree that properly trained psychologists can make general recommendations about medications to physicians or other prescribing professionals while acknowledging that the final choice is up to the prescriber.

Prescribing psychologists will face unique liability issues. Of course, the prescribing psychologists will have to face such issues as warning patients about side effects of medications, prescribing off-label, and monitoring the interactions of medications with other medications and herbal and other alternative remedies. In addition, there may be pressures on prescribing psychologists to treat patients with more serious mental illnesses who have overall treatment needs that differ substantially from the depressed or anxious patients who make up the bulk of the caseload of most psychologists. When treating patients with serious mental illnesses, prescribing psychologists need to be especially sensitive to such issues as competency to consent to treatment, confidentiality with family members (who may be in a caregiver role), and ways to integrate medication with psychosocial treatments.

At this time it is not known how often prescribing psychologists will be involved in *split treatment* in which one professional prescribes and manages medication while a second professional provides psychotherapy. Those arrangements can work well if the prescriber and the psychotherapist communicate freely and frequently. They can work poorly if good communication does not occur.

INNOVATIVE TREATMENTS

Innovative treatments range from those that have real promise of success to those that may have some legitimacy but are misapplied or misused to those that are pure quackery. For example, during the 1940s, many psychiatrists began to practice psychosurgery for a wide range of serious mental disorders. Despite claims of widespread success, the methods used to evaluate the results were crude; patient protection measures were poor or nonexistent; and it is now believed that many patients were irreversibly harmed by these procedures (Valenstein, 1986). Nonetheless, recently there has been a resurgence in interest in the potential effectiveness of psychosurgery with a narrow range of mental conditions.

Many desperate parents saw facilitative communications as a method of overcoming autism and other serious and pervasive disorders, even though the research on this intervention was not supportive (Jacobson, Mulick, & Schwartz, 1995). Other unusual treatments include the orgone box, the love treatment (involving sexual relationships with patients), Z therapy (tying up patients and poking and taunting them), and rebirthing therapy. These and other treatments lack professional or scientific support (Norcross, Koocher, Fala, & Wexler, 2010; Norcross, Koocher, & Garofalo, 2006).

On the other hand, there may be positive developments in the ability to help individuals with innovative techniques. Many conscientious and well-informed psychologists are considering the therapeutic benefits of transcranial magnetic stimulation for depression, light therapy for seasonal affective disorders, or other treatments. More research is needed in these new interventions.

Psychologists must ask when a new treatment is to be considered a fad and when is it an innovation. These decisions require an evaluation of the relevant scientific data and professional evidence. Psychologists should be able to review the evidence (e.g., experimental studies, single-case studies, quasi-experimental designs, case histories, or other sources of data). They should be able to articulate a rationale for why certain techniques were used with a particular patient. It is not sufficient to justify the use of a new technique by saying that the technique helped or was successful in some research study. It is necessary to justify why this technique was used with this particular patient.

Care needs to be used when engaging in alternative or complimentary treatments, such as treatments involving touch. Therapies involving touch raise concerns because the meaning of the touch is always in the eye of the beholder, and the therapist's intentions may be misinterpreted by patients with special needs for affection. If the interpretations are not quickly corrected, touch can lead to charges of inappropriate touching, boundary violations, negligence, or sexual misconduct.

Although touch treatments are not inherently unethical, they do increase the legal risks to the practitioner. Psychologists can decrease those risks by informing patients of the innovative and experimental nature of any new treatments, documenting the treatment and the patient's response in detail, and seeking consultation when indicated. Psychologists should document why they thought that the particular treatment was appropriate for this particular patient. The blanket recommendation of touch therapy for all patients, for example, raises questions as to whether the unique benefits of this therapy for this patient were being considered. Certainly, high caution should be used when recommending these treatments with high-risk patients.

At times, psychologists will encounter patients who are taking herbal remedies or who ask whether to continue or initiate a herbal remedy. Advice about herbal remedies may become problematic because the use of herbal remedies is not commonly taught in doctoral programs and is often seen as outside the scope of practice of psychology. In addition, patients who are taking herbal remedies on their own need to be told that the dose or strength of the pills or tablets sold in stores is not standardized, and the herbs may interact with existing prescription or nonprescription medications the patient is taking. It may be wise to recommend that the patients confer with their physician or other prescribing professional before initiating or continuing herbal treatments.

COMPETENCE APPLIED TO THE DETAILED CASE EXAMPLE

It is useful to review the issue of competence from the standpoint of the case example presented at the end of Chapter 1. Here are some issues that need to be considered before Dr. Doe undertakes to treat this patient.

Does he know enough about serious personality disorders and their treatments, such as dialectical behavior therapy or other professionally derived theories for the treatment of serious personality disorders? Does he have the technical skills for handling relationship and parasuicidal issues that may arise? Does he have the emotional strength to handle the anger that may be directed at him? Is he able to say no to clinically contraindicated requests by the patient? Does he have the outside resources that may be needed in this case, such as access to a psychopharmacologist, partial hospitalization program, or inpatient unit if necessary?

Also, Dr. Doe needs to ask himself if, at this time in his career, he has the emotional and time resources to initiate treatment with a high-risk patient. Does he already have too many high-risk patients on his caseload? Does he have a heavy caseload or heavy personal demands at this time that will tax his energy in the event that this patient gets into a crisis? Has he considered the risks in treating such patients by looking at patient characteristics, context of treatment, and his individual therapist factors?

SEVEN ESSENTIAL POINTS TO REMEMBER

1. Being competent involves knowledge, technical skills, emotional competence, and cultural sensitivity.

2. Competence is situation specific and varies according to characteristics of the patient, context of treatment, and other factors.

3. It is wise for psychologists to protect their emotional health by ensuring that their physical and emotional needs are being met as part of their strategy to avoid impairment.

4. Psychologists should strive to be competent with individuals from diverse cultural or linguistic backgrounds.

5. Psychologists can ensure the quality of their care if they embed systems of protection (redundant systems) into their daily practices.

6. Psychologists who move into new areas of practice should ensure that they have received appropriate training before doing so and ongoing outside consultation and feedback once engaged in the new practice area.

7. All psychologists who treat patients with mental illnesses should have basic knowledge of psychopharmacology.

CHAPTER 4: MULTIPLE RELATIONSHIPS AND BOUNDARIES

Boundary violations are one of the most common sources of disciplinary actions that psychologists face. In some states, sexual contact with a patient may also be grounds for criminal charges. Sexual contacts with patients are especially likely to result in disciplinary actions, although harmful or exploitative nonsexual multiple relationships can as well.

Standard 3.05a, Multiple Relationships, of the American Psychological Association's (APA's) "Ethical Principles of Psychologists and Code of Conduct" (hereinafter referred to as the APA Ethics Code; APA, 2010a) states,

A multiple relationship occurs when a psychologist is in a professional role with a person and (1) at the same time is in another role with the same person, (2) at the same time is in a relationship with a person closely associated with or related to the person with whom the psychologist has a professional relationship, or (3) promises to enter into another relationship in the future with the person or a person closely associated with or related to the person.

On the other hand, not every multiple relationship is improper. "Multiple relationships that would not reasonably be expected to cause impairment or risk exploitation or harm are not unethical" (Standard 3.05a).

Multiple relationships can be concurrent (such as when a psychologist is in two or more roles with the patient at the same time as providing services) or consecutive (such as when a psychologist ends one relationship and begins another with a patient). A psychologist who is in a business relationship with a current patient would be in a concurrent multiple relationship. A psychologist who had a business relationship with a close friend or relative of a patient would also be in a concurrent multiple relationship.

Other concurrent relationships occur when a psychologist is providing individual and group therapy to the same person at the same time or when a psychologist serves as both a treating expert and evaluator for a personal injury case (see Chapter 7, "Psychologists in the Courtroom," for more information on treating experts; see Chapter 5, "Working With Couples, Families, and Children," for more information on multiple relationships when working with families).

Other multiple relationships may be consecutive. A psychologist who assesses or treats a patient with whom he or she has had (or expects to have) a business or social relationship is engaging in a consecutive multiple relationship. A promise of a future relationship is also a consecutive multiple relationship, such as when a psychologist offers to enter into a business arrangement with a patient as soon as therapy ends.

Standard 3.05a, Multiple Relationships, of the APA Ethics Code states that psychologists should refrain from entering into a multiple relationship if it "could reasonably be expected to impair the psychologist's objectivity, competence, or effectiveness in performing his or her functions as a psychologist, or otherwise risks exploitation or harm to the person with whom the professional relationship exists."

It is important to reiterate that multiple relationships are not inherently unethical, and sometimes they are unavoidable. However, psychologists must ensure that any multiple relationships could not be expected to exploit or harm a patient.

UNAVOIDABLE MULTIPLE RELATIONSHIPS

Standard 3.05b of the APA Ethics Code states,

If a psychologist finds that, due to unforeseen factors, a potentially harmful multiple relationship has arisen, the psychologist takes reasonable steps to resolve it with due regard for the interests of the affected person and maximal compliance with the Ethics Code.

Many psychologists in this situation adopt the "you first" rule, meaning that the psychologist will not take the initiative to acknowledge a patient if there is an unexpected encounter in a public place; instead the patients have to decide if they want to acknowledge the psychologist first. Some unavoidable encounters may be more intense than an incidental encounter as shown in this example.

A psychologist belonged to the local Buddhist Temple and received referrals from other Buddhists in the area. Although he did not treat those who regularly attended his own Temple, he did treat other Buddhists even though there was a possibility that they might encounter each other coincidentally through their common religious affiliation. (4.1)

This psychologist discussed with the patients the clinical implications of possible encounters or of having mutual acquaintances or friends.

TREATMENT BOUNDARIES

A crucial feature is whether a multiple relationship would impair the objectivity of the treatment relationship. Relationship factors are extremely important in ensuring the success of psychotherapy. Some may argue that they are even more important than specific therapeutic techniques in producing positive outcomes. The relationship factors related to good patient outcomes could include the ability to form a therapeutic alliance, collaborate in establishing treatment goals, show empathy and positive regard, and collect client feedback (Norcross & Wampold, 2011).

The term *boundary* refers to the context in which this relationship occurs. The salient feature of the boundary is that the focus of the relationship is on the welfare of the patient, not the psychologist. It is helpful to distinguish between the terms *boundary crossings* and *boundary violations* (Guthiel & Gabbard, 1998). Boundary crossings refer to any activity that moves psychologists away from a strictly neutral position with their patients. Boundary crossings may be helpful or harmful. A boundary violation is a harmful boundary crossing.

Common examples of boundary crossings include limited patient-oriented self-disclosures, exchange of token gifts, and nonsexual and socially acceptable touching. The risks of these boundary crossings are generally low. Properly trained psychologists can judge when the disclosure of personal information to patients can have therapeutic benefits, when the exchange of token gifts is a mere social formality or a nonpathological expression of appreciation, or when a gentle touch or a hug could have a therapeutic benefit.

A boundary violation could occur if the patient interprets the boundary crossing as harmful. For example, a patient might construe a gift, therapist self-disclosure, or a hug as a step in moving from a professional to a social or potentially a sexual relationship. Because some patients may interpret boundary crossings as boundary violations, it is important to have a therapeutic rationale for any significant boundary crossings and to note these in the patient's chart.

> A psychologist who worked in a rural and religiously conservative state often has patients or prospective patients ask her if she is a Christian. She anticipates this question from patients or prospective patients and has a response consistent with her comfort zone for self-disclosure. Although she is a not a Christian, she declines to disclose her religious affiliation but states that she is very respectful of the beliefs of her clients. She has learned that most patients or prospective patients are trying to discern if she will allow them to discuss their religious beliefs in a nonjudgmental atmosphere. (4.2)

However, in clinical work, boundary flexibility may be indicated under some circumstances. Boundary decisions are not made in a vacuum but require a consideration of patient factors, context, and therapist factors (Zur, 2007). Perhaps with other patients, under different circumstances, it would be clinically indicated for psychologists to disclose their religious affiliation (as long as the reason for disclosure has a rationale that respects patient autonomy and well-being). Certainly in rural or other small communities it is hard to avoid a patient who might have some connection to the psychologist, even if it is two or more degrees of separation (Younggren & Gottlieb, 2004; Zur, 2007).

Furthermore, it is possible to interpret boundaries so strictly that it becomes clinically contraindicated. There is even a story, perhaps apocryphal, about the psychologist who wanted to analyze what was behind the patient's remark of "how are you today?"

Furthermore, some kinds of services require more flexibility in boundaries. Sport psychologists who help athletes perform up to their potential may show more flexibility in boundaries because the power differential between the participants is less and the ability of the psychologists to do their jobs may require some boundary flexibility (Anderson, Williams, & Kramer, 2012). For example, a sport psychologist may have to meet and discuss performance in a semipublic venue, such as an athletic arena.

A consideration of the risk management factors of patient characteristics, context, and psychologist factors may help to clarify whether or how to modify boundaries in accordance with ethically based risk management principles (Younggren & Gottlieb, 2004).

Boundaries and Patient Factors

Otherwise benign boundary crossings are more likely to be problematic when they are done with patients with high-risk factors. Psychologists encounter some of the most disturbed persons of society. These patients may challenge boundaries, solicit sexual favors directly or indirectly, or react with extraordinary rage to relatively minor events.

In one case a patient became furious when her psychologist took a month off from treatment to give birth. The patient alleged that the pregnancy was a planned event designed to allow her therapist to "abandon" her. Of course, this complaint appears frivolous to us (but they are not to the patients involved). We mention it only to describe how the perceptions of patients can lead to serious results. It is easy to see how these patients could further distort any deviation from strict professional roles. Any touch, no matter how benign, could be eroticized, and any self-disclosure, no matter how discreetly and therapeutically indicated, could be construed as an effort to turn the professional relationship into a social one. Psychologists who choose to cross a professional boundary need to live with its outcome. This reality calls for thoughtful evaluation of the reasons for crossing the boundary and potential risk.

We are not attempting to dissuade psychologists from touching or self-disclosing to all patients. Remember, we considered such advice to be one of the false risk management principles discussed in Chapter 2 ("Key Elements of Risk Management"). However, psychologists need to be aware that a few patients may grossly misconstrue relatively innocuous boundary crossings. Consequently, psychologists need to have a clinical justification for their actions. Some psychologists may, as a result of their therapeutic orientation, eschew all touching (other than handshakes) and reject all gifts, no matter how innocuous or small. Other psychologists engage in limited self-disclosure and accept token gifts. Both, however, should be able to justify their decisions on the basis of clinical and ethical grounds.

Emerging forms of social networking have led to unique issues in self-disclosure. The general rule is that self-disclosure should be intentional, deliberate, and focused on patient well-being. Social media presents unique boundary challenges because postings on social networking sites represent a form of self-disclosure. One survey (Lehavot, Barnett, & Powers, 2010) found that although most psychology students participated in social networking sites, many had not set privacy settings, had included photos, or had content that they would not want their patients to see (See also Gabbard, Kassaw, & Perez-Garcia, 2011). About 7% of the psychology students reported that a client had found information about them on the Internet. Some professionals have used social media to post pictures of themselves using alcohol to excess or being in varying stages of undress or have posted comments about patients, off color jokes, or comments using profanity (Tunick, Mednick, & Conroy, 2011). As expressed by Dr. Stephen Behnke, director of the APA Ethics Office, "Putting something on the Internet is no different than leaving it on a table at a coffee shop at the mall" (quoted in Chamberlin, 2007, p. 14). We recommend that psychologists use privacy protections diligently, scrutinize the content of the social media they use, search their names periodically to see what content is out there, and talk to their supervisees and employees about this issue. These and the other risk management recommendations we suggest later in this chapter will greatly reduce the potential for negative consequences of any boundary crossing.

Boundaries and Context

Any concurrent or consecutive multiple relationship may become problematic if it is accompanied by another high-risk factor. For example, it would be unwise to be in a multiple relationship with a patient who has been diagnosed with a serious personality disorder. Also, if a family is seeking help because of a high-conflict divorce or is seeking assistance in ongoing litigation, a multiple relationship has a greater likelihood of creating problems or being misconstrued. In other words, any time patient or context characteristics suggest high risks, psychologists should be especially prudent about engaging in a multiple relationship or crossing boundaries.

> A psychologist began evaluating a claimant for a court case in which she alleged serious emotional distress as a result of an accident. Shortly after the evaluation began, the claimant announced to the psychologist, "I saw you in therapy ten years ago." The psychologist checked his records, and indeed he had seen the woman ten years earlier. She had a different surname at the time. He discontinued the evaluation and notified relevant parties of the unexpected multiple relationship. (4.3)

This psychologist wisely understood that a multiple relationship in a high-risk context might disqualify him from his current role. Here we provide a slightly different scenario.

> A psychologist started an evaluation with a couple seeking marital therapy. Shortly after the evaluation began the wife announced to the psychologist, "I saw you in therapy ten years ago." Indeed he had seen the woman ten years earlier. She had a different surname at the time. He paused the evaluation to determine if this prior relationship would compromise his effectiveness as a marital therapist. (4.4)

In this case, the husband stated that because the psychologist was so conscientious about respecting his perceptions and feelings, he had more confidence that the psychologist would be a fair and helpful marital therapist. With some marital therapy cases, such a previous multiple relationship might make treatment clinically contraindicated, although the risks are far lower than those found in a forensic case.

Many psychologists provide home-based treatments, such as with older adults who have mobility problems or when conducting behavioral interventions with children in the home (Knapp & Slattery, 2004). No doubt, much clinically indicated work occurs in such settings. Nonetheless, psychologists who work in patients' homes need to be especially scrupulous about boundaries. Patients who receive services in their homes may be more likely to adopt behaviors characteristic of a host–guest relationship as opposed to a professional–client relationship. That is, the patients may be more likely to engage in polite social conversation, offer refreshments, or otherwise drift away from the therapeutic purpose of the visit. Although some latitude may be clinically indicated, it is wise to redirect the interaction to more professional topics. Psychologists need to use discretion when deciding whether to conduct home visits, especially with high-risk patients.

Sometimes neighbors or social acquaintances may challenge boundaries. For example, a neighbor called a psychologist at home about an apparently minor problem dealing with her child's nighttime routine. Although not wishing to be rude, the psychologist was aware that the brief phone conversation with the neighbor was no substitute for a detailed history and that there might be more complications than could be discerned over the phone. Her comments were circumspect, and she noted that some of the mother's questions could only be answered through a more thorough examination.

Similarly, psychologists need to ensure that they do not make casual comments at parties or other social gatherings that could be construed as giving professional advice. Friends of friends or social acquaintances may pressure psychologists for brief and simple solutions to complex interpersonal or psychological problems.

> An assistant pastor asked a psychologist to participate as an instructor in her church's Women's Spiritual Retreat Weekend that was advertised as a weekend of "prayer, reflection, Bible study, and spiritual renewal." However, on Friday night one of the participants threatened suicide and made superficial cuts on her wrist. It later came out that she had displayed these behaviors before and that the assistant pastor had specifically asked the psychologist to come to the retreat to assist with this problem parishioner. Of course, the psychologist had no idea of the hidden agenda behind the invitation to be an instructor for the weekend. (4.5)

The well-meaning pastor did not know that psychological services could only be administered in the context of a professional relationship. The psychologist declined to interview the parishioner but had a long discussion with the pastor concerning professional boundaries and other ways to ensure that a disturbed parishioner does not upset the weekend for the other parishioners.

As we noted in Chapter 3 ("Competence"), numerous studies have demonstrated therapeutic uses for electronic communications with patients. However, psychologists need to establish boundaries with electronic communications with patients in the same manner as with other communications. It is not clinically indicated to "friend" patients in social networking sites because it allows them access to otherwise private information and conveys that this is a social, not a professional relationship, thus opening the way to other potential boundary crossings or violations. Similarly, psychologists should only engage in other forms of electronic communications with patients between sessions, such as texting or emails, when a therapeutic rationale exists for such exchanges and the patient understands and accepts the limits to confidentiality. Some psychologists have found it helpful to have an electronic communication policy that they can share with patients who are especially interested in electronic communications.

Conversely, a question arises as to whether psychologists should conduct an Internet search on their patients. Such a search might be indicated if a psychologist is performing a forensic evaluation in which the patient expects such scrutiny. Or it may be indicated to view the Internet content regarding patients if they specifically request that psychologists look at something for a clinical reason.

Should psychologists look at the Internet content or postings of patients without being invited to do so? According to Kaslow, Patterson, and Gottlieb (2011), psychologists who conduct unwanted Internet searches may find themselves in potential conflicts if they learn things that their clients have not disclosed to them. They argue that the general rule in therapy is to respect patients' decisions, including the decision about what information they choose to reveal in therapy. Others may disagree and insist that treating psychologists should feel as free to search their patients as their patients search them. To date we know of no legal cases that have arisen from uninvited Internet searches of patients; however, like other treatment decisions, this one needs to have a clinical rationale for it. Because this is a relatively new area, psychologists would benefit from keeping current with research, legal cases, and consultation.

Boundaries and Individual Psychologist Factors

Certain psychologist factors increase one's ability to make wise decisions concerning the maintenance of proper boundaries. Perhaps the first is the general knowledge of how to develop and maintain effective relationships. Effective psychologists understand general psychopathology and especially those disorders in which difficulty in maintaining boundaries is likely to occur. Effective psychologists also understand the need for objectivity in making these decisions. This may include the need for "standing back from a potential dual relationship and looking at it, oneself, and one's own motivation" (Younggren & Gottlieb, 2004, p. 257).

Psychologists need to have ethical decision-making skills to judge when a patient, licensing board, ethics committee, or jury is likely to construe a multiple relationship as exploitative or harmful. As noted previously, psychologists living in small communities have fewer options for avoiding multiple relationships than those who live in larger urban areas and often have to decide whether a relationship would be clinically contraindicated.

Technical competence comes into play because effective psychologists have learned through supervised training and experience how to establish and maintain helpful relationships. Emotional competence is important as well. Effective psychologists have the self-awareness necessary to determine when personal feelings may interfere with their relationships. Finally, they are more likely to be embedded in a redundant system of protection whereby others can provide a check on their judgment. Consulting with colleagues on a regular basis provides such a redundant system of protection.

Sometimes the threat to boundaries can be subtle, such as the potential for psychologists to impose their religious beliefs on patients. Obviously, psychologists should not use their influence to proselytize for their own religion. However, sometimes the issue becomes nuanced, for example, when patients present religious beliefs in a manner that seems harmful to their mental or physical well-being as shown in the following example.

> Dr. Green accepted a patient who requested therapy to help her with her depression. In the first session the patient revealed that she was having substantial marital problems that she attributed to her "proud spirit" and her failure to submit to her husband as commanded by her religion. Twice in the session she cited the Biblical passage from Titus 2:4-5 ("young women [should be] . . . submissive to their husbands") to justify her need to be submissive. (4.6)

Dr. Green, who is both a feminist and a Christian, believes that the patient has selected a passage out of context, and she could have quickly cited numerous other passages and themes to contradict the interpretation that Christianity requires women to blindly submit to their husbands. The first interview leaves Dr. Green with the impression that the husband's misogynistic beliefs are fueling the patient's depression.

However, unless Dr. Green knows how the patient is defining *submission*, she cannot tap the depths, complexities, nuances, or contradictions of the patient's belief system. She should not necessarily assume that the wife's report is normative for her denomination, and an interview involving the husband might give important information to clarify the marital situation. Finally, although her religious beliefs appear to be impacting her psychological functioning, Dr. Green is aware that the reverse also could be true.

In proceeding with the case, Dr. Green can respect the religious traditions of her patient and refrain from imposing her beliefs on her patient. In fact, if the patient's religious beliefs do significantly contribute to her depression, Dr. Green can strive to promote a healthier manifestation of faith, rather than try to undermine it (Rucker, Hite, & Hathaway, 2005).

RISK MANAGEMENT APPLICATIONS

The risk management strategies of informed consent, documentation, and consultation can help lower risks associated with multiple relationships. The informed consent process is relevant in that it is important to discuss the potential ill effects of a multiple relationship with patients ahead of time as illustrated in the next example.

> A psychologist had agreed to represent his church in an interfaith council that was established to help victims of a local flood. When he attended the first meeting he saw that one of his current patients was there representing another religious denomination. During the next treatment session the psychologist spoke to the patient concerning any discomfort or potential negative effects that this would create. (4.7)

This psychologist understood that informed consent was not a one-time event but an ongoing process that had to be revisited from time to time as events in therapy unfolded. He understood that according to the higher levels of Bloom's taxonomy, he needed to integrate the informed consent process with other aspects of treatment with the goal of improving patient welfare and increasing patient autonomy.

Of course, the manner in which the autonomy-enhancing discussion occurs is as important as whether it occurs. A genuine concern for the welfare of the patient is conveyed by body posture, nonverbal cues, and the specific choice of words when discussing delicate and potentially difficult topics.

. It is advisable to document all multiple relationships and why each was, was not, could become, or would likely become clinically contraindicated or exploitative. The facts or circumstances of the case should be laid out, and the reasons for the conclusion given. It is prudent for psychologists to always document unavoidable multiple relationships and how efforts were made to act in accordance with the APA Ethics Code. It may be desirable to document all incidental social contacts and how they were handled when the patient or context suggests a high-risk situation. Of course, psychologists should seek consultation when potentially problematic multiple relationships occur (Younggren & Gottlieb, 2004).

Consultations can help psychologists to evaluate the benefits and drawbacks of a proposed boundary crossing or how an unavoidable boundary crossing was handled. Ideally the consultant will consider the characteristics of the patient, the context of the services provided, the goal of the boundary crossing, and the nature of the psychologist–patient relationship. Often the very process of discussing the patient with a consultant will help psychologists to clarify their goals and the advantages and disadvantages of the boundary crossing.

SEXUAL ATTRACTION TO PATIENTS AND SEXUAL VIOLATIONS

At first glance, it would appear difficult to say anything novel or useful about sexual exploitation. Every psychologist knows that sexual violations are unethical, in many jurisdictions illegal, and a major source of disciplinary actions against psychologists. Conscientious psychologists may think, "I would never have sex with my patients; therefore, I can skip over this section." However, sexual violations are only the more extreme manifestations of a more common problem of mishandling sexual attraction toward patients. Even highly conscientious and moral psychologists may find themselves having unprocessed sexual feelings toward patients that may, even subtly, divert their attention away from client needs.

Offenders are more likely to be middle-aged or older male psychologists who have sexual relationships with younger female patients. Nonetheless, some same-sex relationships are reported, and sometimes female psychologists engage in sexual exploitation. Sexual exploitation can also occur when psychologists have sexual contact with former patients or with relatives of patients (such as the parent of a child patient).

Some have argued that whenever boundaries are crossed, the psychologist and patient find themselves on a slippery slope and are likely to move from a social to a sexual relationship over time. Of course, not all boundary crossings are inevitable invitations to sexual exploitation, and we would not want the fear of sexual exploitation to discourage psychologists from engaging in therapeutically indicated boundary crossings. Although every case of sexual misconduct started with a boundary crossing, few boundary crossings actually lead to sexual misconduct (Gottlieb & Younggren, 2009). Correlation does not imply causation.

The frequency of sexual misconduct by psychologists appears to be decreasing, although the reasons for this are not clear (see review by Sonne, 2012). Perhaps it is because licensing boards are becoming more aggressive in prosecuting cases of misconduct that come to their attention. Several states have criminalized sexual contact with patients. Other states have mandated reporting requirements in place that require psychologists to inform the licensing board whenever they treat a patient who had sexual contact with a former psychotherapist. Patients also are more sophisticated about the inappropriateness of such behavior. Perhaps the decrease is an artifact of the shifting demographics of professional psychology wherein more women (who tend to have substantially lower rates of sexual misconduct) are entering the profession. The apparent decrease may be due to the proactive ways that graduate schools, continuing education programs, and consultation services (such as those provided by The Trust or state, provincial, and territorial psychological associations) are addressing patient relationships, psychologists' self-care, and the interrelationship between the needs of the psychologist and the likelihood of the exploitation of a patient. Perhaps all of these factors have played a role in reducing rates of sexual contact.

In any event, the goal is to reduce the frequency of sexual offenses even more. One step might be to look at sexual offenders and determine what common factors appear to be associated with sexual offenses and what can be done to reduce their frequency. Not all psychologists are at equal risk of offending sexually. Certainly a few psychologists have personality flaws that impair their ability to maintain boundaries with patients. Other psychologists have crossed sexual boundaries when they were vulnerable to becoming "love sick," a state wherein they convinced themselves that they acted with the purest of romantic motives. They may find themselves unusually attracted to a patient who is particularly vulnerable or grateful or who uses the idealization or seduction of others as interpersonal strategies.

These psychologists may be especially at risk if they have had inadequate training in handling their personal feelings for patients or have had a recent stressor in their private lives (e.g., spouse has had an affair, spouse or child dies, business failure or severe financial problems, or too much stress in the practice). Serious personal stressors can blind even the best practitioner. Psychologists may be arriving at a dangerous point if their sexual fantasies are aroused or if they have convinced themselves that they can handle a little more closeness with a particular patient. It is with these individuals that proactive educational techniques focusing on handling treatment relationships and self-care can probably do the most to reduce the likelihood of offending.

Another strategy is to focus less on the characteristics of the few who are at risk of becoming offenders and more on the general issues of improving relationships and self-care for all psychologists. The large majority of psychologists who have sexual feelings toward patients do not offend. Nonetheless, the overall quality of treatment may be degraded, even if slightly, because of these feelings. The inability to acknowledge feelings and deal with them so they do not have a negative impact on therapy may result in those feelings going "underground" and being unprocessed. When the feelings are acknowledged in a safe setting, psychologists may be better able to handle those feelings productively.

Individually Focused Risk Management Strategies

On an individual level, the risk management strategies designed to protect one from becoming vulnerable to sexual temptations are similar to strategies designed to protect one from other unhealthy boundary violations. Psychologists should be technically competent in relationship skills, act to ensure their emotional competence, embed themselves in a protective social framework, and have considerable self-awareness.

Ask newly licensed psychologists if they ever expect to have sex with a patient during their career and 99+% emphatically would say no. Yet current data suggest that a few, 2% to 3% of psychologists, will have a sexual relationship with at least one patient sometime during their careers. On the other hand, the vast majority of psychologists will have strong romantic feelings toward certain patients (Pope & Tabachnick, 1993). Although most of these psychologists will not engage in sexual misconduct, those feelings, if left unprocessed, may nonetheless impact the quality of treatment.

Many good teachers of psychologists address the issue of affect forecasting. That is, they help their trainees appreciate that they will have feelings toward some patients that are so strong that they will tempt the psychologist into a boundary crossing or other inappropriate behavior. Sometimes the strong feelings may be hate, anger, fear, or romantic attraction.

Students may fail to appreciate the hot–cold empathy gap (Loewenstein, 2005). That is, when people are in an emotionally neutral state, such as when they are seated in a classroom, they may fail to appreciate how "hot" transient visceral states may influence their behavior in a manner contradictory to their long-term goals.

Properly trained psychologists will also have enough self-awareness that they know that they need to anticipate how to handle these feelings productively and have the technical skills to continue to help patients when strong feelings arise. If the feelings continue to interfere with effective treatment and the issues are not overcome through consultation, personal therapy, or supervision, it is highly recommended that the psychologist transfer the patient to another professional.

Profession-wide Risk Management Strategies

Another way to approach this issue is to move away from the individual dyad level of analysis and look at society-wide or profession-wide interventions. Some might argue that sexual misconduct is a private act with private consequences for both the patient and the psychologist who is at risk of being disciplined. However, every psychologist suffers when one psychologist has sex with a patient, and every current or potential patient can suffer as well to the extent that public confidence in the profession of psychology is decreased. Current or potential patients who learn of this misconduct will be much less likely to trust their psychologists or even to seek psychotherapy in the future. In addition, stories about sexual misconduct often are made public by print and social media and can become a front page issue. This could have deleterious effects on all therapy during the time of the exposé in that patients and psychologists may need to take valuable treatment time to deal with the media coverage.

One might believe that the remedy for sexual misconduct has to come at an individual level. To a large extent this is true. However, every psychologist can contribute to a profession-wide atmosphere that makes sexual misconduct less likely to occur.

It is also possible to view sexual contact as an outgrowth of degraded professional relationships that have lost their focus on treatment and have become a sexualized social experience. If so, then the level of intervention shifts from being just how psychologists can stop this individual from engaging in sex with this patient to include the question of how psychologists can help all psychologists improve the quality of their professional relationships with all of their patients. In other words, how can all psychologists better handle the feelings generated in psychotherapy? There may be a need to shift the culture of psychology so that there is an increased emphasis on self-awareness and relationship maintenance. How can psychologists shift the culture of psychology?

Some psychologists have taken steps to improve the profession's ability to deal with relationship issues.

One psychologist was assertive in keeping in touch with colleagues and reaching out to those who might not be doing well emotionally. She checked on her friends, asked how they were doing, and went out to lunch with them when they appeared to be struggling.

A psychologist participated in the colleague assistance program of his state psychological association. He counseled other health care professionals who were doing poorly and participated in self-care education.

A psychologist served on the continuing education committee of her local hospital's behavioral health unit that presented workshops on relationship management.

A psychologist participated in a study on treatment factors in psychotherapy and in a study on how psychologists responded to sexually inappropriate behaviors.

Another psychologist read books and took continuing education courses on supervision and incorporated self-awareness as an important component of the experience of his supervisees. This included an effort to engage in self-care and normalize sexual feelings when they arose in treatment.

And finally, another psychologist, realizing that countertransference feelings she was having with a particular patient were threatening to get out of control, sought consultation to assist with the treatment and personal therapy to resolve the feeling without additional interference with the therapy. She shared her experience and her problem-solving thinking when she presented continuing education workshops. (4.8)

SEVEN ESSENTIAL POINTS TO REMEMBER

1. Multiple relationships are not necessarily unethical or harmful. Multiple relationships that are exploitative or clinically contraindicated should be avoided.

2. Boundary crossings are deviations from a strictly neutral therapeutic position; boundary violations are harmful boundary crossings.

3. Psychologists should be extremely cautious about boundary crossing or engaging in multiple relationships with patients with high-risk features or when treating patients in high-risk contexts.

4. Psychologists should regulate the content that they reveal on social networking sites, recognizing that any public posting is a form of self-disclosure. Friending patients through social media should be avoided.

5. Psychologists should be especially prudent about informed consent, documentation, and consultation when crossing boundaries or engaging in multiple relationships with high-risk patients or in high-risk contexts.

6. Although the frequency of sexual exploitation is decreasing, it remains a major source of complaints against psychologists.

7. Sexual exploitation can be reduced if individual psychologists focus on technical skills in maintaining boundaries; embed themselves in a system of protection; and recognize that strong feelings, including sexual feelings, will arise with certain patients during the course of therapy. Continuing education programs, graduate training, supervision, consultation, and other venues can be used to help psychologists learn how to control, modify, or channel those emotions to productive ends.

CHAPTER 5: WORKING WITH COUPLES, FAMILIES, AND CHILDREN

Working with couples, families, and children presents unique complications because of the special public policies regulating the treatment of children and because the interested parties, such as the parents, may have competing interests. In this chapter, we review unique issues in working with couples, families, and children. Specifically, we review issues of informed consent when working with couples, consent and confidentiality when treating children, special challenges when working with high-conflict families, and unique considerations when doing child custody work.

INFORMED CONSENT ISSUES WITH COUPLES AND FAMILIES

The American Psychological Association's (APA's) "Ethical Principles of Psychologists and Code of Conduct" (hereinafter referred to as the APA Ethics Code; APA, 2010a) provides guidance when psychologists treat several persons in a relationship. Standard 10.02a, Therapy Involving Couples or Families, states,

> *When psychologists agree to provide services to several persons who have a relationship (such as spouses, significant others, or parents and children), they take reasonable steps to clarify at the outset (1) which of the individuals are clients/patients and (2) the relationship the psychologist will have with each person. This clarification includes the psychologist's role and the probable uses of the service provided or the information obtained.*

The general rule is that psychologists should avoid situations in which they have conflicting loyalties. We provide here an example.

A psychologist is treating a wife individually. During the course of treatment, the wife brings in her husband for conjoint sessions. However, the relationship between the couple deteriorates, and both wish to have individual sessions with the psychologist. The husband was upset when the psychologist declined to work with him individually. (5.1)

Here it is important for the psychologist to have followed Standard 10.02a, Therapy Involving Couples or Families, and to have clarified to all parties the nature of the relationship with each of them. Ideally, when the husband first came in for sessions with his wife, the psychologist would have explained that the wife was his patient and that the husband was there as a collateral contact only to further the treatment of his wife. If this step had been taken, the husband would have been more willing to accept the fact that the psychologist had the primary treatment obligation to his wife and could only refer him to a therapist of his own.

However, a number of other situations may occur when treating families as shown in the next example.

A psychologist was treating a couple for marital problems. However, the relationship between the couple deteriorated. The husband discontinued therapy, and the wife requested individual sessions with the psychologist. (5.2)

Again it is important for the psychologist to follow Standard 10.02a, Therapy Involving Couples or Families, and to clarify to all parties the nature of the relationship with each of them. Ideally, when the couple first came in for sessions, the psychologist would have identified who was the client. Perhaps in this situation the psychologist considered both parties to be his clients, and the marriage was the focus of the treatment. If the husband dropped out of treatment, the psychologist would need to determine if the husband no longer wished to continue in treatment and, if not, to formally terminate the relationship with the husband and then consider the clinical advantages and disadvantages of continuing therapy with the wife as the primary client. Although legally the psychologist may continue treatment with the wife, there may be clinical considerations not to do so. For example, the psychologist needs to ask whether there is a likelihood that couples therapy will resume and, if so, whether seeing the wife individually would create a perception that the psychologist is now biased.

This issue is illustrated in the following example.

A psychologist was treating a couple for marital problems but decided the optimal way to proceed was to provide individual therapy sessions to each of them. At one point the wife decided that she wanted a divorce, whereas the husband was using the individual therapy sessions to help preserve the marriage. (5.3)

Again, Standard 10.02a, Therapy Involving Couples or Families, should guide the behavior of the psychologist. Ideally the psychologist clarified with all parties that he was seeing them individually for their agreed-upon purpose of saving the marriage. Perhaps he cautioned them that he would only provide such treatment if they agreed that he could exchange information obtained in sessions with one to assist in the sessions with the other (although certainly he would use such information with discretion). Consequently, the wife should have known at the point she told the psychologist of her intent to get a divorce that this information would be conveyed to her husband. She should also have understood that the purpose of her individual sessions was to preserve the marriage, and if she no longer shared this goal, the individual sessions with this psychologist might end.

Each of these situations points to the importance of the risk management strategies we have been using and especially of the informed consent process. Unless the informed consent process was implemented scrupulously, there would have been a potential for misunderstandings, ill feelings, or a sense of betrayal. In each of the three scenarios provided previously, it may have been necessary for the psychologist to review the conditions of treatment periodically to ensure that the patients (or the collateral contacts) did not misconstrue the psychologist's role. Documentation of these informed consent procedures is indicated as well.

CHILD AND ADOLESCENT TREATMENT

Informed consent and confidentiality issues will also occur when working with children. Who can consent for treatment varies according to state law. In some states, adolescents, depending on their age, may consent for mental health treatment on their own. In other states, they cannot. In some states, either parent may give consent for a child to receive treatment. In other states, the right of a child to receive treatment may require the consent of both parents if there is court-ordered joint legal custody.

The APA Ethics Code Standard 3.10b, Informed Consent, states, "For persons who are legally incapable of giving informed consent, psychologists nevertheless (1) provide an appropriate explanation, (2) seek the individual's assent, (3) consider such persons' preferences and best interests." Consequently, if the child is not legally able to give consent, psychologists should nonetheless share information about treatment in a manner appropriate for the child's mental and social development. What psychologists would say to the average 5-year-old will differ from what would be said to the average 11-year-old. Also, psychologists should seek to secure the assent (or agreement) of the individual for treatment and consider his or her preferences and best interests. A sample agreement when treating children and adolescents can be downloaded from the The Trust website (www.apait.org).

The informed consent process is especially important in negotiating the boundaries of privacy between an adolescent, the adolescent's parents, and the psychologist.[1] Parents who bring their rebellious adolescents into treatment may feel helpless in the face of apparently intractable problems. They may expect the psychologist to protect their children from their dangerous experimentations with alcohol or other drugs, sex, or criminal behavior. Their anxiety may prompt them to view the psychologist as an extension of their parental control, and they may attempt to intrude in therapy in ways that are understandable but counterproductive.

On the other hand, adolescents may start distrusting their psychologists if they see them as an authority surrogate for their parents. This tension can be confronted constructively through the therapeutic process by negotiating the parents' access to information about treatment. Parents can be encouraged to set aside their legal right of access to information so that the psychologist can provide the adolescent with a protective space where he or she can build a therapeutic alliance and make therapeutic progress.

---

[1] From "Resolving Some Areas of Continuing Confusion," by E. Harris, 2003, Winter, *MassPsych: The Journal of the Massachusetts Psychological Association, 47*, pp. 18–22, 29. Copyright 2003 by the Massachusetts Psychological Association. Adapted with permission of the author.

In doing so, however, psychologists need to clarify to all parties what kind of information they will share and under what circumstances. Sometimes the sharing of information is dictated by institutional policy or state or federal law, such as when a state law permits adolescents to seek treatment on their own in a drug and alcohol facility.

Unfortunately, at times an adolescent may not trust the therapist and may "game" the therapy regardless of the limits placed on confidentiality. This is a difficult clinical situation, especially if the adolescent continues to engage in dangerous behavior, including using drugs, having unprotected sex, or committing other criminal acts. Where parents have a legal right to information, many psychologists only accept adolescent patients with the understanding that they will be able to give general information to parents concerning the overall progress of treatment (and productive use of time) and that they have the discretion to share information with parents when the life or safety of the adolescent or a third party is endangered. Exactly where that line is drawn will depend on the intensity, frequency, and seriousness of the behavior. Such decisions are context-dependent and include questions such as the likely response of the parents, the damage to the therapeutic process, and the willingness of the adolescent patient to eventually disclose and to work on the problematic behaviors.

Even in those settings in which adolescents may control the release of information independently, some psychologists may insist that adolescent patients agree to release information to parents so that the parents will know if the child is using the time productively (e.g., is the adolescent showing up for sessions?) or if the child needs to be referred (e.g., the child is showing manifestations of another disorder that requires a different therapist or treatment modality).

Sometimes these issues become difficult to manage. When, if ever, should psychologists inform parents that their child is cutting himself or herself if the cutting is not likely to be lethal? What about failure to eat? How much risk should there be in sexual behavior before a parent is notified? What about same-sex activity? The parents may agree to treatment with the expectation that the psychologist will encourage heterosexual interests, but the patient may not share that goal.

The Health Insurance Portability and Accountability Act of 1996 Privacy Rule (hereinafter referred to as the Privacy Rule) also allows parents to enter into "agreements of confidentiality," or binding agreements to waive their entitlement to access a child's records to allow more privacy and facilitate effective therapy. If the parents have joint legal custody, the permission of both parents is required. In states that allow minors to independently consent to treatment and/or control the dissemination of treatment information, such a contract can be an effective way to provide parents with access to the information about the treatment that the psychologist considers important to ensure effective parental participation (and payment for) the treatment. Of course, the ordinary exceptions to confidentiality apply to adolescents as they do to other patients. We provide more information on the Privacy Rule in Chapter 6 ("Privacy, Confidentiality, and Privileged Communications").

A psychologist was treating an adolescent who lived in a state where parents had to consent for treatment and controlled confidentiality. As was her usual informed consent procedure, the psychologist made an agreement regarding confidentiality with both the parents and the adolescent present, noting that she would protect the privacy of the adolescent's communications in therapy but would inform parents if the adolescent acted in a manner that threatened her life or safety. The psychologist also noted that these decisions concerning what constitutes a threat to safety can sometimes be ambiguous and that the parents would need to trust the psychologist about when that line was crossed and the parents needed to be notified. "For example," the psychologist stated, "I may learn that your daughter is using drugs or having sex. I may or may not disclose that to you depending on my perception of the risk involved and whether it is a one-time slip or a pattern." Over the course of treatment the girl disclosed an increasingly disturbed pattern of "hooking up" with men she met over the Internet. The psychologist urged her to refrain from this behavior, which she promised to do. But, over the months, she had difficulty adhering to her promise during periods of stress. The psychologist then reminded the girl of their original agreement that she had the option of informing her parents of behavior that threatened her life or safety. After considerable discussion, the psychologist told the girl that she had to develop a safety plan that included using her parents as a resource to curtail this behavior. The psychologist listened to the girl's objections and insisted that she understand the concerns for her safety. Eventually they negotiated the process by which to inform the parents. (5.4)

This psychologist accurately viewed informed consent at the higher levels of Bloom's taxonomy in that it was incorporated into her overall treatment process and relationship. In this case, the informed consent process involved the parents as well as the identified patient. The parents gave their consent for treatment on the basis of the premise that the psychologist would take appropriate action in the event the life or safety of their daughter was at stake. The risks to the daughter were high enough that she needed external controls to protect her from impulsive actions.

The difficulty for the psychologist in this example would become apparent if the psychologist had decided not to inform the parents of this potentially dangerous behavior by the patient and the patient developed a relationship with an individual who seriously harmed her. This was an extremely difficult decision to make, and all relevant information had to be taken into consideration to provide for the welfare of the patient.

No one format for these agreements of confidentiality is appropriate for every psychologist. Psychologists vary in the extent to which they can tolerate dangerous high-risk behavior among adolescents. Some psychologists prefer to have agreements that adopt a lower threshold for notifying parents (such as any time the welfare or safety of the adolescent is at risk), whereas others adopt a higher threshold (such as immediate danger to oneself or others). It is crucial, however, that the patient and parents understand the standards used by the psychologist ahead of time.

TREATMENT OF HIGH-CONFLICT FAMILIES[2]

Naive psychologists who fail to attend to the nuances of treatment issues with high-conflict families may inadvertently deliver substandard therapy (L. R. Greenberg, Gould, Gould-Saltman, & Stahl, 2003). Even assuming that appropriate parental consent has been obtained, psychologists who are legally allowed to treat a child should consider a number of clinical factors before moving forward. At times, it may be clinically indicated to refuse such cases, especially if the marital turmoil created by the very act of entering therapy outweighs any benefit that the child may experience from therapy. Although therapy is generally beneficial, there are some highly charged situations that doom to failure any therapeutic attempts. It is always recommended that prior to initiating treatment of a minor, the psychologist obtain the consent of both parents if required by law to do so. If one parent refuses, the stress related to the conflict between the parents may prohibit any success in the therapy for the child. Also, seeing a child without the knowledge of both parents may inadvertently reinforce the idea that the nonconsenting parent is bad or cannot be trusted, and it may place a barrier between the child and that parent to the detriment of the child.

Of course, in unusual situations it may be legal and clinically indicated to involve only one parent. In those situations, however, prudent psychologists may want to seek a consultation. Nonetheless, experienced psychologists often find that parents will frequently respond favorably to a fair and open invitation to participate in treatment or at least to give consent to treatment. Sometimes the opposition to treatment is not so much opposition to treatment per se but anger at the fact that the parent was not even consulted about his or her opinions concerning the need for or the direction or nature of therapy.

The policy of refusing to treat some families under some circumstances is a good risk management strategy, but more importantly, it is a risk management strategy that is linked to the overarching moral principles of beneficence (promoting the welfare of others) and nonmaleficence (doing no harm). That is, psychologists need to decide whether the potential to help the family exceeds the potential to harm them. When we look at competence from the standpoint of Bloom's taxonomy, we remember that, at the higher levels, the evaluation of competence considers the context in which treatment occurs. Consequently, it is not our intent to cast doubt on the level of psychologists' skill or expertise. It is to recognize that sometimes the best use of skills and expertise is to determine up front if the services can benefit the child and parents or if the situational factors are such that no intervention should be made at the time absent resolution of the more fundamental underlying problem between the parents. Sometimes the correct course of action is not clear. No doubt, many psychologists can do much good for these

[2] From "Treating Children in High-Conflict Families," by S. Knapp and J. Lemoncelli, 2005, October, *The Pennsylvania Psychologist*, 65, p. 4. Copyright 2005 by the Pennsylvania Psychological Association. Adapted with permission of the author.

high-conflict families, and we are not trying to discourage the treatment of such families. We are encouraging psychologists to make an informed decision as to whether to treat them, how to treat them, and what might be considered to pave the way for unencumbered therapy in the future.

Psychologists who decide to treat children from such families should remember that treatment with divorcing families often differs substantially from treatment with typical families. Ordinarily, psychologists assume that the parent is coming to treatment voluntarily. However, some parents in high-conflict cases have been ordered into therapy by a court or have been strongly encouraged to enter therapy by their attorneys.

Ordinarily, psychologists assume that parents try to present information accurately. However, in high-conflict families the presenting parents may give slanted reports and attempt to use the therapy to promote their own agenda. The emotions generated by the divorce may override sound parental judgment.

Ordinarily, psychologists assume that parents are acting in the best interest of the child. However, in high-conflict families parents may request treatment for benign-sounding reasons, but their real agenda may be to improve their relationship with the child in preparation for a pending custody evaluation or to use the child to get information against the other parent in the upcoming custody evaluation. In addition, one parent may be on his or her best behavior in hopes that the psychologist will "side" with him or her during the custody hearing.

This is not to say that divorcing parents are always coerced into treatment, lie, or put their personal needs above those of the child. Very often divorcing parents are magnanimous in how they relate to each other and the child. They put their ill feelings aside and focus on doing what is best for the child. However, the risks for these problem behaviors increase when families are divorcing, usually as a direct function of the level of acrimony between the parents.

Regardless of whether both parents agree to treatment, it may be desirable to establish parameters of treatment ahead of time. These include an understanding that the purpose of therapy is for treatment only and not for making custody recommendations. Psychologists may inform parents that they will not be discussing the case with any attorneys or any court (some psychologists say they will only discuss the case with a court-appointed custody evaluator on receipt of a court order or the appropriate releases from all the necessary parties). In addition, some psychologists require parents to pay for all services, even for time spent talking to a custody evaluator and time spent talking to an attorney explaining that they will not make a custody recommendation.

In Chapter 11 ("The Reluctant Business Person"), we discuss payment issues, and we suggest that psychologists should ordinarily refrain from "nickel-and-diming" patients with charges even if they are covered in the psychologist/patient therapeutic agreement. Nonetheless, we believe that it is often clinically indicated to be firm about insisting on payment for forensic or forensic-like services when treating high-conflict families.

Requiring payment for such services substantially cuts down on clinically contraindicated or frivolous requests for information.

Finally, when the custody conflict is especially vicious, it may be prudent to get a court order for treatment. This ensures that neither parent can waffle on consent or use the threat of withholding consent to advance a clinically contraindicated agenda. Nonetheless, psychologists who agree to see families on the basis of a court order need to clarify who will be paying for services; what, if any, unusual confidentiality limits apply; and to whom (if anyone) to send reports.

The treatment of high-conflict families takes on special considerations as shown here.

A child's therapist was asked to do a custody evaluation by one or both of the attorneys involved because he already knew the family situation and was liked by both parents. (5.5)

Of course, in this situation the psychologist would reject the offer, noting that the "Guidelines for Child Custody Evaluations in Family Law Proceedings" (APA, 2010b; hereinafter referred to as the APA Child Custody Guidelines) generally prohibit such a change in roles (there are narrow exceptions, such as in isolated or frontier areas where the availability of mental health professionals is limited). Ideally, the requesting parent would understand the therapeutic reasons behind the rule (e.g., the quality of therapy is compromised when forensic and treatment roles are mixed; there is a high risk of alienating one or more of the parents by participating in such roles; and such opinions by treating psychologists are based on less information than opinions expressed by custody evaluators). Nonetheless, at times some parents seem unable to appreciate these reasons, and it may be prudent to reference the APA Child Custody Guidelines which admonishes psychologists to vigilantly maintain boundaries.

A psychologist was treating a child in a high-conflict family. During the course of treatment, the psychologist received a phone call from the mother asking him to send a summary of the treatment to her attorney.

Because the psychologist was a covered entity under HIPAA, the mother had a right to receive a summary of treatment. However, the psychologist was concerned about actions that would compromise the neutrality of therapy. Consequently, as part of his informed consent procedure he informed both parents that he would not be releasing information to third parties unconnected with treatment (except for a court-appointed evaluator with the consent of the parties controlling confidentiality). He also informed parents again that they would be billed for all time spent related to the custody case, even if it included speaking to parents or attorneys about why he would not be involved in the custody dispute.

> The psychologist believed that the child would benefit most from a therapeutic setting in which the child felt safe and removed from the turmoil of the custody decision. Although he was normally generous in providing incidental services to patients without charge, the psychologist billed the mother $30 for the 15-minute phone call in which he explained again the reason he would not be involved. He strongly believed that such bills would discourage the parents from nontherapeutic demands on his time. (5.6)

It is important to remember the risk management factors (patient characteristics, context, and psychologist factors). Psychologists will often find high-risk patients in this high-risk context.

High-conflict families include patients in litigation and often patients with serious personality disorders. Some argue that the patients in high-conflict families are only manifesting behaviors representative of personality disorders in the context of the stressful custody fight. Others might say that the conflicts are expected manifestations of the underlying personality disorders of each parent. In any event, the family members are expressing projection, rigidity, splitting, and other behaviors that seriously interfere with healthy functioning. Consequently, it is very important to use the risk management strategies (informed consent, documentation, and consultation) in these situations.

CHILD CUSTODY

Child custody evaluations are the most frequent context in which parents complain to licensing boards. Bow, Gottlieb, Siegel, and Noble (2010) found that 63% of custody evaluators had licensing board complaints filed against them. About 20% of custody evaluators have had three or more complaints filed against them (Ackerman & Pritzl, 2011). A very high percentage of these complaints are dismissed without an adverse action against the psychologist. Fortunately, some states, such as Pennsylvania, have enacted legislative barriers to frivolous complaints against court-appointed evaluators.

However, complaints also are lodged against psychologists who perform court-ordered therapy, parent education, or other services. In addition, psychologists who are treating patients who are involved in custody disputes in some way may sometimes get involved, albeit unwillingly or unknowingly, in an allegation of misconduct.

Psychologists often evaluate children in anticipation of custody litigation.[3] Who gets custody of children when a marriage dissolves is a difficult legal and moral question. For better or worse, the U.S. system of government delegates the decision making on child custody to local courts in the event that the parents cannot reach a parenting

---

[3] From "Some (Relatively) Simple Risk Management Strategies" by E. Harris, 2004, Spring/Summer, *MassPsych: The Journal of the Massachusetts Psychological Association, 48*, pp. 27–28. Copyright 2004 by the Massachusetts Psychological Association. Adapted with permission of the author. Also from "Child Custody and Custody-Related Evaluations and Interventions: What Every Psychologist Should Know," by S. Knapp and R. Baturin, 2003, March, *The Pennsylvania Psychologist, 63*, pp. 3–4. Copyright 2003 by the Pennsylvania Psychological Association. Adapted with permission of the authors.

arrangement voluntarily. Courts may order parents to mediation or another alternative dispute resolution. If none are available, or if those means fail, the courts may order psychological evaluations to assist in making those determinations.

Typically, the court or a private party arranges for an evaluation to help the court decide the custody arrangement that is in the best interest of the child. The process used to conduct these evaluations should correspond to the APA Child Custody Guidelines. Among other things, these evaluations should address the needs of the children, not the parents. Custody evaluations typically involve psychological testing and interviews with all relevant parties (parents, stepparents, relatives, significant others, the children, and sometimes the teachers and neighbors, as appropriate). Related to custody evaluations are *focused evaluations*, which may be an update of a previous evaluation or a record review in which a psychologist reviews the work of a previously conducted custody evaluation.

Many contested cases bring about the worst in the individuals involved, and the behaviors of the parents may appear similar to those found in patients with serious personality disorders. In such situations, interpretations of the behavior of another person may be governed by the principle that "the friend of my friend is my friend, and the friend of my enemy is my enemy." If one parent perceives that the psychologist is more favorable to the other parent, the parent may vilify the psychologist and have no hesitation about reporting him or her to a licensing board.

Many psychologists note that attorneys involved in custody disputes may leverage their cases by encouraging and assisting the client to file a licensing board complaint against the psychologist evaluator if it appears that the recommendation will not be favorable to the party the attorney represents. Although such a complaint may not impact the current case, when the judge makes the final decision as to the adequacy of the evaluation and testimony, having a history of licensing board complaints can significantly damage one's reputation and practice.

Psychologists do make errors that are likely to engender disciplinary actions. The most common reasons for complaints being filed are allegations of bias, inadequate procedures, failure to investigate an issue, and billing or collection problems (Bow et al., 2010). Other allegations include sending out information without having a release of information form or court order, failing to get consent of parents or a court order when conducting an evaluation, making substantial scoring errors on tests, or not performing the work in a timely manner. The use of projective tests (e.g., Draw-A-Person, Thematic Apperception Test, Children's Apperception Test, and Rorschach) can open the psychologist to severe cross-examination. Psychologists who use these tests need to be sure that they know them well enough to justify them as valid for some meaningful purpose in this situation.

Custody evaluators, of course, like other psychologists, have to report suspected child abuse. We urge psychologists to interpret their state laws literally. Psychologists should not assume that because another health care professional is involved in the case that they do not need to report suspected or known abuse. Such laws typically require reporting when the psychologist suspects or believes that abuse has occurred. Thus the threshold for reporting is low. It does not necessitate certainty, nor does it require the psychologist to verify the accuracy of the report. Even if, on a statistical basis, the probability of founded reports is substantially lower when they are made in the context of a custody dispute, child abuse does occur and must be reported when the necessary threshold is reached. Unfortunately, in highly charged custody cases it is not unusual for one parent to accuse the other of child abuse.

Some parent support groups are very aggressive about reporting psychologists who do custody evaluations to the point that such allegations are used as a tactical weapon designed to intimidate evaluators or create an apparent conflict of interest that will result in removing the psychologist from the case. Some parents have been coached to plant inaccurate information in the child's history so that they can have grounds for alleging negligence on the part of the psychologist if they do not like the conclusions in the report. They may, for example, report that the child started a private school in February 2005, when in fact the child started the private school in March 2005. Although this fact may be irrelevant to the issues facing the court, it nonetheless creates an impression of sloppiness on the part of the psychologist. More importantly, websites now provide parents advice on how to respond to the psychologist's questions and tests that are part of the custody evaluation. Unfortunately, some of these websites do not focus on the well-being of the child, nor do they encourage transparency and self-reflection. Instead, they appear to represent custody proceedings as life-and-death struggles with no holds barred, with winning being the primary (or only) goal.

Attorneys vary considerably in the manner by which they handle custody disputes. It has been said that clients pick the attorneys most likely to reflect their personal styles. However, the obligation of attorneys is to their clients, not to the psychologist. Some attorneys attempt a more restrained and moderate approach, recognizing that the long-term welfare of the family will be best ensured by fair play during the divorce and custody proceedings. Others, sometimes with an exaggerated sense of self-righteousness, demonstrate unrestrained aggression toward the other parent or the custody evaluators if it suits their purposes, even if it means harming the child in the process.

Special Risk Management Strategies for Custody Evaluators

Good risk management strategies both protect the psychologist from allegations of misconduct and, at the same time, help reduce the harm that may occur to the litigants or the children as they go through the custody process. Custody evaluations are inherently stressful for the litigants, and the process itself may increase the tension between the litigants. It is hard for a parent to be vilified in court one day and then deal respectfully with the spouse the next day on a matter related to parenting. As a result many custody evaluators do what they can, within the limits of their role, to reduce the likelihood of harm to the litigants or the children during the process.

In this section we review the unique risk management strategies that custody evaluators can use, such as ensuring competence and maintaining boundaries. Because every custody evaluation occurs in a high-risk context, psychologists should always keep the three universal risk management strategies (consultation, documentation, and informed consent) in mind.

Competence

It takes special skills to be a child custody evaluator. Simple competence as a child clinical psychologist is necessary but not sufficient. Some skills of child clinical psychologists are relevant, such as knowledge of child development (including normal developmental stages), family systems, parenting skills (including the match between parents and children), psychological testing (including the degree of confidence to place in the sources of data and information on the psychometric properties of the tests), child and adult psychopathology, report writing, knowing how to testify, and basic professional ethics. In addition, competent custody evaluators know the basic workings of the legal system, professional ethics as applied to forensic practices, the unique clinical features that are likely to occur in high-conflict families such as serious allegations of misconduct by one parent against the other, exaggeration of small concerns into major issues, and similar features that occur when parents are locked in battle. Custody evaluators need to know how to identify and respond to domestic abuse or child-alienating strategies on the part of parents. Some families will make up or exaggerate allegations of domestic abuse or parent alienation as a tactic. However, abuse and alienating behaviors do occur in some divorcing families and can have a profound impact on the life of the child. Although most evaluators are skeptical of parental alienation as a "syndrome," they do acknowledge alienating behaviors or dynamics (Bow, Gould, & Flens, 2009). Given the extent of knowledge needed to conduct child custody evaluations, it is best to consider them as a subspecialty of forensic psychology.

Whether conducting child custody evaluations or evaluating sexual abuse, psychologists may find their personal biases influencing their professional decisions (Everson & Sandoval, 2011). Some psychologists, because of personal histories, may—without conscious awareness—lean toward giving greater credibility to fathers (or to mothers) or toward giving greater weight to the wishes of the children. However, psychologists can greatly reduce the impact of these biases if they have thought through their reactions to divorce carefully and embedded themselves in a supportive professional environment.

Furthermore, it is necessary to have the personality to tolerate the stresses of child custody work including resilience, comfort and confidence in one's work, problem-solving abilities, conflict tolerance, and a sense of humor. The average competent clinician should not enter the custody arena without substantial additional education, supervision, or consultation.

Prudent psychologists will follow the APA Guidelines on Child Custody Evaluations meticulously. In addition, other guidelines, although not necessarily binding on psychologists, such as the APA *Specialty Guidelines for Forensic Psychology* (2013b) and standards of the Association of Family and Conciliatory Courts (AFCC, 2006) can provide useful guidance. Custody evaluators have a difficult job. They are dealing with families at a time when emotions are high and when some otherwise decent parents are not always acting at their best. In that context psychologists must ask highly personal questions and report candidly what they observe and conclude. They may face many unexpected and unusual questions, for example, What should be my relationship with collateral contacts (individuals who are not the subject of the evaluation, but provide information useful to the evaluator)? How should I handle attorneys who want to engage in ex parte communications? How should I structure the informed consent process so that it helps mitigate potential iatrogenic effects of the custody process? How do I handle the request of a parent for me to listen to a tape of his spouse that he made surreptitiously? Professional guidelines address many of these issues. It also is essential to have a cadre of professionals for backup and support.

Finally, psychologists can improve their effectiveness as custody evaluators by appreciating the formal and informal rules governing the local court. The rules and procedures of a child custody court vary from state to state, and even within the same state, they may vary from county to county. There are also informal or unwritten preferences of particular judges on how they want a report written.

Client Relationships

We noted in Chapter 4 ("Multiple Relationships and Boundaries") that not all multiple relationships are inherently unethical. However, greater sensitivity to potential harm should be adopted for multiple relationships in the context of child custody evaluations. The mere appearance of a conflict of interest may be sufficient to undermine confidence in the custody evaluator. As noted in the APA *Specialty Guidelines for Forensic Psychology* (2013b), "forensic practitioners are encouraged to identify, make known, and address real or apparent conflicts of interest" (1.03).

In Chapter 4 we gave an example of a psychologist who realized, after marital therapy had started, that he had seen one of the spouses in individual therapy 10 years earlier. Similar discoveries have been made by psychologists who have completed child custody evaluations. In a custody evaluation, the court (if it is a court-ordered evaluation) and attorneys must also be consulted on whether the evaluation can continue.

Evaluators should adopt a polite but reserved stance with the parent litigants. These situations contain the risk that anxious or angry litigants will misconstrue otherwise innocuous comments or use them maliciously. One custody evaluator told a parent that she "looked nice today." Her complaint against the custody evaluator included allegations of sexual advances. Another custody evaluator told a parent that he was doing custody evaluations because he was tired of dealing with managed care. The parent later cited this comment in his complaint that the evaluator was untrained for custody work.

Finally, care must be taken to ensure an appearance of fairness. In one instance, a complaint was based on the fact that the psychologist spent more time interviewing one parent than the other. Although the time differential was entirely justified by the circumstances, the mere appearance of unfairness was sufficient to prompt a complaint.

Consultation

Every custody evaluator needs to have a resource for advice on unusual clinical or legal situations that arise. Even the most skilled custody evaluator will encounter some unusual family pattern or custody related issue that requires consultation with another professional. The consultation services offered by professional liability insurance companies such as The Trust are one source for advice on high-risk situations.

Documentation

Custody evaluators work in a fishbowl where everything they do must be documented carefully, and every decision they make needs to be justified. Without sacrificing accuracy, psychologists can reduce the likelihood of harm by using language about the litigants in their reports that is as tactful as possible. It is prudent to assume that the parents will eventually read the report. A survey by Bow, Gottlieb, Gould-Saltman, and Hendershot (2011) showed that 40% of attorneys gave their clients copies of the custody report, and another 47% allowed their clients to read the reports.

Informed Consent

Psychologists can also reduce harm to litigants by being especially scrupulous about the informed consent procedures to ensure that the litigants understand the nature of the custody evaluation process and the role of the evaluator. Also, A. Shienvold (personal communication, February 2012) reported that he uses "affective informed consent," which means part of the informed consent process involves informing the litigants of common emotional reactions that they may experience as they move forward with the custody process. Other custody evaluators point out the importance of ensuring that the litigants feel their concerns have been heard. That is, evaluators should be able to repeat to the litigants the general nature of their interpretation of the salient issues involved in the custody dispute. A balance needs to be made, however, so that custody evaluators do not act so friendly that they inadvertently convey agreement with the parent's perspective.

Other Risk Management Comments

Risk management practices for custody evaluators include having professional liability insurance that covers licensing board complaints. Surprisingly, Bow et al. (2010) reported that one half of custody evaluators did not have professional liability insurance that covered licensing board complaints. Custody evaluators also benefit when they are court appointed because the court appointment provides some limited immunity for lawsuits, but not licensing board complaints.

ALTERNATIVE DISPUTE RESOLUTION AND OTHER ROLES

Many people have become dissatisfied with using litigation to resolve disputes because of the time and cost involved. In addition, litigation tends to force parents into adversarial roles. Consequently, several methods of alternative dispute resolution (ADR), such as arbitration or mediation, have been applied to family disputes. These

ADRs differ in terms of their degree of confidentiality, the extent to which they are legally binding, and the qualifications of the persons who perform them. The particular ADR used depends on the state laws and local rules. Mediators have their own training programs and standards of conduct. Often mediators are attorneys, but they may also be psychologists and other mental health professionals.

Collaborative divorce is another alternative to the adversarial process. In a collaborative divorce, the attorneys and their clients work toward a mutually agreeable settlement. If they are unable to reach a settlement, the attorneys may not be involved in any future litigation (Tesler & Thompson, 2006). Collaborative attorneys sometimes hire psychologists as consultants to facilitate the collaborative process or to act as child development consultants to the parents.

Some courts have appointed psychologists (or other professionals) as parenting coordinators whose goal is to resolve disputes between the parents if they are consistently unable to agree on day-to-day decisions regarding parenting. The parenting coordinator may not alter the custody order. Parenting coordination is a specialized type of service that requires in-depth training (APA, 2012d).

Court-Involved Therapy

Parents in high-conflict families will often seek the services of psychologists, or the court may order them to receive these services. The services may be called parenting classes, co-parent education, therapy, or family therapy. However, judges may use these terms differently, so psychologists responding to court orders for services need to ensure that they understand the nature of the services that the judges want.

Parenting classes are generally conducted in an educational format and are designed to address common problems encountered by families. Some parenting classes may be tailored to families that are undergoing a divorce. In co-parent counseling, psychologists meet with the parents to help them consider the best manner in which to work together to promote the welfare of (or minimize the harm to) their children. Of course, psychologists may provide therapy to the child, either of the parents, or to the family. When judges refer a family for therapy, it is desirable to identify the specific issue that prompts the judge to make the referral. Whenever possible, a psychologist who is providing therapy to a child in a custody dispute should attempt to get an agreement from all parties to protect their neutrality in providing treatment for the child.

Whenever a judge or attorney refers a parent for therapy or parenting classes, it is desirable for the judge to clarify the goals and nature of services ahead of time and whether the judge wants a report, how frequently he or she wants the report, and to whom the report should be sent.

Psychologists who provide court-ordered services to parents or children should ensure that the court order allows them to structure the relationship in a manner that they believe will be effective. Some of the issues that need to be clarified include what information, if any, can be released and to whom; whether one or both parents may be or have to be involved in therapy; whether the psychologist must give copies of the treatment records to the parents; whether the court expects the psychologist to testify in court; and who pays for services (L. R. Greenberg, Gould-Saltman, & Gottlieb, 2008). The "Guidelines for Court-Involved Therapy" from the Association of Family and Conciliatory Courts even recommends that psychologists include the fee arrangement in the court order (AFCC Task Force on Court-Involved Therapy, 2011). Although the treating psychologist should not make custody recommendations, the court may request feedback on the parents' or child's progress in therapy or relationship dynamics (AFCC Task Force on Court-Involved Therapy, 2011).

The agreement should allow psychologists to bill for all the time they spend on matters outside of actual therapy, such as communicating with attorneys or other third parties; all legal work, including reading reports, reviewing records, traveling to court, speaking to attorneys, and getting consultation; and all other time. If psychologists spend only a small amount of time on matters outside of therapy, they can always decide after the fact to waive the costs of such services. On the other hand, we know patients who have requested services from their psychologists that resulted in dozens of hours of time. As long as psychologists make the payment arrangements known ahead of time and the parents agree to them, they have the right to bill and collect for such services. In addition, psychologists who require payment for such services discourage patients from impulsively requesting clinically contraindicated third-party involvement.

> A psychologist agreed to treat a child in a high-conflict family. After the first session one parent gave the psychologist a box with more than 1,000 pages of court transcripts, letters, previous medical records, and other information, and told the psychologist that "you really cannot help my child unless you understand the background which is contained in these records." (5.7)

Reading through these papers and understanding the full implication of everything would have probably taken the psychologist 100 hours. After briefly reviewing the documents, the psychologist contacted the parent, reminded him of the payment arrangements (which required compensation for all extra-therapy time spent on the case), and asked him if there was a better way for him to communicate his perception of the child's needs.

Whether a psychologist should apply for third-party reimbursement for these services depends on the nature of the service. A parenting class will probably not qualify for reimbursement, whereas therapy might. It is very unwise to "relabel" something to gain access to insurance coverage. Whether co-parent counseling or reunification counseling qualifies for insurance reimbursement depends on whether the intervention is designed to alleviate a mental disorder in the identified patient and if the services are covered under the parent's health insurance policy by the managed care company.

Reunification Therapy

At times, children will become emotionally detached from a parent and resist or refuse to visit a parent even when the court determines that such a relationship would be indicated. In deciding how to respond to these situations, judges need to consider the long-term benefits of having a relationship with one parent versus the short-term resistance of the child. Often the favored parent views himself or herself as the protector of the child and will sabotage efforts at reconciliation.

The courts may order reunification or reintegration therapy in which the child and alienated parent receive therapy with the goal of achieving some reconciliation. These may be the most difficult therapy assignments that a psychologist will ever have. The favored parent may undermine therapy by missing appointments, continually demanding a change in therapists, encouraging the child to reject the other parent, or encouraging the child to resist court-ordered visitations or meetings. Despite a small body of literature showing success for some programs (Johnston & Goldman, 2010; Sullivan, Ward, & Deutsch, 2010; Warshak, 2010), "it is prudent to have modest expectations for change" (Johnston & Goldman, 2010, p. 114).

Other Services to High-Conflict Families

At other times the parents may have sought treatment on their own, and there is no court order to direct how information is to be released. Ellis (2010) argued that psychologists should not routinely turn over notes to custody evaluators but may do so under unusual circumstances, such as if there is a strong need for the custody evaluator to have the records and the information cannot be obtained elsewhere.

On the other hand, custody evaluators may claim that they routinely need to have access to all sources of information, including psychotherapy records to ensure the thoroughness of their evaluation. At times courts have issued orders for therapists to release records to the custody evaluator. In the hands of good custody evaluators, notes or conversations with custody evaluators will be only one of many sources of information on the parent, and they treat these notes with the sensitivity they deserve. Conscientious custody evaluators know that seeking therapy is often a sign of strength and insight, and they commend parents for having the insight and strength to take care of themselves or to seek services for a child in distress.

Psychologists with patients who are litigants in a custody case should expect to receive a request (or even a court order) for treatment records. Psychologists can minimize harm to the therapy relationships by informing patients ahead of time that such a request may be made and clarifying what the communications with the custody evaluator will or will not include.

Often litigant patients will want the psychologist to include information in the notes or a separate report that will advocate for them and tell the custody evaluator that they are a fit parent or endorse the parenting plan favored by the parent. However, psychologists should inform patients at the start of treatment that they are not, by virtue of their role as a treating professional, competent to make such comments. Most treating psychologists will have an inherent bias toward their patients. Furthermore, they will not have evaluated the parenting skills of the other parent (or perhaps even the parent being seen in therapy) and will not have conducted the tests or parent–child observations, contacted collateral sources, or taken the other steps that custody evaluators typically take to determine parenting competence.

However, even treating psychologists who do not intend to provide a custody recommendation may inadvertently do so, thinking that they are performing a good service. For example, sometimes attorneys request a report and phrase it in a deceptively innocuous manner, such as asking the treating psychologists to comment on visitation arrangements. Naive treating psychologists may do so without realizing that any comment about the custody arrangements is crossing the line into a custody evaluation.

Psychologists can reduce problems with releasing notes to custody evaluators if they write the notes carefully to reduce the likelihood that their records could be misconstrued. When custody evaluators have access to therapeutic information (either by speaking to the psychologist directly or reviewing notes), the psychologists can ask the evaluator to fax a written summary of how this information will be used in the report to ensure that the evaluator correctly understands the content of the conversation or therapy notes. In addition, they need to be candid with their patients about what was said.

SEVEN ESSENTIAL POINTS TO REMEMBER

1. It is important to clarify obligations whenever treating more than one person in a relationship (see APA Ethics Code Standard 10.02, Therapy Involving Couples or Families).

2. The treatment of children and adolescents involves special issues regarding assent, permission, informed consent, and confidentiality. The rules may vary from state to state or even within the same state depending on the treatment setting.

3. The treatment of high-conflict families requires a special awareness of the unique clinical features that such families are likely to manifest.

4. The risk management strategies of informed consent, documentation, and consultation are very important when treating high-risk families.

5. Psychologists who perform child custody evaluations should follow the APA Child Custody Guidelines and relevant state laws and receive specialized training.

6. Participation as a custody evaluator requires special skills, training, and temperament in addition to those held by otherwise competent child clinical psychologists.

7. Psychologists may perform valuable roles in alternative dispute resolution or other roles helping divorcing families. However, these roles involve disciplinary risks as well.

CHAPTER 6: PRIVACY, CONFIDENTIALITY, AND PRIVILEGED COMMUNICATIONS

Privacy is the constitutional right of individuals to choose for themselves whether or when to reveal private information. Privacy overlaps but is distinguished from confidentiality and privileged communications. Confidentiality is the duty imposed on professionals to keep information disclosed in professional relationships in confidence. It is embedded in ethics codes and state laws but also in the federal Health Insurance Portability and Accountability Act of 1996 (HIPAA) Privacy Rule (hereinafter referred to as the Privacy Rule). Privileged communication is a legal term that refers to the legal right of individuals to withhold information in judicial proceedings under limited circumstances.

Throughout this book we have emphasized the importance of therapeutic discretion in applying the risk management strategies. However, in this chapter we give relatively more emphasis to understanding basic information about the legal system and its impact on the practice of psychology. Of course, psychologists still must use their professional judgment on many important issues such as how much effort to place on preventing accidental breaches of confidentiality and how to handle patient requests for records.

BASIC FACTS ABOUT CONFIDENTIALITY

Privacy and confidentiality are cornerstones of effective psychotherapy. As stated by the United States Supreme Court in *Jaffee v. Redmond* (1996),

> *Effective psychotherapy... depends upon an atmosphere of confidence and trust in which the patient is willing to make a frank and complete disclosure of facts, emotions, memories and fears. Because of the sensitive nature of the problems for which individuals consult psychotherapists, disclosure of confidential communications made during counseling sessions may cause embarrassment or disgrace. For this reason, the mere possibility of disclosure may impede development of the confidential relationship necessary for successful treatment. (p. 340)*

Psychologists are required to protect patient privacy by virtue of the American Psychological Association's (APA's) "Ethics Principles of Psychologists and Code of Conduct" (hereinafter referred to as the APA Ethics Code; APA, 2010a), provisions of their state's licensing law (many of which adopt the APA Ethics Code or a version of it or the Association of State and Provincial Psychology Boards' *ASPPB Code of Conduct*), and other statutes and case law. The general rule is that psychologists must keep patient information confidential. They do not gossip about patients or permit the unauthorized release of patient information except in specific situations as required or permitted by law. This means, among other things, that psychologists take special care in how they create, store, and dispose of records. There are also rules regarding patient access to records.

The special rules governing the release of patient information in court proceedings are referred to as privileged communication laws. These laws deal with the limited circumstances in which courts will permit patients to withhold confidential information from legal proceedings. Other rules regarding patient releases, subpoenas, or court orders deal with the circumstances under which psychologists are required to release information into court.

Most rules governing confidentiality are found in state laws. However, the Privacy Rule, which went into effect in April 2003, established minimum nationwide standards for confidentiality of patient information. Moreover, the Privacy Rule contains a preemption clause; it holds that any state law that is more protective of patient privacy trumps the minimum standards in the Privacy Rule. Because mental health laws tend to be more protective of patient privacy than other laws dealing with health care records, the Privacy Rule has had little impact on the day-to-day manner in which psychologists handle confidential information. We describe these minimal changes in the discussion that follows.

The Privacy Rule requires each covered entity to appoint a Privacy Officer who is responsible to develop and implement privacy protections. Among other things, Privacy Officers ensure that each patient receives a Privacy Notice, all staff members are trained in confidentiality issues, and the other confidentiality requirements are met. Because certain aspects of HIPAA are scalable (meaning that the measures to implement it vary according to the size and needs of the organization), most solo practitioners serve as their own Privacy Officer, and in small practices, one owner or employee can be appointed the Privacy Officer.

Exceptions to Confidentiality

The exceptions to confidentiality are determined by the standards in the APA Ethics Code and the relationship of these standards to the peculiarities of state and federal law. The exceptions to confidentiality may occur either through the actions of the patient (such as by signing an authorization to release information) or through an exception created for public policy reasons. The public policy exceptions include consultations with other professionals or the mandated reporting of suspected child abuse. Other mandatory reporting laws found in some but not all states include reporting of elder abuse, medical errors, impaired professionals, professionals who have sexually abused patients, professionals who have committed serious ethical violations, and impaired drivers. More details on these mandated reporting requirements are found in Chapter 9 ("Assessing and Treating Patients Who Are Potentially Suicidal or Dangerous to Others"). The point is that psychologists need to know their state laws.

The APA Ethics Code permits psychologists to consult with other professionals concerning a patient as long as they "do not disclose information that reasonably could lead to the identification of a client/patient" and limit the disclosure "to the extent necessary to achieve the purposes of the consultation" (Standard 4.06, Consultations). Most psychologists prefer a broader right of consultation that allows them to identify the patient if it is appropriate to the consultation, such as with the referral sources, the patient's primary care physician, or the patient's psychiatrist. The laws and regulations in some states permit such consultations, as does the Privacy Rule. However, the laws and regulations in other states are silent with regard to such consultations. The Trust recommends that even when permitted by state law, psychologists include a consultation policy as part of the informed consent agreement that patients sign.

There is an exception that permits psychologists to review information with workers' compensation referees in some states. Discretionary disclosures when clinically indicated may include a breach of confidentiality when needed to protect a patient with a high risk of suicide or in most states to protect an identifiable third party from violence (we discuss this topic in greater detail in Chapter 9, "Assessing and Treating Patients Who Are Potentially Suicidal or Dangerous to Others"). Other narrow exceptions include collections for payment of bills and giving confidential information to the executors or personal representatives of the estates of deceased patients (in most states).

Confidentiality rights of minors vary from state to state. Psychologists need to consider who controls the confidentiality of minors. If parents control the information, psychologists need to consider how much to involve the parents in the information exchange and whether to use an agreement of confidentiality (see Chapter 4, "Working with Couples, Families, and Children").

Breaches of Confidentiality

Most psychologists are scrupulous about the protection of patient privacy. Seldom do they gossip or talk about their patients in public places or display identifiable confidential patient information openly. However, a few psychologists are indiscreet about patient information and may tell stories about patients at parties or to their close friends. Even though they may believe that the patient is not identifiable, such an assumption might not always be warranted. Furthermore, such "entertaining" stories may give an impression that these professional psychologists are not taking the problems or privacy of their patients seriously.

Also, an accidental breach of confidentiality can occur in any professional setting. When psychologists have their offices in their homes, professional mail may get mixed up with personal mail, or messages from the answering machine may be played too loudly and be overheard by members of the family. The conversations of psychologists meeting for a lunch consultation may be overhead by others sitting nearby. In large institutions, extra protections for patient records stored on computers may be needed. In any setting, voices may sometimes bleed through the office walls and ceilings, patient charts may be left unattended, and staff members may forget that they need permission before leaving messages on the answering machines of patients.

According to the Privacy Rule, the Privacy Officer is responsible for training support staff members (and documenting that training). Within the office, patient privacy should be everyone's business. In the ideal environment, all of the staff members (clerical, billing, and professional) will be looking out for the welfare of the patient and each other. When threats to patient privacy arise, each staff member should feel comfortable addressing the issues with each other. All psychologists are human and may be unaware of how their behavior presents a threat to confidentiality.

Psychologists should also have *business associate* agreements. Business associates are non-healthcare professionals with whom psychologists have contracts but whom they do not employ and who have a legitimate reason to get protected healthcare information. Business associates include billing services, bookkeepers, and attorneys. A business associate agreement ensures that these associates will respect the confidentiality of the information provided to them.

PRIVILEGED COMMUNICATIONS

The term *privileged communications* refers to a limited right to withhold information from a court (Younggren & Harris, 2008). Within the United States the first privileged communication laws were developed to ensure that clients would be able to share all relevant information with their attorneys without fear that the attorneys could later be required to testify against them in court. However, in creating privileged communication laws, the legislatures balanced the interest of fairness in justice against other social policies to determine the exception to the general rule of admitting all evidence into court. That is, the likelihood that a court could reach an erroneous conclusion increases every time evidence is withheld from the court because of a privileged communication law. Because fairness in dispute resolution is a high social value, legislators have been reluctant to create privileged relationships, and courts have tended to interpret them narrowly.

Although some may argue that privileged communication laws are based on a constitutional right to privacy, courts have been reluctant to accept such arguments (Knapp & VandeCreek, 1987). Instead, most legislatures have enacted psychologist–patient privilege laws primarily out of utilitarian concerns. That is, the overall public good is promoted when patients can receive therapy without unnecessary worry that their communications will be made public. Some degree of privacy is necessary for effective psychotherapy.

Privilege laws exist in every state for the attorney–client, husband–wife, and priest–penitent (or clergy–communicant) relationships. Many states also have privileged communication laws for the social worker–client, sexual assault crisis counselor–client, domestic abuse counselor–client, counselor–client, physician–patient, and journalist–source relationships.

All states have a privileged communication law for psychologist–patient relationships, although the scope of these laws varies greatly from state to state. In some states the protections are quite extensive; in other states they are very limited. In any event, in every state these laws all have some exceptions and, unless their application is clear, will be narrowly construed by the courts. Privilege laws are enacted state by state and usually profession by profession so that patients of different mental health professionals in the same state may have quite different protections. A psychotherapist–patient privilege exists in all federal courts. Here are some exceptions that apply in some states, depending on the privilege statute or the common law interpretation that the courts have given to the statute. There is no substitute for learning the relevant state rules.

Most state privilege laws include an exception when patients place their mental status into litigation as part of their claim or defense. In addition, once they have made their mental health a part of the litigation, patients may not selectively edit what gets admitted without special permission from the court. In some states, courts hold that any time parents seek custody of a child, they are entering their mental health into litigation, and the privilege would not apply. The privilege typically does not apply during a hearing for a civil commitment to a hospital or when individuals enter their mental health into litigation, such as when they present a plea of insanity or diminished mental capacity or if they initiate a suit alleging emotional harm (such as a malpractice suit). The privilege does not apply to court-ordered examinations. The courts in many states have carved out additional exceptions for when a patient self-releases information about the treatment or when the patient's behavior is inconsistent with an expectation of privacy. Most state laws allow psychologists to pursue patients who do not pay their bills but limit the information that they may release to collection agencies to that which is necessary to collect the debt. Another exception occurs if psychologists seek restraining orders against patients who threaten their safety.

In some jurisdictions the privilege may only apply to those professional relationships that involve the diagnosis and treatment of a mental or nervous disorder; other professional communications may not be covered. In some jurisdictions the privilege may apply only to the information shared by the patient, whereas in others it will include collateral contacts with family members or others who are present to further treatment. In some jurisdictions it covers supervisees; in other jurisdictions, it does not. In many jurisdictions judges have discretion to waive the privilege if it is necessary for the administration of justice.

This list of potential exceptions is not given to imply that the privilege is completely toothless. Indeed, it provides meaningful protection for many patients. Not all of the exceptions apply in all states, but this list of exceptions illustrates the idiosyncratic manner in which privilege laws are written or the manner in which courts interpret the privilege laws under similar circumstances. Although psychologists should be familiar with the privilege statute and its exceptions in their state, they should always refer patients to a mental health attorney when they have questions about unique circumstances such as whether their communications will be protected if they are involved in an unrelated lawsuit.

> The privilege exists for the benefit of the patient and belongs to the patient. A psychologist received a court order to testify but refused to do so, noting that she was invoking the "psychologist privilege" even though the patient wanted her to testify. She did not realize that she had no standing to invoke the privilege (except in some states in which psychologists have a narrow obligation to invoke the privilege on behalf of the patient if the patient cannot be located). (6.1)

The privilege only deals with the circumstances under which patients may block psychologists from sharing information with the court. It is not up to the psychologist to determine that a patient has waived the privilege. It is up to the judge, after hearing arguments from attorneys, to make a final determination. Psychologists, for their part, can only release records with a signed patient release of information form (authorization) or court order.

> A psychologist received a phone call from an attorney who told him that he was sending a subpoena to turn over patient records, that the patient had waived her privilege by introducing her mental health into litigation, that the subpoena was binding on the psychologist, and that the failure of the psychologist to honor the subpoena would be construed as contempt of court, and he could be subject to imprisonment or fines if he refused to comply. The psychologist, who had neither a release from his patient nor a court order, sent the records. He was later disciplined by his state licensing board. (6.2)

This psychologist failed to appreciate that privileged communication laws deal only with the criteria that the courts use for admitting evidence into court. These laws do not permit psychologists to make the decision about whether to release such records. Of course, the psychologist also failed to realize that the attorney was not acting on the psychologist's behalf and had no legal obligation to ensure that he understood the relevant state laws governing his profession. Unfortunately, such misrepresentations by attorneys are common.

Patients should be given some information about privileged communications at the start of treatment, presumably in a Privacy Notice or another informed consent document. The amount of information given needs to be tailored to the needs of individual patients. More extensive information should be given to patients who are involved in litigation or when it is anticipated.

Subpoenas and Court Orders

In general, a psychologist may only disclose information with the consent of the patient or in response to a court order.[1] The receipt of a subpoena alone without the consent of the patient does not override this requirement. A court order, however, overrides the need to obtain patient consent. *(See How to Handle Subpoenas and Depositions,* available at http://www.apapracticecentral.org/update/2008/12-17/subpoena.aspx).

A subpoena is a document issued by an attorney instructing the recipient to provide documents or to be present to give oral testimony. The exact form of a subpoena may vary from jurisdiction to jurisdiction, but it typically includes a signature or stamp of the clerk of court, prothonotary (court clerk), or an attorney.

A court order is a document issued by a presiding judge that instructs the recipient to provide documents or oral testimony. The exact form of the court order may vary from jurisdiction to jurisdiction, but it typically includes identification of the case and the signature of the judge.

Psychologists are required to respond to a subpoena, but they are prohibited from releasing records merely upon the receipt of a subpoena. In most instances the psychologists should inform the other party, in writing, that the receipt of a release of information form (authorization) signed by the patient is required prior to releasing information in response to a subpoena. If no such release is forthcoming, the psychologists should advise the requesting party that he or she is waiting for further instruction from the presiding judge. California, a state that is often imitated legislatively, allows a "Notice to Consumer" to be delivered to the patient or his or her legal representative with a subpoena. If the patient does not formally object within a specified period, they are deemed to have waived their privilege rights. This does not change the psychologists' responsibility in most cases to claim the privilege on the patient's behalf, but a California psychologist should be aware that this provision could be invoked by the requesting attorney. In that case, psychologists should seek consultation

Unfortunately, many attorneys do not understand that psychologists have limited discretion for releasing records. Attorneys representing patients (or sometimes attorneys representing parties adverse to the patient's interests) may misinform psychologists of their legal obligations and instruct them to release records in response to a subpoena alone. Psychologists should not allow themselves to be bullied by these tactics. It is best to seek legal consultation when the requirements are unclear.

A court order issued by the presiding judge does compel the release of records or testimony as specified in that order. Although psychologists may feel very strongly about the obligation to protect patient privacy, they need to remember that there are other competing social values in play, and judges, with their wealth of experience in the law

[1] From "Practical Considerations When Responding to Subpoenas and Court Orders," by S. Knapp, A. Tepper, and R. Baturin, 2003, August, *The Pennsylvania Psychologist, 63,* pp. 5, 16. Copyright 2003 by the Pennsylvania Psychological Association. Adapted with permission of the authors.

and the social obligation to ensure the administration of justice, are entrusted to balance competing demands and make such choices. Our experience is that judges, as a whole, are conscientious (often impressive) public servants who will consider the welfare of the patient and the overall public good. As a rule, they have no desire to cause needless harm to anyone. If a psychologist has a good reason to challenge a court order, most judges will want to learn of this concern.

When dealing with the courts, the first risk management rule is "Treat all judges with respect." In the rare situation in which psychologists wish to challenge a court order, we recommend that they obtain legal counsel to avoid any behavior that gives direct or indirect appearance of contemptuous behavior. Some battles are best left to others.

> A psychologist received a subpoena from an attorney asking for the release of patient records. The attorney followed up the subpoena with a phone call in which he claimed that the psychologist would be in contempt of court if she failed to send the requested information. The experienced psychologist was not intimidated by such tactics. She called her patient, and the patient, upon consultation with his attorney, decided that he did not want the information released. The psychologist then sent a brief letter to the attorney who sent the subpoena that stated she would only release patient information with a release signed by the patient or a court order. (6.3)

If the patient, upon consultation with his attorney, had wanted the information to be released, the psychologist would have acquired the appropriate release from the patient and sent the records. This experienced psychologist was wise enough to ensure that the patient had consulted with his attorney before any decision was made. If the patient had been a child, the psychologist would have contacted the parents and/or ascertained if a guardian ad litem had been appointed for the patient.

HIPAA PRIVACY RULE[2]

The Privacy Rule applies to any licensed health care provider who electronically transmits or hires someone to electronically transmit protected health care information in one or more covered transactions. All transactions involving communications with insurance, managed care, or third-party payer entities are covered. Once an electronic transmission occurs, the Privacy Rule thereafter applies to all of the psychologist's activities involving protected health care information. For now, psychologists who have not transmitted information electronically in one or more covered transactions are not covered by HIPAA. However, psychologists who receive reimbursement from third-party payers electronically are likely to be covered in the future if and when electronic billing or electronic utilization reviews are required.

---

[2] From "Resolving Some Areas of Continuing Confusion," by E. Harris, 2003, Winter, *MassPsych: The Journal of the Massachusetts Psychological Association, 47,* pp. 18–22, 29. Copyright 2003 by the Massachusetts Psychological Association. Adapted with permission of the author.

For those who are not covered entities but who bill clients directly with the expectation that they will pay out of pocket or seek reimbursement from third parties on their own, the future is uncertain. For those with an entirely self-pay practice or who exclusively engage in non-healthcare activities, such as forensic services or coaching, the Privacy Rule will most likely not apply. However, as soon as a psychologist transmits a bill or other covered information electronically, *the entire Privacy Rule will apply to the entire practice*. In addition, as more and more HIPAA rules are promulgated, it is possible that some future court will rule that some of the standards of HIPAA, such as a Privacy Notice at the start of therapy, will become mandatory for all health care providers. As the electronic creation and storage of records becomes more prevalent, it is increasingly important to consider the special protections required for electronic records (See discussion in Chapter 2, "Key Elements of Risk Management"). Because it is difficult to implement the Privacy Rule suddenly, we recommend that all psychologists understand the Privacy Rule and assume that it will apply to them in whole or in part at some point in the future.

The Privacy Rule has been in effect since April 15, 2003. The current APA Ethics Code has been in effect since June 1, 2003, with minor modification in 2010. Many psychologists have tried to understand and integrate these complex regulatory changes into their practices. However, the implementation process has exposed confusion and uncertainty concerning (a) informed consent, (b) psychotherapy notes, (c) forensic services, and (d) psychological testing. We review each of these four areas next.

Informed Consent

We have already reviewed informed consent as a risk management strategy in Chapter 2 ("Key Elements of Risk Management"), and we discuss the application of informed consent as a risk management strategy throughout other chapters. However, here we are just referring to the informed consent requirements found in the Privacy Rule.

The Privacy Rule mandates that covered entities must give patients a Privacy Notice (Notice Form) that details their rights involving the release of information. It is important to note that although some aspects of the Privacy Rule are scalable, the requirement to give patients a Privacy Notice and all that the notice must contain is not scalable. Obtaining the patient's signature by the end of the first professional contact showing that the Notice Form was received generally satisfies this requirement. If patients refuse to sign the acknowledgment that they received the Privacy Notice, the psychologist can note that the patient was offered and refused to sign the acknowledgment. The Notice Form must comply with both the Privacy Rule and state law according to the preemption analysis prescribed within the Privacy Rule. Therefore, the actual content of the Notice Form will differ from state to state. In addition to the notice requirement under the Privacy Rule, the Ethics Code requires that psychologists obtain the informed consent of patients before initiating professional services or as soon as feasible (Standard 3.10, Informed Consent).

These informed consent requirements are not very different from what always has been considered to be essential for effective psychotherapy (see Chapter 2, "Key Elements of Risk Management"). Psychologists, perhaps more than other health care professionals, are well aware that confidentiality serves as the foundation of therapeutic services. However, the Privacy Rule substantially adds to the amount of information that should be presented to patients.

The Trust and the APA Practice Organization (APAPO) developed the home study product, *HIPAA for Psychologists*, as a resource tool to assist in meeting these requirements (Psychologists can access this information at www.apait.org). *HIPAA for Psychologists* includes three important downloadable documents: (a) the required Notice Forms researched to comply with the specific requirements of statutory law and regulations in each state; (b) the Explanation Form; and (c) the Psychologist–Patient Agreement, a document addressing the major informed consent issues that should be provided at the end of the first session so patients can read, discuss, and sign it at the next session. The use of these documents will vary depending on the modality of services and types of patients seen. The rationale for developing two separate informed consent documents rather than one more elaborate document was that the Psychologist–Patient Agreement (which is a redesigned form of a sample generic informed consent document that has been distributed by both organizations for some time) is more user friendly and is much more relevant to what actually takes place in most psychotherapy than the Notice Form, much of which concerns issues that rarely arise in most practices.

HIPAA requires psychologists to give the Privacy Notice to patients and receive acknowledgment by the end of the first professional contact in which the psychologist receives protected health care information. We recommend that psychologists give the Psychologist–Patient Agreement, which is a more user friendly informed consent document, to the patient at the same time as the Privacy Notice, but that they do not seek a signature until the beginning of the second session after they have given the patient an opportunity to review and discuss its terms and conditions. In practice, few patients read the document carefully, and few ask questions. This approach requires a brief verbal statement about the limits of confidentiality at the beginning of the first contract to prevent uninformed and potentially damaging statements.

If the patient is a child, psychologists should give to and discuss the documents with the parent or legal guardian who brings the child for services. If the state allows minors to consent to treatment independently, they should receive the Notice Form instead of the parent or legal guardian. More information on privacy and confidentiality with adolescents can be found in Chapter 5 ("Working With Couples, Families, and Children").

The Explanation Form provided with *HIPAA for Psychologists* provides the basic information that psychologists need to know about the interaction of the laws in their jurisdiction and how these laws interface with the provisions of the Privacy Rule. Unfortunately, this is a complicated area of psychology–law interface, and the relevant documents require careful reading. Nonetheless, as we discussed in Chapter 2 ("Key Elements of Risk Management"), when done properly, a careful discussion of the salient issues in these documents can augment treatment and strengthen the therapeutic relationship.

Psychotherapy Notes

A second area of confusion caused by the Privacy Rule involves psychotherapy notes. We reviewed the risk management features of documentation in Chapter 2 ("Key Elements of Risk Management"), and we discuss the use of documentation as a risk management strategy in several other chapters. Here we only address the special topic of psychotherapy notes as defined by the Privacy Rule. The Privacy Rule provides special protection of confidential mental health information by permitting the practitioner to keep some types of confidential information in psychotherapy notes. Under the Privacy Rule, insurance companies may not require the patient to release information contained in psychotherapy notes as a condition of coverage. In addition, the psychologist may not be required to release information contained in psychotherapy notes to the patient unless mandated by state law. Unfortunately, there is much confusion in the field regarding the advantages and disadvantages of psychotherapy notes.

Initially there was confusion as to whether creating psychotherapy notes was required or optional. On the one hand, it could be argued that such notes should be required to fulfill the obligation to maximize patient confidentiality. On the other hand, it could be argued that such an obligation would not make sense in states whose laws give patients access to their complete records, including psychotherapy notes. Keeping psychotherapy notes would seem unnecessary for psychologists who provide primarily behavioral therapy and do not depend on analysis of relationship factors or for psychologists who are performing evaluations. Further, if psychotherapy notes were obligatory, it could stimulate disputes between patients and psychologists about the location of specific patient information. These disputes could develop into licensing board complaints with patients alleging that the psychologist should have placed more or less information in clinical records as opposed to psychotherapy notes. Fortunately, conversations between The Trust, the APAPO, and the U.S. Department of Health and Human Services (HHS) confirmed that HHS intended that the separate designation of records entitled psychotherapy notes is at the discretion of the practitioner.

The confusion regarding the appropriate use of psychotherapy notes is partially a result of poor regulatory draftsmanship as well as a lack of guidance for when to use and when not to use psychotherapy notes. The Privacy Rule itself is somewhat vague about psychotherapy notes, stating only that they include

> *notes recorded (in any medium)... documenting or analyzing the contents of conversation during a private counseling session or a group, joint, or family counseling session and that are separated from the rest of the individual's medical record. (45 C. F. R. 164.501)*

Psychotherapy notes do not include documentation related to the

modalities and frequencies of treatment furnished, results of clinical tests, and any summary of the... diagnosis, functional status, the treatment plan, symptoms, prognosis, and progress to date. (45 C. F. R. 164.501)

Accordingly, the Privacy Rule allows patients access to the results of their psychological evaluations (this issue is discussed in more detail in the section that follows on Psychological Testing). However, the Health Information Technology for Economic and Clinical Health Act of 2009 recently passed by Congress requires a reexamination of the rule allowing patient access to psychological testing. As we go to press, the results of that reexamination have not been finalized. If read expansively, psychotherapy notes would seem to include all information that describes what took place in any psychotherapy session. However, it is clear that psychotherapy notes must be kept separate from the general medical record so, for example, the notes written in the log on the ward of a medical hospital as part of a consultation would not be considered psychotherapy notes because they are not separated from the rest of the medical record.

A psychologist working in a nursing home two days a week knew that the information he wrote in the patient's chart in the nursing home would be read by the entire staff. Although Medicare laws required him to document his meetings in the nursing home chart, he was circumspect about what he placed in those records. On the other hand, he kept more detailed patient records in the patient charts that he kept in his private office. (6.4)

Some practitioners have suggested that the option of keeping separate records permits them to keep very sparse clinical records, putting the meaty information about treatment in the more confidential psychotherapy notes. This seems a very attractive option given practitioners' well-founded concerns about privacy and the intrusiveness of managed care companies into the psychologist–patient relationship. The clinical records could be limited to an initial treatment plan, dates of treatment, changes in the treatment plan, and session notes (e.g., "June 10, psychotherapy, 50 minutes, discussed problems with parents"). This may be poor advice for a number of reasons. First HHS, in its commentary accompanying the Privacy Rule, provided guidance that would be inconsistent with this strategy.

The rationale for providing special protection for psychotherapy notes is not only that they contain particularly sensitive information but also that they are the personal notes of the therapist, intended to help him or her recall the therapy discussion and are of little use or no use to others not involved in the therapy. Information in these notes is not intended to communicate to or even to be seen by persons other than the therapist. Although all psychotherapy information may be considered sensitive, we have limited the definition of psychotherapy notes to only that information that is kept separate by the provider for his or her own purposes. It does not refer to the medical record and other sources of information that would normally be disclosed for treatment, payment, or health care operations.

It is reasonable to conclude that the clinical record, excluding psychotherapy notes, must at least be adequate to meet professional documentation guidelines. The records must be comprehensive enough to adequately document and share what transpired in the treatment with a future treating professional and with other health care providers who might be treating the patient for some other condition. As discussed in Chapter 2 ("Key Elements of Risk Management"), if psychologists are seeking insurance reimbursement, their records (or the treatment report forms of the patient's managed care organization [MCO]) must include sufficient information to justify medical necessity and to survive a retroactive utilization review.

Another way to determine what information should be kept in the clinical record and what should be kept in psychotherapy notes is to consider the rules that determine access to both sets of records and determine how much patient privacy psychotherapy notes actually provide. On the basis of the 20-year experience of The Trust Risk Management Program, access to provider records is most commonly sought (a) by the patients and/or their guardians or legal representatives to examine and/or receive a copy of the records, (b) for release as potential evidence in litigation in which the patient is a participant, and (c) by health insurers or MCOs for eligibility and accountability purposes. The more access a state law provides to psychotherapy notes in these three situations, the less sense it makes to keep them.

PATIENT REQUESTS FOR INFORMATION

Although there are a few exceptions, in most states the Privacy Rule provides either the same or greater access by patients to protected health information (i.e., the clinical record) as does existing state law. According to the preemption doctrine, the statute or rule that provides the patient with the greatest level of access preempts (or overrides) the more restrictive statute or rule. Under the Privacy Rule, the primary ground for refusing patients' request for copies of their clinical records is that in the professional judgment of the provider it is "reasonably likely to endanger the life or physical safety of the individual or another person" (45 C. F. R. 164.524 (a) (3) (i)). Providers who withhold records under this provision must justify the decision in the record and provide an appeals process that may be difficult and expensive to implement.

Because the Privacy Rule does not require psychologists to provide patients access to their psychotherapy notes, current state laws governing patient access to medical and mental health records would take precedence and regulate access to psychotherapy notes. A few states have no laws governing record access. Most commentators believe that in these jurisdictions the actual records (i.e., the content of the records and the paper on which it is written) belong to the provider, who could restrict or deny patients access to them. However, patients could almost always obtain a copy of their complete record through the legal process.

Many states have laws that provide patient access to mental health records unless in the professional's judgment the release would damage the patient. Often, these states require that the threatened damage be "substantial" or "serious" and that providers document their reasons for refusal in their records. Many also give patients the right to forward the records to another provider of their choice. Some states require that a summary of the record be provided to the patient as an alternative to the actual record. However, others have laws that give patients complete access to their records including both clinical records and psychotherapy notes. The more access to records a state law provides to a patient, the less privacy protection psychotherapy notes enjoy. In states where access is greater than that provided by the Privacy Rule, the rationale for keeping psychotherapy notes is diminished. We encourage psychologists to know the law in their states about patient access. Psychologists may obtain this information from their state association, a local mental health attorney, or *HIPAA for Psychologists* for their state.

Clinical Features of Patient Access to Records

Up to this point we have discussed only the legal requirements concerning patient access to the records. However, these requests have clinical implications as well, which require some judgment on how to respond. When patients request access to their records, it is often helpful to think clinically first and to ask, Why does this patient want the record? Often the request for records is an indirect way of asking other questions, for example, What does my psychologist really think of me? or Am I really crazy?

When possible, it is best to address the underlying clinical issue first and ask about the patient's goal. Often psychologists can address the clinical issue without giving the patients access to the records or by showing them a limited portion of the records.

The harm from the occasional request by patients for their records can be avoided either by keeping a second set of psychotherapy notes for certain patients who appear especially vulnerable or by being very tactful in the manner in which clinical notes are written. However, in some situations patients will insist on seeing their notes and have the legal right to them, although seeing the notes may be harmful to them. For example, some patients may request to see their records, which will include, among other things, the patient's presenting problem and diagnosis. Because patients have a right to know their diagnosis as part of their protected health information, psychologists need to consider the consequences of providing the patient with the diagnosis. The conditions under which providers can withhold the protected health information from patients are exceedingly narrowly defined as explained previously and are unlikely to be met in the large majority of clinical situations. Given that reality, should psychologists, for example, give the diagnosis of borderline personality disorder or a similar diagnosis indicating a serious mental disorder, especially if they work in a state that grants patients full access to all their records? On the one hand, it could be argued that giving such a diagnosis to a patient might harm the patient. For example, it may limit the patient's ability to purchase life insurance or be accepted into the military or a high-security occupation, prejudice future health care providers, or be upsetting to the patient. On the other hand, it can also be argued that such a diagnosis should be given if it is accurate, regardless of whether it is upsetting to the patient, just as a medical diagnosis should be given even if it is upsetting to the patient.

To ease the potential burden on the patient and assist the psychologist in making decisions about assigning such diagnoses, it may be useful to consider the risk management factors here. The decision making should include awareness that assigning an inaccurate or inadequate diagnosis is a common disciplinary complaint (it is often included as negligent practice in the list of common disciplinary complaints reported to ASPPB). If the diagnosed condition, such as borderline personality disorder, is the focus of treatment, it may be desirable to find a way to fulfill the potentially incompatible obligations to present information accurately, respond to the request by the patient, and minimize harm. For example, it may be possible to involve the patient in the development of the treatment plan, including a behavioral description of the presenting problems in a manner that is consistent with borderline personality disorder. It may be better to share the diagnosis with the patient up front and describe it and its implications in therapy, rather than to have the patient learn the meaning and implication of the diagnosis from a website or other informal source of knowledge. The general rule for psychologists in dealing with patients is to be transparent about what they are doing and why they are doing it. However, at times, transparency may need to yield to other considerations, depending on the unique context. These situations require clinical judgment as shown in the next example.

One patient periodically asked the psychologist, "What do you think of me?" "What are you going to put in your notes about me?" The patient showed other signs of suspiciousness and self-consciousness. The psychologist suspected that her patient might eventually request the records, so the psychologist was careful in how she phrased her thoughts in her notes, clarified the diagnosis with the patient in lay terms, and offered to show her notes to the patient on occasion. (6.5)

Requests for Information to be Released as Potential Evidence in Litigation

All states have psychologist–patient privilege statutes that allow patients to prevent information in their psychologist's records from being admitted as evidence in a legal proceeding. However, these privilege laws typically include exceptions, such as when patients place their mental health at issue in a case or when a court has ordered an examination (more detail on privileged communication laws can be found earlier in this chapter).

Privileged communication laws do not distinguish between clinical records and psychotherapy notes. When psychologists receive information requests in the early stages of litigation, they may want to offer a summary of the record to protect their patient's privacy at least to some degree. In general, this is not a good strategy. Attorneys are rarely going to be satisfied with a prepared summary; they usually want to examine the actual content of the record to see how they can use it to their advantage and to prepare for its use by their adversaries. Furthermore, attorneys, particularly attorneys opposing a patient, are likely to believe that the material was edited in ways that reflect the bias of the psychologist in favor of the patient or the work with the patient and interfere with the best legal arguments. Psychologists who are compelled to turn over records in a legal proceeding will undoubtedly end up turning over the entire record including psychotherapy notes. Offering a summary may actually hurt the patient because the opposing side is likely to request the entire record, and if the psychologists are called to testify, the opposing side may attempt to discredit their testimony by pointing out differences between the summary and the original record.

Requests by Third Parties for Reimbursement

Perhaps the most confusing aspect of the release of psychotherapy notes occurs when trying to ascertain what information a health insurer or MCO can require as part of its claims review or utilization management process to determine whether requested services are within the policy contract or are medically necessary. (Note that this restriction does not apply to health insurance requests to determine coverage eligibility or to requests from other insurers such as disability or life insurance companies.) Health insurers and MCOs cannot require patients to turn over their psychotherapy notes as a condition of coverage. However, they can refuse to pay claims or even demand recovery of funds already paid if the documentation in the clinical record cannot establish medical necessity on a prospective or retrospective basis.

If the clinical record is insufficient to demonstrate medical necessity, psychologists will have to go back to the patient and ask permission to submit the information contained in the psychotherapy notes, in whole or in part, or ask the patient to pay for the service out-of-pocket. Further, if the clinical record is insufficient to establish medical necessity on its own, the initial impression of the insurance company may be that the documentation was inadequate to justify services, thus making the review process more onerous. Psychologists are more likely to be targeted as outliers if their clinical records are inadequate to justify services in the first place.

Many psychologists have been subjected to Medicare audits. Often, the sole problem is that these audits identified inadequate documentation, but this is sufficient to allow Medicare to recover all payments for those sessions for which adequate documentation does not exist. Most MCOs regularly audit participating providers, and if the records of these providers are deemed inadequate, the company can also demand repayment. Since the audits often take place after the treatment is over, psychologists may not be able to obtain from the patient the separate authorization required to release psychotherapy notes to use in those audits. Recently, an insurance company audited the records of many mental health professionals and determined that many of the records were inadequate. The company initiated claims for repayment, many of which were based on extrapolation formulas and involved many thousands of dollars. Although these demands were withdrawn as part of a settlement because of the lack of established standards for record keeping, they point out the need to have adequate clinical records that can independently establish medical necessity. Providers would have a difficult time using their psychotherapy notes to establish that. Unfortunately, other psychologists have had to repay money. The repayment and any associated legal costs are not covered by professional liability insurance (see Chapter 13, "Professional Liability Insurance").

Given the limited privacy protection accorded psychotherapy notes and the additional administrative time required to keep two sets of notes, many psychologists have decided to forgo keeping psychotherapy notes and to keep a single record. Psychotherapy notes would seem to make the most sense for psychodynamically oriented psychologists in states that do not allow patients access to these notes or who wish to keep the analysis of the process of the therapy relationship and other psychodynamic formulations separate from the more behavioral descriptions of what happened in the session. These types of notes were often referred to as *process notes* before the advent of the Privacy Rule. If the records adequately document the presenting problem, treatment plan, and progress, MCOs should not need the additional information contained in psychotherapy notes. The primary interest of the MCO is in clinical necessity and not in embarrassing personal details or transference and countertransference issues.

Forensic Psychological Services

We discuss forensic psychological services in more detail in Chapter 7, ("Psychologists in the Courtroom"). Here we discuss the application of the Privacy Rule to forensic services. The Privacy Rule has also caused confusion concerning the extent to which it applies to forensic services. One could argue that those who provide only forensic services are unlikely to be covered by the Privacy Rule because their services do not generate protected health care information. However, many psychologists have mixed practices and the provision of one single covered transaction triggers the application of the Privacy Rule to one's entire practice, including one's forensic work.

The Privacy Rule defines protected health information so broadly that it would be very difficult to argue that forensic psychological services do not involve protected health information. Although the Privacy Rule mandates a sweeping right of patients to access protected health information (45 C. F. R. 164.24) and to request amendments (45 C. F. R. 164.526) of protected health information contained in a health care professional's records, it specifically exempts "information compiled in reasonable anticipation of, or for use in, a civil, criminal, or administrative action or proceeding" (C.F.R. 164.524 (a) (ii)). When forensic psychologists are hired directly by attorneys, their work, in almost all cases, can be deemed to fall within this exception because any other interpretation would be in conflict with the very strong attorney–client privilege that includes materials prepared by retained experts as attorney work products. Such information, therefore, would be governed by state laws relating to access to information, and forensic psychologists could impose the same limits to access forensic information that existed before the Privacy Rule went into effect.

Therefore, the Privacy Rule has not greatly impacted forensic practices for psychologists working for attorneys. Regardless, forensic psychologists need to give a Notice Form or an Informed Consent Contract to the person being assessed before services are provided.

Such a form needs to meet the formulaic requirements of the Privacy Rule and would probably include more information about the exceptions to confidentiality than was previously included in such contracts. A sample forensic contract (pre-HIPAA) can be downloaded from The Trust website (www.apait.org). Most forensic psychologists would probably need a similar contract for the attorney requesting the services.

Of course, many psychologists present information in court as fact witnesses, as treating experts (see Chapter 7, "Psychologists in the Courtroom"), or in other roles in which they are not covered by the attorney–client privilege. Psychologists would arguably then be covered by the Privacy Rule, assuming that they are an otherwise covered entity.

Also, psychologists who perform nonforensic third-party evaluations, such as independent medical examinations, in which there is no reasonable anticipation that the services will be involved in administrative or legal proceedings are subject to the Privacy Rule access to information requirements. Psychologists who perform Social Security disability determinations have been informed that the previous federal rules prohibiting patient access to psychologists' records have been preempted by the Privacy Rule.

It is important to note that our conclusions about the Privacy Rule, along with the conclusions of many others, are subject to differing perspectives. Some commentators have come to different conclusions and, for example, believe that all information collected for third-party evaluations that do not contain protected health information are not covered by the Privacy Rule.

Psychological Testing

We provide more information on psychological testing in Chapter 8, ("Psychological Assessment and Testing"). However, here we review the impact of the Privacy Rule on psychological testing. Among the most significant changes of the 2002 Ethics Code are the standards pertaining to patient access to test data and test materials. The 1992 Ethics Code (APA, 1992) stated that psychologists should not give test data or materials to individuals who are not qualified to use them. This standard (2.02b, Competence and Appropriate Use of Assessments and Interventions) was designed to protect patients from receiving confusing or potentially misleading information and to protect the reliability and validity of psychological tests by limiting the publication and distribution of test questions and answers.

The 1992 provisions created several problems for psychologists. In most states, court rules considered this material, if not protected by privilege, as admissible evidence, particularly if the report was based in part on testing. Many judges were reluctant to grant a request that the material be released only to another psychologist or another mental health professional or to issue protective orders requiring that the parties not further release information beyond what was required for the specific case. Psychologists who refused to turn over raw data in response to a valid subpoena or court order faced credible threats of contempt motions from the requesting attorneys.

In some states, patient access laws require psychologists to release all materials to patients, including raw data, although some have argued that federal copyright laws override state record access laws. Other states prohibit release to untrained individuals and prohibit courts from issuing court orders to obtain the information. Furthermore, forensic psychologists who were retained by attorneys to do testing or to analyze testing by someone else could not very well refuse to provide the hiring attorneys with as much of the testing as was necessary to help the attorneys understand how they reached the conclusions and to defend them in court, if necessary. Finally, with the advent of the Internet, many test protocols or manuals can be obtained online. Many websites provide sophisticated advice on how potential test takers can "beat" the psychological tests. It is not unusual to see test manuals in used book stores or for sale on eBay.

Although agreeing to turn over test data to another psychologist was a plausible solution to ensure appropriate review, interpretation, and copyright protection, some commentators recommended that courts and attorneys have greater access to copyrighted tests (e.g., Lees-Haley & Courtney, 2000). The question remained how one was to determine that another provider had the requisite skill and knowledge to review and interpret the test results. The idea was to keep the material out of the hands of lawyers who, it was thought, would use test materials to coach their patients. This also overlooked the fact that some mental health attorneys frequently knew more about psychological testing than many psychologists. Attorneys have argued that they need direct access to test information to represent their clients effectively. At times it was difficult for attorneys to find a qualified psychologist to interpret the test results, and retaining a second psychologist placed a financial burden on patients. Furthermore, the extant draft of the Privacy Rule held that the test report and test data must be available to patients and their attorneys on appropriate request, unless release would cause serious physical harm to the requester. This was the context of developing law when the APA Ethics Code Task Force redrafted the APA Ethics Code.

The 2002 APA Ethics Code (see the amended version, APA, 2010a) changed long-standing ethical policy on this issue. The Ethics Code first established new definitions for test data and test materials to help clarify what had formerly been an almost epistemological debate. Standard 9.04, Release of Test Data, in the 2002 Ethics Code states,

> the term test data refers to raw and scaled scores, client/patient responses to test questions or stimuli, and psychologists' notes and recordings concerning client/patient statements and behavior during an examination. Those portions of test materials that include client/patient responses are included in the definition of test data.

This last sentence means that if patient responses are written on the test protocols, such protocols are converted to test data. The term *test materials* refers to "manuals, instruments, protocols, and test questions or stimuli and does not include *test data*" (Standard 9.11, Maintaining Test Security). Unless prohibited by law, test data must be provided to the client/patient unless to do so would cause "substantial harm or misuse or misrepresentation of the data or the test" (Standard 9.04, Release of Test Data).

Psychologists were required to make reasonable efforts to maintain the integrity and security of test materials and other assessment techniques consistent with law and contractual obligations. One gray area left unresolved by the 2002 APA Ethics Code and the 2010 amended version was how to address the conflict between the requirement of release of data and the contractual obligations to test publishers that prohibit release in cases in which state law does not directly resolve the question, especially when the test stimuli or questions appear on the same page as patient responses and turn the test materials into test data.

It is not surprising that test publishing companies are greatly concerned about these developments, particularly the provision that would convert test materials, which the companies consider proprietary, to test data in which data and materials are merged. A series of communications between and among test publishers and HHS has failed to resolve all of the issues to everyone's satisfaction, and conscientious readers can still find uncertainty in the response given by HHS. The legal issues are complex. Nonetheless, the test manufacturers have interpreted the response of HHS as permitting psychologists to withhold test materials (protocols and other stimuli) as legally protected "trade secrets." Under this analysis, materials could not be converted to data by the inclusion of client/patient answers or other identifying data.

Harcourt Assessment, Inc., one of the largest test publishers, sought an advisory opinion as to whether either federal copyright law or legislation protecting trade secrets overrode the Privacy Rule. They were told that copyright law did not negate the access provided by the Privacy Rule. However, HHS responded,

> *Any requirement for disclosure of protected health information pursuant to the Privacy Rule is subject to Section 1172 (e) of HIPAA, "Protection of Trade Secrets." As such, we confirm that it would not be a violation of the Privacy Rule for a covered entity to refrain from providing access to an individual's protected health information to the extent that doing so would result in a disclosure of trade secrets. (Campanelli, 2005)*

Pearson (then Harcourt) interprets this letter as requiring psychologists to comply with their contracts with test publishers that prohibit dissemination of test record forms or protocols to attorneys, patients, or others who claim that they are entitled to these documents under HIPAA. If Pearson is correct, the part of the Ethics Code that states that including patient answers on test protocols converts the protocols to test data would violate federal law and thus be invalid. Unless a court decision overrules Pearson's interpretation, we believe that psychologists should comply with it.

We advise psychologists to act in accordance with their contracts with test publishers and refrain from sending copyrighted test materials to patients. Noncopyrighted materials would not qualify as trade secrets and would be governed by the 2002 Ethics Code and would need to be sent to patients. This means that patient answers to copyrighted materials should, to the extent possible, not be included on question sheets or other test protocols because that arguably converts the entire document to test data.

The Privacy Rule gives patients a right to receive all test data. Practically, this would require a psychologist to manually separate the answers and questions. When test data are requested by a patient, psychologists can respond either by whiting out the questions or stimuli or putting the answers on a separate sheet of paper before sending them. If one adopts this latter approach and the material is subpoenaed, whiting out the questions and stating why they have been redacted is the only appropriate response. Photocopying the answers on a separate sheet of paper and submitting that paper rather than a redacted original would be problematic under the rules of evidence in most states because the photocopy is not the original document demanded by the court.

Psychologists who receive a subpoena with appropriate authorization from their clients/patients should not send test questions and test stimuli to the requesting attorney, citing the fact that these materials are protected by the Federal Trade Secrets Act and stating that they, therefore, can only be supplied in response to a court order. Psychologists should keep a copy of their contracts with test publishers as well as the test publisher's legal interpretation. These documents should be sent to the subpoenaing attorney to substantiate the position and to thereby avoid threats of contempt actions. It is very unlikely that a state court would cite a psychologist for contempt for a good faith attempt to conform to state law. Also, forensic psychologists can include in their business associate agreements with the lawyers that the lawyer will not voluntarily redisclose any test materials given to them by the psychologist unless required to do so by law.

Of course, the problem of who gets access to test materials can also be addressed through a protective court order that could say, among other things, that the attorneys may have access to the test materials only for the purpose of the immediate litigation and must return originals, destroy copies, and otherwise be prohibited from further use of the test materials.

Obviously this will take time to sort out. The Trust will monitor developments closely and provide information on its website as soon as more definitive information is available. At this time, patient requests for test data should be honored and requests for test materials resisted.

HIPAA SECURITY RULE

For covered entities, the Privacy Rule applies to all communications of patient information, whether they are through oral, written, or electronic means. However, the HIPAA Security Rule (hereinafter referred to as the Security Rule) applies to the manner in which information is stored electronically. The APAPO developed a home study course on the Security Rule as a resource tool to assist psychologists in meeting these requirements. Psychologists may access information regarding this course at www.apait.org.

The Security Rule requires providers to determine the risks to the accessibility and privacy of patient records that they store electronically and to take precautions to minimize those risks. As such, they need to analyze their existing storage systems, identify where there are gaps, and close those gaps (Holloway, 2005). Electronic information storage includes electronic organizers, cell phones, computer records, and other electronic devices.

The Security Rule consists of three types of standards, some of which contain specific implementation standards and others that do not. Administrative standards involve questions such as how to protect privacy in the office. They ask, Do you have rules and procedures, training, and consequences for persons who violate the rules and procedures? Physical standards refer to limits of access to the places where information is stored, including such things as locks on doors, passwords, virus protection, and firewalls. Technical standards refer to the actual format or structure of records, such as whether they are encrypted and which staff members have access to this information (such as through the use of passwords).

The Security Rule has two different types of specifications. "Required" specifications must be implemented as written. "Addressable" specifications allow providers more discretion to tailor the particular standard to their own practices. Providers may implement the standard as it is, or they may implement an alternative standard, but providers must explain in writing why the alternative standard accomplishes the objective better. Psychologists should look at each issue, think about what they are doing, and document how they are trying to comply with it.

Just as the Privacy Rule was more flexible for smaller practices, the Security Rule also invokes the principle of scalability that allows smaller practices to choose implementation strategies that are appropriate to the size and sophistication of the data storage system. For example, a small office with limited storage of patient data might not need to purchase an encryption program. As long as providers make a good faith effort to comply with the Security Rule and document the reasons for their decisions, they will be in compliance.

Providers must do a risk analysis, which means they must look at the ways that they store electronic information and how they protect it. They need formal written policies and procedures. They have to document how they looked at these risks and how they are complying with the law, although they have a lot of discretion about how to comply.

Although there is no inherent prohibition against storing records electronically (and many advantages to doing so), such decisions need to be made carefully with an attentive eye toward protecting patient records. A considerable amount of damage can be done if electronic records are lost, accidentally deleted, or otherwise compromised (See Chapter 2, "Key Elements of Risk Management," for more information on the electronic storage of records). Similarly, emails from patients need to be protected.

Finally, many institutions have developed electronic health records and extensive health information exchanges that permit sharing of electronic records created in different electronic platforms. These recordkeeping systems typically have special precautions to protect the privacy of mental health or substance abuse records. Nonetheless, the quality of the protections can be undermined if protocols are not followed or if staff members are not trained adequately. Psychologists who store records in institution-wide recordkeeping systems should be alert to any breaches or potential breaches to confidentiality.

SEVEN ESSENTIAL POINTS TO REMEMBER

1. Most violations of confidentiality occur when psychologists accidentally allow the confidentiality protection mechanisms to break down. Responding to a subpoena for records without proper consent or legal authority represents a major breach of confidentiality. When confronted with difficult or confusing confidentiality issues, psychologists should refrain from any action until they have sought consultation.

2. Psychologists are responsible to train and monitor their employees on procedures to protect patient privacy.

3. State and federal laws generally permit patient access to at least some portion of their records. Attempt to handle most requests for patient records clinically.

4. Privileged communication laws, which have numerous exceptions, deal with the right of patients to withhold information from court.

5. Except in narrow circumstances specified in law, psychologists should only release patient information upon receipt of a valid patient release or a court order.

6. The Privacy Rule has certain ambiguities regarding its application to forensic services and access to test materials.

7. The Security Rule provides standards for protecting the security of electronically stored data.

CHAPTER 7: PSYCHOLOGISTS IN THE COURTROOM

Forensic psychology is one of the specialties in professional psychology. The demand for forensic psychologists has expanded substantially in recent years. In part, this expansion has occurred because the courts believe that psychological testing provides important information that assists them in their decision-making processes.

Many psychologists find court involvement stressful and will go to great lengths to avoid it. Nonetheless, most psychologists will, at some time in their careers, have some involvement with the judicial system. Those who have no knowledge of the judicial process run an increased risk of exposing themselves to legal liability.

Otto and Heilbrun (2002) classified psychologists into those who are forensic specialists (have a high level of intensive and in-depth training in forensic psychology), those who are proficient (have some training in forensic activity related to their areas of practice), and those who are legally informed clinicians (know basic information about the legal system and know when they are moving into a forensic role). It may be realistic to add a fourth category, the legally naive clinician who is rarely called on to work with attorneys or do forensic work and who knows very little about forensic issues or the experience of testifying. In this chapter we review the basics of practicing within the legal system as legally informed clinicians.

According to a recent study, about 5% of psychologists reported forensic psychology as their major area of practice (S. Greenberg, Caro, & Smith, 2010), thus putting them into the first group of forensic specialists as identified by Otto and Heilbrun (2002). However, many more psychologists fall into the second group of being forensically proficient in that they perform competently in a narrow forensic area, such as a child psychologist who provides evaluations for the local juvenile court, but have no other forensic involvement. Nonetheless, all psychologists should become forensically informed because they (or their clients) are likely to be involved with the judicial system at some time through circumstances largely out of their control. All psychologists need to be informed enough to determine whether they are entering into a forensic area and whether the role is more appropriate for a forensic specialist.

Historically most forensic psychologists were trained as generalists and cobbled together specific skills through readings, continuing education programs, consultation, or their own experiences. For example, most child custody evaluators got into that work as an extension of other forensic work or work with children and adolescents (Bow & Martindale, 2009) and got their training post license through seminars and workshops (Ackerman & Pritzl, 2011).

Although many psychologists will still acquire forensic expertise in that way, the standards for judicial work are increasing, and more value is given to formal training and credentials. Now many forensic psychologists have had internships or practicum placements that involve forensic work; some have attended doctoral training programs with forensic specialties or attended one of the few doctoral programs that combine

JD and doctoral degrees in psychology; and a growing number are earning a diplomate in forensic psychology offered by the American Board of Professional Psychology (DeMatteo, Marczyk, Krauss, & Burl, 2009).

The forensic roles that psychologists are asked to perform vary enormously and include but are not limited to evaluating prisoners to determine if they meet the criteria for the jurisdiction's definition of insanity at the time of the crime or if they are competent to stand trial, to determine clients' capacity to manage their own affairs, to determine eligibility for workers compensation or Social Security Disability Income, to comment on whether (or how much) a plaintiff was damaged in a civil suit, to determine the optimal parenting plan for a family that is divorcing, or to determine if parental rights should be terminated. Also, attorneys may hire psychologists to review the work of other psychologists. Although they have not evaluated the individual themselves and cannot comment on the questions before the court, they can opine as to whether the proper methodology was used and whether the conclusions were justified by the information provided. The identities of many such experts are protected from disclosure by the attorney work product.

In addition, other psychologists may provide court-involved therapy, either appointed by the courts or hired outside of the court with the expectation that they may have some involvement with the court system. Court-involved therapy can occur in many different venues, not only when families are divorcing (as covered in Chapter 5, "Working With Couples, Families, and Children"). For example, multisystemic therapy involves intense treatment of juvenile offenders in the community (Sawyer & Borduin, 2011). In the past, many of these children would have been placed in residential treatment facilities. Multisystemic therapy has been identified as an efficacious treatment; however, to be done properly, it is time intensive and requires well-trained staff.

Court-ordered treatment with adolescent offenders is more complicated than other forms of outpatient treatment because it requires special sensitivity to the potentially competing formulations of the presenting problem (because parents, child, and court may disagree on the presenting problem), attention to interests of several parties (including the court, parents, and the child), and the identification of limits to confidentiality (Dewey & Gottlieb, 2011). Finally, if third-party reimbursement is being sought, psychologists need to ensure that the therapy meets the medical necessity requirements of the insurance company. Some insurance companies automatically exclude court-ordered treatment from coverage. Those insurance companies that allow reimbursement for court-ordered therapy would still require that the child has a covered disorder and that treatment is directed toward alleviating that disorder.

As noted in Chapter 5 ("Working With Couples, Families, and Children"), which deals with court-ordered therapy in child custody cases, psychologists are not required to accept any case ordered by the court. However, if psychologists do accept such cases, they should review the court order to ensure that it covers the salient issues that arise and allows them to have an effective structure for treatment. Court involved psychologists should not be asked to comment on the legal issues before the court but may be asked by the court to comment on the "patient's reported history or other statements, mental status, diagnosis, progress, prognosis, and treatment" (*Specialty Guidelines for Forensic Psychology,* American Psychological Association [APA], 2013b, Section 4.02.02). For example, in a hearing concerning termination of parental rights, a court-involved psychologist could comment on his or her history and treatment of a patient but would not give an opinion concerning the legal issue before the court (i.e., whether the patient's parental rights should be terminated).

More information on the court system and forensic roles can be found in Chapter 5 ("Working With Couples, Families, and Children"); Chapter 6 ("Privacy, Confidentiality, and Privileged Communications"), which includes discussions of the Health Insurance Portability and Accountability Act Privacy Rule and forensics); and Chapter 8 ("Psychological Assessment and Testing").

Patients who are involved in legal cases are a high-risk group because of the inherently adversarial nature of forensic proceedings. Also, as we noted in Chapter 2 ("Key Elements of Risk Management"), patients who litigate may have a more adversarial orientation toward handling problems; the litigation itself may produce more aggressive or narcissistic behavior on the part of the patient; or the role of being in court may place psychologists in a position where they are, or appear to be, acting against the best interests of their patients.

THE AMERICAN LEGAL SYSTEM

The American legal system is adversarial. It seeks truth by presenting and evaluating positions and arguments from opposing points of view. This process is known as dialectic dispute resolution and is governed by a complex set of formal and informal procedural rules (known as the Evidence Code). In jury trials, the judge's role is to be a referee who ensures that the appropriate rules are followed, to instruct the jury about the legal rules governing the dispute, and to consider and rule on the attorneys' motions and objections. When serving in a proceeding that has no jury, the judge also becomes the trier of fact, making decisions on guilt or causation along with making determinations as to an appropriate sentence in a matter.

Within this system, the attorney's role is to convince the jury by providing them with the narrative of his or her client's case concerning the events that happened. To do this, attorneys may present evidence in the form of witness testimony, documents, and demonstrations that support this narrative. The attorneys may argue for an interpretation that supports their client's narration. They may refute evidence and interpretations presented by the other side. They also act to protect their clients by objecting to what they perceive to be unfair practices by the other side's attorney. Attorneys may also advocate with the judge for appropriate instructions to the jury.

Within this system, the role of the jury is to consider all of the evidence and assign appropriate weight to it. The jury decides what most likely happened and which narrative to believe. They apply the legal rules contained in the instructions from the judge to the facts, and they reach a decision as to which side prevails. The jury may also determine the consequences, such as what damages will be awarded or what penalties will be imposed.

Within this system, the psychologist's testimony, records, and opinions are considered as evidence and are governed by the rules of evidence. It is wise to remember that any involvement with the legal system and lawyers, whether voluntary or involuntary, is considered a forensic activity. The activities of psychologists in the forensic arena are governed by several standards within the American Psychological Association's (APA's) "Ethical Principles of Psychologists and Code of Conduct" (hereinafter referred to as the Ethics Code; APA 2010a), such as Standard 2.01f, Boundaries of Competence, which states, "When assuming forensic roles, psychologists are or become reasonably familiar with the judicial or administrative rules governing their roles." Psychologists who work in the forensic arena need to become familiar with the *Specialty Guidelines for Forensic Psychology* promulgated by APA (2013b). Psychologists do not need to be forensic experts. However, when they act in the forensic arena, psychologists need to make some effort to have a working knowledge of the rules governing their participation.

To facilitate the fairness of judicial proceedings, the doctrine of testimonial immunity protects a witness's testimony. Except under the most unusual circumstances, witnesses cannot be sued for giving testimony. In addition, psychologists who are appointed by the court to perform certain functions such as custody evaluations are protected from suit by the related concept of judicial immunity. This immunity is limited to litigation, however, and does not protect a psychologist from a licensing board complaint. As noted previously, psychologists can perform many functions as experts by addressing questions before civil or criminal courts. These roles require a high level of expertise, and psychologists performing these roles should ensure that they have an adequate skill set before performing these duties and that they adhere to risk management strategies scrupulously.

Psychologists hired to address specific forensic questions before the court, such as whether an individual was insane at the time of the crime or competent to stand trial, should avoid conducting therapy with those individuals. The APA *Specialty Guidelines for Forensic Psychology* (2013b) state that "providing forensic and therapeutic services to the same individual or closely related individuals involves multiple relationships that may impair objectivity and/or cause exploitation or other harm" (Section 4.02.01).

PSYCHOLOGISTS AS WITNESSES

Although mental health professionals appear in court for many reasons, they are frequently called as expert witnesses. Many psychologists do not want to appear in court at all and may go to great lengths to avoid doing so. Some may even require patients to sign a contract at the start of therapy stating that the patient will not require them to appear in court. Others may want to avoid being in a potential dual role with patients in which they must answer questions in court that may interfere with a productive treatment relationship. Some psychologists have had a bad experience in court in which they felt attacked and humiliated. Or they are afraid of losing a day's income or more by having to appear in court. Some psychologists have heard stories from colleagues and believe that providing such services will be too stressful.

We sympathize with these psychologists. Certainly some attorneys have taken liberties and acted without proper concern for the welfare of the patient or the treating mental health professional. At times attorneys will call a psychologist as a fact, percipient, or lay witness (for which the psychologist receives a nominal fee for travel or parking) and then ask questions that try to elicit expert testimony. At other times attorneys have been insensitive to the schedules of psychologists and have bullied them into canceling a day's worth of appointments, without informing them that the judge might, in fact, be more considerate of their time demands and willing to reschedule their testimony or allow them to testify over the phone or make other accommodations.

Some attorneys have misrepresented the legal obligations engendered by a subpoena and threatened the psychologist with legal action for failing to respond to a subpoena when, in fact, the subpoena from an attorney alone does not permit the psychologist to reveal information. Some attorneys may act out of ignorance and be unaware that state laws typically grant greater legal protection to the records and testimony of mental health professionals than they do to the records of other health professionals. Other attorneys may deliberately try to mislead psychologists and rationalize their behavior by stating that they are only zealously advocating for their client and are not responsible for representing the interests of nonclients.

Attorneys vary considerably in their knowledge of mental health law, tactfulness, and sensitivity to the legitimate needs of other professionals. The great majority of attorneys act with highly commendable virtue when dealing with their clients, other parties, and psychologists. Usually psychologists are able to educate these attorneys on the differences between an expert and a lay witness and other features unique to the role of a psychologist. On the other hand, a few attorneys will, either deliberately or because of ignorance, attempt to induce psychologists to violate the law and place them in jeopardy of disciplinary actions. Typically, the attorney working on behalf of the patient will treat the psychologists of their clients with courtesy. However, these attorneys are not working for the psychologists, have no fiduciary relationship with them, and have no obligation to work to reduce their discomfort or protect their interests. Psychologists can better protect themselves if they know the basics of the legal system.

Basic Information About Psychologists Serving as Witnesses

During the course of his or her career every psychologist will probably appear in court on behalf of a patient, probably more than a few times. The *no-court* provisions in contracts are not foolproof. Although they may dissuade patients from trying to get the psychologist involved in a court case, they cannot prevent a judge from ordering the psychologist to testify. A court may view a no-court contract as contrary to public policy and fail to recognize it (Woody, 1997). Furthermore, because psychologists are professionals with obligations to their patients, there may be times when the welfare of their patients requires them to testify in court.

The reasons that some psychologists give to avoid testifying may not, in the opinion of the court, represent good policy reasons.

> A patient was seriously injured in an automobile accident during the time she was in therapy. She entered her mental health into litigation, alleging that the automobile accident caused mental as well as physical damage. She signed a release that permitted her psychologist to release her treatment records to her attorney so the attorney could determine if the records would support her claim of mental damage from the accident. The psychologist refused, noting that "sharing the notes in court would harm the patient because of public embarrassment," and that "these notes are mine." (7.1)

The psychologist failed to consider the patient's right to decide about sharing records about her (principle of respect for patient autonomy). As an autonomous individual, the patient has to decide, albeit with input from the psychologist and the patient's attorney, whether pursuing the case for mental damage is worth more than whatever embarrassment might occur from admitting the evidence into court. Furthermore, the psychologist is wrong in stating that the "notes are mine." Although the psychologist may own the paper on which the notes are written, the patient has an interest in what happens to those notes and may, with informed consent, authorize their release to a third party. Finally, the release of the records is to the patient's attorney who, like the psychologist, is in a fiduciary relationship with the patient and bound to act to promote the welfare of the patient. To represent the patient properly, the attorney needs to know the content of those records.

> A psychologist was treating a patient with a serious personality disorder who became involved in a traffic accident during the course of therapy. The patient sued the other driver, alleging that she was seriously harmed mentally by the accident. However, the treating psychologist believed that the patient had a long-term mental condition and that the accident only slightly aggravated her mental health issues. The psychologist had to tactfully but clearly convey to the patient and her attorney the general nature of his prospective testimony. His patient was furious with him. However, it was better that he told the patient up front rather than have the patient learn about his opinions in court. (7.2)

Nonetheless, we present some suggestions that will greatly reduce the negative aspects of an occasional appearance in court. First, when treating high-conflict families for whom participation in court would be clinically contraindicated (see the discussion in Chapter 5, "Working With Couples, Families, and Children"), we suggest that psychologists specify in the psychologist–patient agreement their unwillingness to testify in court (although do not expect this to be binding in all circumstances). Also, psychologists can clarify with all patients that they will be charged a forensic rate for all time spent on work for a court case (including but not limited to phone calls, preparation for the case, record copying and mailing, time traveling to and from the court house, travel and parking expenses, time testifying, and time spent at court waiting to testify). This provision will do more to reduce frivolous requests to be in court than anything else. Finally, psychologists can reduce their worries by understanding basic information about courtroom procedures (We provide more information about payment under the heading Getting Paid for Services).

It is extremely important to remember that being named in a court order to perform therapy with a child, couple, or an individual patient does not require the psychologist to perform that therapy. More than one psychologist has been surprised by a prospective patient who appears with a court order specifying that he or she is to do therapy with so and so. One psychologist had a patient appear with such an order and then announce, "The court may order you to appear, but I am not going to pay you a penny." In another case, a patient verbally abused a psychologist accompanied by the explanation that "The judge has ordered me here, so you have to take this abuse from me."

Of course, psychologists do not have to treat such patients. If no specific treatment provider is named in the court order, it is not incumbent on the psychologist to treat that individual. If a psychologist is specifically named in the court order and does not want to accept the case, we recommend that the psychologist write a courteous letter to the court to explain why he or she will not be treating the individual. Any reason given is adequate. Perhaps the needs of the patient are outside of the areas of expertise of the psychologist, or the schedule is already filled, or the case is too demanding at this time.

One psychologist interviewed a man who announced that he could not pay for any of his court-ordered therapy. The man explained that he had to pay the attorney a retainer of $5,000 and could not afford any more expenses. The psychologist elected not to see the patient. (7.3)

Another psychologist accepted a court-ordered patient even though it meant adding to an already heavily booked schedule. However, he wanted future referrals from the court and took the case as a courtesy to a potential future referral source. (7.4)

Fact and Expert Witnesses

A psychologist may be called on to serve in one of several roles as a witness. In a trial, both sides present a narrative of events that supports their desired resolution of the dispute. The decision maker (the jury or a judge in a bench trial) evaluates the factual evidence and decides the dispute on the basis of judicial instructions provided about the relevant law in that jurisdiction. Each of the attorneys will call witnesses to present facts that they know from their personal experience and experts who have been qualified on the basis of their ability to provide guidance in areas in which a layperson does not have sufficient knowledge or expertise to reach a conclusion. *Fact witnesses* have firsthand knowledge of facts that are relevant to the case at issue before the court. They are only allowed to testify about what they know firsthand and cannot opine as to what the facts mean in the case. A pure fact witness cannot give opinions or testify about something that was said to them by another person. Such hearsay testimony is generally prohibited because the person who communicated the knowledge is unavailable to be cross-examined.

Expert witnesses constitute an entirely different category. State or federal law will determine which professionals qualify as expert witnesses on specific topics. However, the general rule is that an expert witness has knowledge in an area that is directly relevant to the dispute and is beyond the knowledge base of the average layperson. In addition, expert witnesses can take the factual situation and draw conclusions related to the issue in dispute. Expert testimony is allowed to assist the trier of fact to interpret scientific evidence. Therefore, expert witnesses are expected to bring information on a specialized branch of knowledge to the court. What qualifications an expert should have and what subject matters are appropriate subjects of their expertise are questions that forensic specialists and courts regularly debate. A psychologist who has been qualified as an expert by the court is allowed to give a full range of opinions within areas of expertise as designated by the court, including speculative or hypothetical opinions. Expert opinions are not personal opinions; they should be opinions based on scientific evidence. According to the Supreme Court decision *Daubert v. Merrell Dow Pharmaceuticals* (1993), courts must evaluate both the qualifications of witnesses and the scientific basis of their testimony. If the psychologists cannot provide scientific evidence for their opinions, they should respectfully decline to offer an opinion.

Many psychologists have treated patients and have become a witness in litigation in which their services were relevant to their patient's lawsuit. The patient may have brought suit against other parties in which the patient asserted that as a result of the other party's negligence, the patient experienced emotional damage. Another common situation is a highly contested divorce involving child custody issues with a family or child previously treated. Sometimes patients are involved in a criminal proceeding, and psychologists are called to challenge the patient's veracity. When psychologists provide professional services to a patient and are later called to be a witness in a lawsuit, their role is neither purely that of a fact witness nor an expert witness. They are either a *percipient expert* or a treating expert. Percipient experts are "those individuals who have specialized training and experience but who are not retained for the purpose of litigation" (Caudill & Pope, 1995, p. 104). What distinguishes expert witnesses from fact witnesses is that expert witnesses have relevant specialized knowledge beyond that of the average person; this knowledge may qualify them to provide opinions as well as facts.

Psychologists and psychiatrists who provide patient care can usually qualify to testify as treating experts in that they have specialized knowledge not possessed by most individuals to offer a clinical diagnosis and prognosis (S. A. Greenberg & Shuman, 2007). However, when psychologists testify as a treating expert, they are only allowed to opine about issues that are directly related to the services that they provided. In addition, the hearsay rule does not apply because the communications between the therapist and patient constitute much of the data on which the treating expert bases his or her professional opinions.

To clarify the responsibilities of a treating expert, we provide the following example:

> A psychologist is treating a patient for depression and for problems at home and work. The patient reports and believes that he became depressed after a recent traffic accident. During treatment he brings suit against the other driver, asserting that the other driver negligently caused the accident. Because the patient has placed his emotional state at issue in this litigation, he has waived his privilege, and either his attorney or the attorney representing the defendant may want to find out what the psychologist knows about the patient's history of depression. The psychologist can, as a treating expert, answer questions about his treatment. He can state that his patient displayed symptoms of depression and some impairment. The psychologist can say that the patient presented as depressed and identified the traffic accident as the cause of the depression. He can also state that as the treating psychologist, it was not his role to determine the accuracy of the patient's narrative. The psychologist can state that nothing he observed or heard was inconsistent with the patient's narrative. (7.5)

However, the patient's attorney may want to persuade the psychologist to opine as to whether the accident caused the depression. The psychologist cannot give an opinion on that question; he cannot state that the accident caused the patient's depression or whether the patient had depression prior to the accident because he did not know the patient prior to the accident. In this instance, the psychologist can report that the patient stated that he believed the accident caused the depression.

In addition, the defense attorney may want to question the psychologist about the patient's history in hopes that he will prove that the patient was already depressed at the time of the accident. The psychologist will have to answer honestly on the basis of his interviews of the patient or past medical records, if he has reviewed them. However, the psychologist cannot be asked to review the records and opine as to whether the depression was a preexisting condition. He can only provide data that he was given and state how he used those data to diagnose and treat the patient.

Often attorneys will try to manipulate a treating expert into providing opinions that go beyond the diagnostic and prognostic judgments. The attorney may be unfamiliar with the differences or may try to manipulate the psychologist to assist his or her client. The attorney for the patient/litigant will often be willing to brief psychologists prior to their testimony, but the attorney's primary purpose will be to assist his or her client, not to protect the interests of the psychologist. If psychologists raise issues with attorneys about protecting their own interests, the advice likely will be that they need to retain their own attorney to advise them. Psychologists need to be aware of the types of questions that are appropriate for them to answer and what types are not appropriate. Attorneys, although expensive, can be hired to assist. This is particularly important for psychologists who are participating in a deposition and there is no judge to appeal to if lawyers raise questions that they have doubts about answering. In many cases, if psychologists make a good faith attempt to stay within the appropriate role, going beyond the role will not have serious disciplinary consequences. One exception occurs in child custody proceedings in which psychologists are at risk for a licensing board complaint if they provide opinions that could be construed as recommendations on custody or visitation without having conducted an evaluation in which both parties had given appropriate consent.

COOPERATING WITH ATTORNEYS

At times, the attorney for a current or former patient may contact psychologists for their records. Assuming that a proper release is obtained, psychologists can legally send the information to that attorney. Sometimes psychologists may be aware of the litigation and understand the general nature of the issues involved. At other times, they may not know why the patient or former patient wants the records sent to an attorney. If psychologists believe that the material might be clinically or legally damaging, they should contact the patient to discuss the situation.

Testifying as a witness for a current patient runs a risk of damaging the treatment relationship. To a certain extent, successful treatment requires psychologists to have some esteem in the eyes of their patients, and that is difficult to sustain when an attorney is trying to discredit them on the witness stand. Patients typically will want their treating psychologist to be their advocate, but the responsibility of a psychologist as a witness is to tell the truth. Patients will want their psychologists to be strong and competent, whereas in reality some psychologists may be anxious and uncertain. Psychologists should discuss this in advance to prepare the patient for the potential downsides of their testimony.

If psychologists learn that their patients are in litigation and they suspect that they may be called to testify or release records, it is prudent to discuss this situation with the patient and perhaps the patient's attorney ahead of time. There is a danger if the nature of the testimony will vary from what the patient would want. Also, it is desirable for psychologists to clarify payment arrangements with the patient ahead of time if they do not already have a payment agreement with their patients for the time psychologists will spend on the legal case.

Some psychologists may advise patients that the content of their records will hurt them in court or that the content of the records is not appropriate for admission into court. However, psychologists who make these comments risk giving patients bad legal advice. If psychologists believe that the admission of the records will hurt the patient's case in court, the best advice is to discuss what is in the record with their patients so that the patients can consult with their attorney on the matter, or the psychologists can discuss it with both their patients and their patients' attorneys.

Getting Paid for Services

Often psychologists participate in court proceedings on the initiative of a party who has brought a lawsuit against their patient. They will discover this when they are served with a court order or a subpoena for their testimony or records, accompanied by a release from their patient. In this situation, the subpoenaing party is not obligated to pay professional rates for the considerable time required to comply. States typically have laws that set a nominal statutory witness fee for fact witnesses; treating experts are usually considered fact witnesses with regard to compensation. California, for example, statutorily recognizes the special nature of the treating expert witness role. Court decisions in many jurisdictions have awarded expert witness fees to treating experts. Psychologists who receive subpoenas by opposing counsel can petition the court to require payment of professional fees, but this usually requires the assistance of counsel and the expenses involved often exceed what the psychologist could reasonably expect to recover.

Even though the opposing party initiated the participation of the psychologists, their involvement is an indirect result of providing professional services to their patients. These services are typically not covered by health insurance. Nonetheless, it is perfectly appropriate for psychologists to bill patients for their professional time, providing that the patient has agreed to be responsible for payment. This requires that psychologists include a provision in the initial treatment contract signed by the patient that states something like "You understand that if I am subpoenaed or otherwise required to participate in a legal proceeding as a result of providing professional services to you, you will be responsible for paying me at the rate of $XXX an hour for all time expended on preparation, transportation, and testimony." Many psychologists charge more than their regular clinical fee for forensic participation because of the extra work and possible external resources (such as an attorney) that are needed. The fee must also be agreed to in writing as part of the initial contract.

We recommend that the informed consent agreement require patients to pay the full professional fee for all services provided, including fees for work on legal issues. As a general rule in everyday practice we recommend being generous with time and refraining from nickel-and-diming patients for brief incidental services. However, for both personal and clinical reasons, we recommend being very strict when it comes to charging for all forensic time. The charges could include, for example, talking to the patient about the case between sessions, talking to the patient's attorney, retrieving and reviewing records from other sources, reviewing the patient's chart, preparing for testimony, travel to and from the courtroom or deposition, long distance phone charges, parking costs, time spent waiting to be called to testify, and so on. For personal reasons, psychologists need to appreciate that the time commitment may be very substantial. Although the patient or the patient's attorney may frame the request in terms of "taking a morning off," in reality the preparation and travel time could easily escalate into dozens of hours with no guarantee that the hearing might not be postponed or that the psychologist might not be asked to return on another day. Furthermore, it may be desirable to spend time reviewing the general nature of the testimony or conclusions with the patient's attorney and the patient ahead of time for clinical reasons.

Testifying in Court

Many times psychologists will be asked to participate in a deposition that is part of the discovery process. To make a proceeding as fair as possible, each side is allowed to discover what evidence the other side will be presenting to be better able to prepare for or refute it. When psychologists are deposed, they are part of the discovery process. The lawyer for the person opposing the patient wants to find out what the psychologist would say if called to testify in court. A deposition is taken outside the presence of a judge. With no judge around, some lawyers will take liberties in their questioning and comments that they would not take in a trial. They may be unusually aggressive or offensive to discern how far they can push the witness. The attorney for the patient will be present but will usually remain silent. He or she will save questions for the trial so as not to expose his or her strategy in advance. A deposition can be the most difficult part of a psychologist's participation in the legal process. It can be damaging to the treatment relationship. In many situations, after consultation with their attorneys, we have advised psychologists to avoid these negative impacts by encouraging their patients not to attend the depositions. Some liability policies will pay for an attorney to be present at a deposition to represent the interests of the psychologist and assist in avoiding any negative outcomes.

As we described previously, we urge psychologists to consider billing for all of their time spent on these cases. If they do not bill for their time, they may not be as committed to putting in the necessary time to ensure that they are well prepared for the deposition. However, testifying without preparation can engender substantial risks. Psychologists may confuse the patient with someone else, misstate an important point, or otherwise fail to present themselves clearly or accurately. They need to address the issues before the court, which may include justifying the content of their notes, identifying their treatment or diagnostic hypotheses, and presenting the data to substantiate them.

Any time psychologists testify, they also run the risk of saying something that would offend their patient and harm the treatment relationship. If the patient's case depends on demonstrating the extent of psychopathology or impairment, the psychologists could offend the patient by emphasizing the degree of the impairment. Conversely, if they fail to describe the impairment as sufficiently severe they may offend the patient as well. Therefore, psychologists might consider discussing the general nature of their testimony with the patient ahead of time, debriefing the patient after their testimony, or as previously recommended, requesting that the patient refrain from attending the deposition.

Psychologists should not accept contingency fees (i.e., any fee tied to the outcome of litigation); such fees are considered a conflict of interest. When on the stand, their primary obligation is to speak the truth. Any contingency fee would give a financial incentive for the psychologist to weigh the testimony in a manner consistent with their financial interests rather than the truth.

Generally psychologists should avoid letters of protection, which are promises from attorneys to pay for services once the case has been settled. Although they are not inherently unethical, they present problems in that often attorneys simply do not pay, or if the settlement is less than anticipated, they do not pay the promised amount. Also, it may have the same incentive as a contingency fee in that a successful outcome would increase their likelihood of being paid (Woody, 2011).

Generally, in preparation for testifying, psychologists do not need to hire their own attorneys. Sometimes the experience is unpleasant, but it does not typically generate legal risks. Here are some general suggestions about how to testify.

- Psychologists should get a briefing from the patient's attorney prior to their deposition or testimony. They should understand relevant information about the case, the attorney's strategy, and where their testimony fits. They should be aware of the conflicts between roles of experts and advocates. From the beginning and throughout the process, they may need to clarify their role with attorneys retaining their services.

- Psychologists should review their records carefully and review and know the literature concerning the services they provided. They may wish to rehearse their testimony or to ask an experienced colleague to role play with them.

- Psychologists should beware of manipulation by the opposing attorney. The attorney for the patient may provide assistance regarding the opposing counsel's strategy. Psychologists should limit testimony to matters that they can address in a meaningful manner. They should not assume that they know more than the attorneys about the legal system. It is reasonable for psychologists to expect that their testimony will be challenged, sometimes vigorously.

- When on the stand, psychologists should listen to the questions and respond carefully. Prudent psychologists ensure that they understand the questions and may reflect on them before they testify. If they do not understand a question, they will ask the attorney to repeat it. An excellent response to a confusing question is, I don't understand the question; could you rephrase it? Sometimes attorneys will ask a question with many parts to it. In such cases, do not hesitate to ask, Which part of that question do you want me to answer first?

- Psychologists should feel free to say, "I don't know" or "I have no opinion" if that is accurate. At times, psychologists may feel compelled by the social pressure of the courtroom to give some response to a question.

- Psychologists should limit their testimony to data regarding their own patient and opinions related to the services they provided. They do not comment on family members or others whom they have not evaluated. If they must answer a question for which they have little information or data, psychologists will qualify their answers and note their bias or limitations (Standard 9.02b, 9.02c, Use of Assessments).

- Experienced psychologists do not allow themselves to get baited by the opposing attorney into responding emotionally. They explain but do not argue. They give a competent, confident response in a neutral, unemotional tone and avoid hyperbole and being defensive.

This experience can create great stress for psychologists who lack control over the process and may feel that the questions are unfair or highly biased. Psychologists who are at a deposition with no judge to monitor the process may encounter an attorney who wants to bait them to determine if they will be a good witness in court. After the deposition, psychologists have a right to review their transcript and should not be afraid to make amendments. They do not have to pay for the transcript of a deposition. At times they will be asked to sign a copy of their deposition attesting to its accuracy. In such cases, psychologists should read the document carefully, make corrections as needed (although it is not recommended to change too much), and charge for their time in doing so.

TAKING FORENSIC CASES

Some psychologists enjoy forensic work; they may work with attorneys to evaluate a defendant for an insanity defense, do neuropsychological testing for a case involving a head injury, be involved in child custody cases, or otherwise provide expert opinions related to psychology/legal issues. Indeed forensic psychology is a rapidly expanding area of practice.

Those psychologists who do forensic work can make their experiences less stressful by trying to be very clear with the referring attorney on the issues as soon as first contacted or as soon as possible. They may, for example, need to clarify as many details as possible. Who is the client? Where is he or she? What role does the attorney want the psychologist to fill? Will the psychologist need to see or test the client personally or is this a record review? What type of services and skills are needed (and do the psychologists have those skills)? What are the legal issues to be considered? Does the attorney want a written report? Will testimony be required? What is the time frame? Who are the opposing attorney and judge (if psychologists do much forensic work they may need to screen for potential multiple relationships)? How will the psychologist be paid (Gottlieb & Coleman, 2012)? Some psychologists find the experience of being an expert witness exciting and rewarding (albeit at times frustrating). They may see themselves as public servants whose goal is to provide information to empower the juries to make better decisions (Brown, 2000). They may also have a good sense of themselves and their roles and have confidence (but not too much confidence) in their abilities. They do not view themselves as "opinions for hire" in which they will delete, overemphasize, or shade the evidence to support the position of the attorney who hired them. Instead, they view themselves as committed to being honest and accurate in all of their representations.

SEVEN ESSENTIAL POINTS TO REMEMBER

1. Psychologists who perform forensic roles need to have a reasonable familiarity with their roles, including the procedures followed in the justice system.

2. The roles and functions of fact, expert, and treating expert witnesses vary.

3. When working as an expert witness, psychologists clarify their role with the attorney who has hired them.

4. Informed consent and documentation are especially important when working with clients in the legal system.

5. The hybrid role of treating expert presents unique ethical and legal demands that require consideration of the psychologist's roles and obligations.

6. Psychologists will be able to withstand the stress of testifying if they understand some basic rules about the process and proper decorum. For example, always treat judges with high respect.

7. Psychologists should never be afraid to say "I don't know" or "I have no opinion" in a courtroom when that is the truth.

CHAPTER 8: PSYCHOLOGICAL ASSESSMENT AND TESTING

Psychological assessment is a broad term. For our purposes here, it refers to the integration of a wide range of information into a comprehensive report. That information may be obtained from an interview, review of archival records, collateral contacts, questionnaires, checklists, standardized psychological tests, behavioral observations, or other sources. Psychological testing is a narrower term that refers to the use of standardized stimuli or testing procedures to gather information. Although some legal risks can come from psychological assessments, on the whole many of the ethical and risk management challenges of psychological assessments come from the manner in which psychological tests are selected, administered, scored, and interpreted. Consequently, in this chapter, we give a disproportionate amount of attention to psychological testing. Issues related to patient access to test results or data are covered in Chapter 6 ("Privacy, Confidentiality, and Privileged Communications").

Psychological testing may be used for vocational, educational, health care, or employment purposes. Test are frequently used to measure academic progress, predict academic achievement, clarify vocational interests, assist in career planning, identify psychopathology for health care purposes, or assist in employee selection or promotion. The use of psychological testing to plan for mental health treatment has declined substantially over the years in part because of refusal of third-party payers to reimburse for these services. However, as we describe subsequently, the use of psychological testing at the request of other third parties (often called testing with third-party consequences, testing with external consequences, or high-stakes testing) has increased substantially. Of course, any testing, even for planning mental health treatment, can have ramifications beyond its immediate purpose. The possibility always exists that some third party at some time or under some circumstances could get access to the testing that was done for treatment planning and use it for another purpose. For example, testing done for treatment might find itself admitted into evidence in a legal proceeding sometime in the future.

TESTING FOR TREATMENT PLANNING

Testing patients for the purpose of treatment planning carries some legal risk. However, such complaints are relatively rare. First, the lack of payment for such tests by third-party payers makes the overall use of psychological testing for treatment purposes less common. Second, psychologists tend to have good relationships with their therapy patients, and these relationships tend to discourage patients from filing complaints. There is a good general principle here, of course, namely, that patients who experience good relationships with their psychologists, even when the focus is on assessment, are less likely to initiate complaints. So, a good risk management strategy with assessment is to develop a collaborative relationship with patients and pay careful attention to informed consent principles.

A movement within psychology called *consumer-focused* assessment or a similar term (Brenner, 2003; Finn, 2011; Fischer, 2004) represents a series of strategies that attempt to maximize patient involvement in the assessment process as much as is clinically indicated. Some of the activities could include involving patients in the phrasing of the referral question, selection of the tests to be given, wording in the social history, or phrasing of the conclusions in the final report.

This perspective on assessment has risk management advantages and disadvantages, depending on how and under what circumstances it is used. On the one hand, it could increase the legal risks to psychologists if it compromised the accuracy, reliability, or validity of the report. This could occur, for example, if the testing involved unjustified deviations from standardized test administration procedures or interpretation or the deletion of clinically relevant information from the social history.

On the other hand, it could decrease legal risk to the psychologist if it increased the accuracy, reliability, validity, or usefulness of the report and increased the extent to which patients felt invested in and confident in the assessment process. For example, a discussion of the referral question or the wording of the report may help clarify an important point that the psychologist had originally misunderstood or may lead to the phrasing of a sensitive topic in a manner that avoids unnecessary embarrassment to the patient.

When assessing a patient and determining a diagnosis, the psychologist may be confronted with difficult issues. On the surface, it would appear straightforward: The psychologists assign patients whatever diagnosis is warranted by the facts. However, the issues are more complex, especially if the diagnosis may have an unintended negative consequence, such as making it more difficult for patients to qualify for life insurance, negatively biasing any future but unanticipated legal action involving the patients even if the legal action has no connection to the patients' current or past level of functioning, or stigmatizing the patients when they seek treatment from subsequent health care professionals.

It would, for example, be appropriate to give a patient a diagnosis of borderline personality disorder if the facts warranted the diagnosis, if it was the focus of treatment, or if the Axis II diagnosis was integrally involved in the Axis I diagnosis that was the focus of treatment. However, it need not be given if it is not the focus of treatment. Indeed some insurers, such as Medicare, do not pay for the treatment of personality disorders, and any Axis II diagnosis would be meaningless from the standpoint of insurance reimbursement. If the information was to be shared with another service provider, it would be important to give comprehensive and accurate information. Again, accuracy is paramount, but if there is uncertainty, it may be prudent to give the diagnosis in terms of ruling out certain disorders (often called a *rule out*).

In addition, the information provided in a report should be relevant to the referral question. Psychologists should not include irrelevant information out of a false sense that they are being thorough.

ACCOMMODATING CULTURAL AND LINGUISTIC DIFFERENCES

Historically, most psychological tests were normed with English-speaking European Americans and may not have been appropriate for use with individuals who did not have English as a primary language or who were from other cultural backgrounds. Over the past decade or more, however, most tests have incorporated members of many cultural and ethnic groups into their norms and the research on these instruments suggests that some tests are valid for members of the major ethnic minority groups. Nonetheless, decisions about which tests to use with any particular member of a minority group rest, in part, on the degree of acculturation of patients or their proficiency in English. Unless the test is designed to measure English-speaking ability, consideration should be given to using a translated test. Even then, psychologists should be sure that the translated test has been assessed for equivalency because some psychological constructs that are meaningful to European Americans are not relevant to members of other cultures and language groups. Similarly, members of some cultural groups are not accustomed to sharing their problems with strangers, especially in an objective test format. In such instances, formal testing may be inappropriate, or the psychologist may need to spend additional time with the patient to establish a more trusting and supportive relationship. Regardless, whenever psychologists decide to use a test for which there are no standardized norms for the target population, they should always acknowledge that fact in their report and present the results cautiously.

Sometimes, it may be necessary to modify the administration or interpretation of a test to account for the cultural or linguistic background of the patient. Any change in standardized administration or interpretation should have a professional basis and should be noted in the test report. More information on working with diverse populations is found in Chapter 10 ("Other Areas of Concern for Psychologists: Consultant or Supervisor, Diversity Issues, Conflicts in Institutional Settings, Referral, and Termination and Abandonment").

DEBRIEFING PATIENTS ·

According to Standard 9.10 of the American Psychological Association's (APA's) "Ethical Principles of Psychologists and Code of Conduct" (hereinafter referred to as the Ethics Code; APA, 2010a), psychologists take steps to ensure that they go over the test results with the person being tested or a representative, such as the parent of a minor child. Exceptions can occur when psychologists conduct forensic, pre-employment, or security evaluations or engage in organizational consulting, and the psychologist explains to the person ahead of time that the test results will not be explained to them.

TESTING WITH EXTERNAL CONSEQUENCES

Most complaints about psychological assessments or testing occur when the assessment is requested by third parties. We refer to these assessments as testing with external consequences because the test results may have significant implications for the person being tested. This can occur, for example, when psychologists test an applicant for an executive position or promotion in a corporation, for the legal right to use lethal weapons as a security guard, for eligibility as a law enforcement officer, or for entrance into a clergy position in a religious denomination; when they conduct an evaluation with health consequences, such as eligibility for bariatric surgery or organ transplants; when they examine an individual for intellectual disabilities, which could assist in determining eligibility for rehabilitation programs; when they evaluate a child for placement into a special education or gifted program; or when they conduct a child custody evaluation (special issues related to custody evaluations were covered in Chapter 5, "Working With Couples, Families, and Children"). Psychologists may also be asked to evaluate sexual offenders, juvenile delinquents, or others to make determinations of public risk. Although all testing should have consequences, we are discussing here the instances in which testing can be expected to have significant consequences outside of treatment planning and psychotherapy.

These types of high-risk assessments have increased substantially in recent years, and we expect the demand for testing with external consequences to increase. For example, we have seen a very rapid increase in morbid obesity in the United States and an increase in bariatric surgery to address that problem. The standards of bariatric surgeons require a psychological or psychiatric assessment before they perform surgery on such persons. Similarly, recent scandals have led many religious denominations to require psychological testing before individuals can enter religious training or be employed by a religious denomination. Courts have increasingly relied on psychologists to provide information on the risks of releasing individuals convicted of sexual offenses or violent crimes. Many school districts will not allow a child who has threatened violence to return to school unless that child has undergone a psychological evaluation.

Assessments of this type have major consequences for the persons being examined, and in some of these circumstances, the test results or conclusions may be unwelcome by the person being tested (or the parents). Given the seriousness of negative consequences, these clients may be more likely to question the professional competence of the psychologist and to file a complaint.

To reduce their legal risk, psychologists need to know basic information about psychological testing, specific information about the domain of assessment in which they are engaging, and the application of risk management strategies. It is important to know the APA guidelines appropriate for the area of assessment, such as the "Guidelines for Assessment of and Intervention With Persons With Disabilities" (APA, 2012a), "Guidelines for the Evaluation of Dementia and Age-Related Cognitive Change" (APA, 2012b), "Guidelines for Psychological Evaluations in Child Protection Matters" (APA, 2013a), and "Guidelines for Child Custody Evaluations in Family Law Proceedings" (APA, 2010b).

BASIC INFORMATION ABOUT PSYCHOLOGICAL TESTING

Here are some general rules about testing that require special vigilance. Some of these comments may appear elementary. Nonetheless, the report of a psychologist may be challenged on these elementary or basic points. Prudent psychologists familiarize themselves with the standards of the Ethics Code (APA, 2010a) that deal with assessments along with other relevant documents such as *The Standards for Educational and Psychological Testing* (American Educational Research Association, APA, & National Council on Measurement in Education, 1999; as we go to press, this document is undergoing revision). Fortunately, some quality comprehensive reviews concerning competence in psychological testing have appeared recently (Butcher, 2009; Krishnamurthy et al., 2004; Moreland, Eyde, Robertson, Primoff, & Most, 1995; Turner, DeMers, Fox, & Reed, 2001).

When testing for external consequences, psychologists should be able to defend why each test was selected and was appropriate for the referral question. We recommend that psychologists defer heavily to the test manual or professional literature for guidance on this question. Psychologists should ask themselves if the test has been validated for this purpose. Is this test appropriate to the patient in terms of reading level, language skills, or cultural background? Most psychological tests require at least a fifth-grade reading level. If the client does not have the necessary reading skills, it may be necessary to give the test orally and note the modification in the administration in the report. At very low levels of cognitive ability, even an oral administration of a test may exceed the patient's ability to comprehend the meaning of items and psychological constructs.

The test must be administered and monitored according to standardized procedures or the deviations from standard procedures must be noted. Factors influencing the test findings should be noted in the report and accounted for in the test interpretation. Other sources of measurement error should be noted.

Prudent psychologists will double-check for scoring errors. Even minor or inconsequential errors in administration and scoring may lead critics of psychological testing to view the entire testing process with suspicion. Prudent psychologists remember that when test results are challenged, another psychologist will review with a magnifying glass the procedures, scoring, and interpretation of the testing psychologist.

A psychologist made several minor scoring errors in an intelligence test. None of these scoring errors altered his basic conclusions. Nonetheless, an opposing attorney emphasized these scoring errors and suggested that they represented an overall pattern of sloppiness. (8.1)

Good reports include the sources of data on which conclusions are based (i.e., test data, past reports, and interview data). Some possible questions that may be posed are, Did the psychologists integrate the test data with other sources of information? Is the written report understandable and free of unnecessary jargon? A general rule is, when doing an evaluation with external consequences, it is essential for psychologists to have a strong professional rationale for anything unusual that they do.

> A psychologist administered the MMPI–2 (Minnesota Multiphasic Personality Inventory) in a forensic case without using the forensic scoring option. The results were consistent with other sources of data. Nonetheless, the fact that she failed to use the forensic option was criticized by the opposing attorney, who suggested that she was using "shortcuts" in her assessment. (8.2)

Nothing is wrong with using computerized test interpretations appropriately. In fact, computerized tests eliminate hand-scoring errors. However, computer-generated interpretations only present hypotheses for psychologists to consider and cannot usurp their judgment in reaching their own conclusions. Psychologists retain the ultimate responsibility for writing the report and supporting the conclusions.

> A psychologist used a quote from the computer-generated test to represent his conclusion rather than using it to fortify his conclusion. Although the quotation represented his professional opinion, the way it was presented gave an impression that he was blindly following the computerized printout. (8.3)

Psychologists should not use tests that are obsolete for the purposes of the assessment. Although typically psychologists should use the latest version of a test, this may not always be clinically indicated.

> A licensing board complaint was filed against a psychologist, alleging that he violated professional standards by administering an older form of the MMPI to a patient instead of the MMPI–2–RF. The psychologist responded by noting that the patient had taken an older version of the MMPI 15 years earlier, and he believed that comparative results would be helpful in treatment planning. A consultant for the licensing board reviewed the response of the psychologist and recommended that the case be dismissed. (8.4)

Although some might argue that the psychologist would have obtained more useful data from the MMPI–2–RF, his decision to use the MMPI was based on sound clinical reasoning. If a licensing board reviewed the decision, it could look to the test manual to determine how the test developers intended the test to be used, or it could look at whether the psychologist could provide a sound justification for the decision.

DOMAIN SPECIFIC KNOWLEDGE

Each of the areas of testing for external consequences requires detailed information about a specific area of psychology (specialized information on child custody evaluations is provided in Chapter 5 ("Working With Couples, Families, and Children").

Bariatric Surgery Assessments

Bariatric surgery has the potential to greatly improve the physical health, psychological health, and quality of life for patients. However, it also involves substantial risks, especially if the patients are not compliant with the recommended post operation lifestyle changes. According to a report prepared by the American Society of Bariatric Surgeons, successful applicants for bariatric surgery will need "sound psychological resources, resiliency, effective coping strategies, and willingness to access meaningful support from others" (LeMont, Moorehead, Parish, Reto, & Ritz, 2004, p. 1). Consequently, most bariatric surgeons require an overall evaluation of all prospective candidates for bariatric surgery to determine those for whom surgery is indicated and those for whom surgery is too risky.

Between 14% (Walfish, Vance, & Fabricatore, 2007) and 18% (Zimmerman et al., 2007) of applicants have had their surgery delayed or denied as a result of their performance on preoperation psychological evaluations. Some rejected applicants may undergo mental health treatment or participate in other activities that will eventually prepare them sufficiently to receive the operation. The reasons for denial include a serious and untreated psychopathology (such as psychosis or bipolar disorder), an active and untreated eating disorder, a lack of understanding of the risks and postoperative requirements of the surgery, an active substantive abuse disorder, a chaotic lifestyle or unusual situational stressors, or a questionable ability to comply with post-surgery requirements (Bauchowitz et al., 2005; Walfish et al., 2007; Zimmerman et al., 2007).

Although psychologists varied in how they performed these evaluations, Walfish et al. (2007) reported that almost all evaluators (85%) did more than a clinical interview; a majority used the MMPI–2; and others used other psychological tests or screening instruments specific to eating disorders (such as the Weight and Lifestyle Inventory, Wadden & Sarwer, 2006). Applicants for bariatric surgery often feel desperate for the surgery and view the psychological testing as an annoying and unwanted barrier that they must overcome. Psychological testing is especially important with these patients because their strong desire for surgery may lead them, even if unwittingly, to selectively report information that places them in a more positive light (LeMont et al., 2004).

Prudent psychologists carefully explain the purposes of the testing and how it is geared toward benefitting the patient. If psychologists decide to recommend against surgery, it is important to have convergent data for that decision. That is, psychologists should make the decision on the basis of multiple sources of information and, if possible, make specific recommendations as to how the patient may eventually reach the benchmarks necessary for approval.

Screening for Religious Occupations

When psychologists test applicants for religious occupations, they must understand what the denomination wants the evaluation to assess. Although it may be obvious that the denomination wants to screen out individuals who have pedophiliac inclinations or serious and pervasive mental disorders, some denominations may also want to identify persons with personality disorders or traits that may interfere with their job performance. In some instances, the denomination may use the results of these assessments to reject the applicant; in other instances, they may use the results to encourage the applicant to address the personal issues and then seek admission again. Still other denominations may want psychologists to identify candidates with "homosexual tendencies." Aside from the moral issues involved in such requests, this last request represents a misunderstanding of what psychological testing can and cannot uncover (Glassgold & Knapp, 2008). There is no substitute for clear and frank discussions with the referral source concerning the nature and scope of the inquiry.

A middle-aged minister had given commendable service to her denomination for many years but then displayed substantial problems getting along with parishioners and was seen drinking heavily in public on several occasions. The denomination ordered the minister to undergo a psychological evaluation as a condition of retaining her ordination. The denomination used the report and other sources of data to develop a program designed to rehabilitate her. (8.5)

A psychologist routinely did psychological testing for a local theological seminary. As part of her assessment protocol, she ensured that she was given the opportunity for a feedback session with each applicant. Although almost all of the applicants passed the screening, she wanted the opportunity to give them useful feedback on how they might capitalize on their personality strengths and compensate for their personality weaknesses to make their religious career more rewarding. (8.6)

Testing for Educational Placement

The educational testing of children can be quite controversial. Some parents have a great personal investment in having their children placed in the district's gifted program. Other parents are quite concerned that their children with special needs receive the optimal school placement. When testing such children, psychologists can be of more service to the parents if they understand the conditions under which children may be granted entitlements under state and federal law.

One neuropsychologist in independent practice opined that a child he tested needed special accommodations in school. Another psychologist who worked for the school did not believe that the educational placement recommendations found in the report were in the best interest of the child. The two psychologists and parents met, discussed the needs of the child, and agreed on an educational program. Although the assessment of the neuropsychologist in independent practice was valuable, the school psychologist knew more about the local resources of the school. (8.7)

Risk Assessments for Sexual Offenders

Few assessments can have as much impact on a client's life as a risk assessment for being a sex offender. This specialized area of assessment requires extensive training and expertise.[1] Fortunately, a number of screening instruments have been developed for assessing the risk of reoffending among sex offenders.

Psychologists risk giving misleading or inaccurate information to the court if they fail to use or interpret these tests appropriately. First, psychologists must ensure that they use an assessment instrument appropriate for the individual being tested. A screening instrument for pedophilia, for example, may have little usefulness for other forms of sexual offenses. Some instruments have only been normed with reoffenders and have not been studied with first-time offenders.

Also, some test developers conveniently provide guidance on how to place individuals into dichotomous categories such as high risk or low risk for reoffending. Psychologists should not naively accept these categories and fail to consider the psychometrics behind them.

Psychologists need to know the criterion variables that the test developers used for predicting risks. For example, a study that used re-arrest records for sexual offenders is likely to underestimate the extent to which the individuals will reoffend because most sex crimes are never reported, and some that are reported do not result in arrests. Gender, age, ethnic, and linguistic factors also influence the applicability and interpretation of the test data.

Furthermore, Boccaccini, Murrie, Caperton, and Hawes (2009) noted that the validity of risk assessment instruments may vary according to local jurisdictions. For example, the validity of an instrument used in a state that monitors sex offenders closely will differ from the validity of an instrument used in a state that monitors sex offenders less closely because the degree of monitoring may influence the criterion variable (e.g., re-arrest rate). There is no substitute for knowing the normative data and other psychometric properties of the test that was used.

---

[1] Portions from "Ethical and Professional Issues in Assessing Sexual Offenders," by B. Mapes and S. Knapp, 2005, December, *The Pennsylvania Psychologist, 65,* pp. 3–4. Copyright 2005 by the Pennsylvania Psychological Association. Adapted with permission of the authors.

Psychologists' ability to interpret tests accurately improves if they consider the strengths and limitations of the statistical methods used to generate conclusions. This requires an understanding of null hypothesis testing, Type I and Type II errors, among other things. However, the field of statistics has changed considerably since the older generation of psychologists (at least the generation of the psychologists who wrote this book) was trained in the 1970s. Now a thorough understanding of statistics may include the need to understand Bayesian analysis, effect sizes, and other things. For example, Beauregard and Mieczkowski (2009) found that Bayesian analysis helped in their understanding of the STATIC-99, and Mokros, Stadtland, Oseterheider, and Nedopil (2010) found it useful in their understanding of the Psychopathology Checklist (PCL-R).

The usefulness of psychologists to the court will improve if they can explain to the court the statistical factors used to obtain their interpretations including how randomness can influence predictions. Popular books such as *The Drunkard's Walk* (Mlodinov, 2008) or *Calculated Risks: How to Know When Numbers Deceive You* (Gigerenzer, 2002) provide helpful examples that psychologists can use to explain randomness to the judge or jury.

Psychologists who fail to indicate the psychometric qualities of tests and the statistics used to generate interpretations risk giving the court misleading or inaccurate information. The purpose of noting these limitations is not to bog the court down in psychometric details but to help the court understand the complexities and uncertainties involved in predicting future behaviors. The concerns about test limitations apply not only to pencil-and-paper tests but also to assessments that involve phallometry (changes in size of penis in response to stimuli).

Some of the methodological issues related to the prediction of dangerousness are relevant here. The prediction of recidivism or dangerousness is improved when psychologists use standardized measures of violence prediction. However, these tests often have high rates of false positives. As a result, psychologists should also look at individual factors that are not found in the risk assessment measure (DeMatteo, Batastini, Foster, & Hunt, 2010). These factors could include the self-reported circumstances of the offenders' last or most recent antisocial acts, their insight into the factors that led to this act, and the desire to avoid such behaviors in the future.

For example, one set of test materials reported that individuals who fell into the low-risk range had only a 2% chance of reoffending, whereas individuals who fell into the high-risk range had a 50% chance of reoffending. However, psychologists need to go beyond that basic statistic and ask, Although Mr. Jones fell into the group that had a 2% chance of reoffending, is he one of those 2% who will reoffend? Then psychologists can describe why Mr. Jones's chances of reoffending are higher or lower than the 2% figure indicated by the test score. A common error is to misinterpret group data as applied to individual cases. In the preceding case, the fact that 2% of the persons who obtained a certain score reoffended does not necessarily mean that Mr. Jones has a 2% chance of reoffending. Reports should carefully explain how that 2% figure should be interpreted.

Often psychologists are asked to predict the likelihood that a prisoner will be a risk to the community if released. At one time it was the conventional wisdom that predictions of dangerousness by mental health professionals were no more accurate than "flipping coins" (Monahan, 1981). Subsequent research, though, has suggested that psychologists can exercise greater skills in predicting violence, although these predictions can best be compared with meteorological (weather) forecasts in which the likelihood of violence has to be represented in terms of probability as opposed to absolute chances (Monahan & Steadman, 1996). Helpful reports address idiosyncratic factors or life circumstances that could increase or decrease the risk of violence for this particular person.

Several screening or predictive instruments for violence have been developed, but they have the same limitations as screening instruments for sexual offenders. Violence is a relatively infrequent event; it is often not reported to authorities; predictive scales may be limited to certain populations such as former prisoners or former mental patients; and these scales may have a high rate of false positives (Norko & Baranoski, 2005). There is a dearth of psychometrically validated assessment instruments to determine the risk of violence among children and adolescents.

These comments are not designed to denigrate the use of these scales. Indeed, the scales are generally far more effective than clinical intuition alone. However, these cautions speak to the importance of psychologists clearly clarifying the basis of their judgment to the decision maker. Psychologists who fail to delineate the limitations of their assessment instruments risk an allegation of incompetent practice or incorrect diagnosis.

Pre-employment Testing and the Americans With Disabilities Act

Many psychologists perform screening for employers who are interested in hiring or promoting the most qualified applicants. When testing for external consequences, psychologists should be aware of and trained in the unique domain of knowledge necessary for effective functioning in the position. Under some circumstances, pre-employment testing may involve not so much the use of psychological tests that have been standardized with normative populations but the development and validation of specific tests on the basis of a job analysis unique to that work setting. Training as a clinical psychologist usually is not sufficient to qualify psychologists to do pre-employment testing.

In addition, psychologists who do pre-employment testing need to pay special attention to the Americans With Disabilities Act of 1990 (ADA), which prohibits discrimination in hiring and employment screening for persons with physical and mental disabilities. Factors used in determining whether a person is disabled include whether he or she "has a physical or mental impairment that substantially limits one or more major life activities, has a record of such an impairment, or is regarded as having such an impairment" (U.S. Equal Employment Opportunity Commission & U.S. Department of Justice, Civil Rights Division, 2002, p. 2).

Of course, employers are allowed to select the most qualified applicant for a position, and the ADA does not require employers to hire otherwise unqualified persons. But employers must offer a position to qualified individuals with a disability if they can perform the essential functions of the position with or without reasonable accommodations. A reasonable accommodation "is any modification or adjustment to a job or the work environment that will enable a qualified applicant or employee with a disability to… perform essential job functions" (U.S. Equal Employment Opportunity Commission & U.S. Department of Justice, Civil Rights Division, 2002, p. 5).

During the pre-employment selection process, psychologists may not ask about the presence of a mental disability, and using a test that is commonly used to diagnose mental illnesses (even if they do not actually intend to use it to give a diagnosis) is problematic. In *Karraker v. Rent-a-Center* (2005), for example, the 7th U.S. Circuit Court of Appeals (Chicago) ruled that an employer violated the ADA by using the MMPI as a pre-employment screening instrument. The court noted that the MMPI is administered and interpreted by a health care professional, was designed to reveal a mental impairment, and is normally given in health care settings. Some employers delay conducting the mental health evaluation until a job offer has been made; after that point it is permissible to require the prospective employees to "pass" a medical and psychological evaluation as long as that evaluation is tied closely to specified job duties. Also, some specific disorders, such as most sexual disorders, gambling, or kleptomania, are not covered by the ADA. Substance abuse is covered by the ADA, although the employer may prohibit the use of alcohol on the premises and may dismiss employees if their job performance falls below acceptable standards. Also, employers may refuse to hire (or may fire) anyone who presents a threat to the safety of the workplace.

The pre-employment screening may take into consideration personality traits related to the job under consideration. For example, chronic lateness, poor attendance, and rudeness are personality traits that may be relevant to the job, but in and of themselves, they are not indications of mental illness and, therefore, may be considered in the employment decision.

RISK MANAGEMENT STRATEGIES

It is time to recall the three risk management strategies: informed consent, documentation, and consultation. Although the person being assessed is not always the client when the assessment is at the request of the third party, it is still important to treat such persons with as much respect and courtesy as if they were the client.

A psychologist who did employment testing always included comments about the strengths of the applicants at or near the beginning of her report. She did so because she believed that this accurate information presented a more balanced view of the applicant for the employer. Also, she reasoned, even if the applicant did not get the job and eventually saw the report (perhaps as part of discovery in a lawsuit), any personal injury to the applicant would be reduced by reading these positive statements. Finally, from a risk management perspective, it would show that she was trying to be fair and balanced in her assessment of the applicant. (8.8)

It is prudent to always have a written informed consent agreement when doing evaluations with external consequences. Psychologists should go over the informed consent agreement with the persons being evaluated ahead of time. They should clarify who is requesting the evaluation, who is paying for it, the general nature of the evaluation, the right of access to records, the potential consequences of the evaluation, and other topics. After ensuring that the client understands informed consent and does not have further questions, psychologists obtain the person's signature. If the person refuses to sign, the psychologists may want to terminate the testing.

According to the Health Insurance Portability and Accountability Act Privacy Rule, patients have access to test reports and test data (their own answers and or productions). More information on access to testing information is provided in Chapter 6 ("Privacy, Confidentiality, and Privileged Communications") in the discussion of the Health Insurance Portability and Accountability Act. In some evaluations, such as when evaluating religious professionals, Malony (2000) recommended that psychologists ensure the opportunity for a feedback session with the individual being tested. That way, psychologists can have assurance that the individual will have the option of getting clinically useful information.

When testing for external consequences, it is very important for psychologists to document the basis for every conclusion or recommendation they make. Ideally they will be able to identify the specific sources in the test or their interview notes to substantiate each conclusion. We recommend that psychologists keep copies of the raw notes they take during the interview. If a case goes to court, psychologists should assume that all of their notes will be subject to discovery by the other side.

Prudent psychologists seek clinical consultation as indicated. Psychologists should not assume that they will know everything about every situation that arises.

A psychologist routinely did assessments for individuals applying to be security guards. One applicant showed soft signs of a neuropsychological impairment. The psychologist spoke to a neuropsychologist about this applicant before he completed his evaluation. (8.9)

This psychologist was working at Bloom's higher levels of professional development and understood that consultations can take different forms and be done for different purposes. Sometimes the consultations focus on the clinical features of the patient, the context of professional services, the items in the psychologist's skill inventory, the disciplinary consequences, or more than one calculation of risk. In this case, the neuropsychological signs were irrelevant to the question that the third party wanted to have addressed. However, the psychologist did receive permission from the third party to review the implications of the soft signs and encouraged the applicant to receive a more specialized evaluation from a neuropsychologist or neurologist. This consultation was easily defended in that it helped improve the quality of services provided.

SEVEN ESSENTIAL POINTS TO REMEMBER

1. Legal risks are more likely to occur when psychologists are engaging in testing with significant consequences for the person being assessed.

2. When testing psychologists should ensure that they make accommodations for the cultural or linguistic backgrounds of their patients or clients.

3. Psychologists will become a target for criticisms if they make rudimentary errors in psychological testing, such as making scoring errors, or if they are unable to justify their choice of tests.

4. When testing for external consequences, it is important to have a clinical rationale for any procedures that deviate from usual or customary practice.

5. When testing for external consequences, psychologists should consider the psychometric properties of the test in interpreting the test results.

6. When testing for external consequences, psychologists should emphasize the informed consent process and documentation.

7. When testing for external consequences, psychologists should ensure that they have specialized knowledge about the area in which they are providing an opinion.

CHAPTER 9: ASSESSING AND TREATING PATIENTS WHO ARE POTENTIALLY SUICIDAL OR DANGEROUS TO OTHERS

Patient emergencies are a stressful part of working as a psychologist. The most frequent mental health emergency is the threat of suicide. However, most psychologists will also experience the stress of dealing with patients who threaten to harm third parties (Kleespies & Dettmer, 2000). Psychologists should know their legal obligations and mandatory reporting requirements when evaluating or treating high-risk patients such as those who have HIV/AIDS or other infectious diseases and present a risk to infect identifiable third parties, children who are being abused, older adults who are being abused, or drivers who are impaired.

ASSESSING AND TREATING PATIENTS WHO HAVE A RISK OF SUICIDE

Suicide is the 10th leading cause of death in the United States. One survey found that the odds of losing a patient to suicide are 1 in 2 for psychiatrists and 1 in 5 for psychologists (Chemtob, Bauer, Hamada, Pelowski, & Muraoka, 1989). Of course, psychologists who work with high-risk populations, such as returning war veterans, have an increased risk of having a patient die from suicide. Simon (2000) has commented that "there are only two kinds of clinical psychiatrists—those who have had patients commit suicide and those who will" (p. 399). Suicides take an emotional toll on treating professionals as well as their families. Chemtob et al. (1989) reported that therapists experienced high rates of psychological distress following a patient suicide.

In addition, patient suicides or attempted suicides are a frequent cause of malpractice suits against psychiatrists (17% of all malpractice suits for psychiatrists; Bender, 2005) but a less frequent cause of malpractice suits against psychologists (4% of all malpractice suits for psychologists according to the most recent data from the The Trust Sponsored Professional Liability Program) Malpractice complaints arising from a patient suicide occur more frequently in inpatient settings. Of the few outpatient suicide malpractice cases, most result in settlements because insurance companies are afraid of emotional jury verdicts. In such situations psychologists have only a limited ability to resist the demands of the insurance company to settle (Chapter 13, "Professional Liability Insurance").

It is difficult to obtain reliable data on suicide. It is an infrequent event for the population in general; there is a tendency to underreport suicides; and the samples used for research might not necessarily generalize to the population as a whole. Nonetheless, on the National Comorbidity Survey (a study of the prevalence of mental disorders), 13.5% of the respondents reported suicidal ideation; 3.9% had a plan; and 4.6% had made an attempt sometime during their lives (Kessler, Borges, & Walters, 1999).

Although females attempt suicide more often than males, males are three times more likely to die from suicide. Most, but not all, persons who die from suicide have communicated their intent in advance, primarily to family or significant others. Multiple attempters represent a clinically more severely troubled group with an elevated risk of suicide compared with those who report just suicide ideation or a single attempt (Rudd, Joiner, & Rajab, 1996).

STRENGTHENING INDIVIDUAL THERAPIST FACTORS

Psychologists will be better prepared to deal with patients who have a risk of suicide if they have studied the core competencies required for assessing and managing suicidal risk (Rudd, Cukrowicz, & Bryan, 2008). Among other things, it is essential to understand how to assess and manage potentially suicidal patients. This includes the ability to collect relevant information, formulate the degree of risk, develop a treatment plan, and manage care, including anticipating crises and patient noncompliance. In addition, it is desirable for psychologists to know the involuntary hospitalization or civil commitment laws in their states; know the local crisis intervention program, if any; and have a professional relationship with an inpatient unit. If it is necessary to hospitalize a patient, the process will be easier for psychologists who already have a relationship with the hospital staff, know the admission procedures, and can discuss the procedures with the patient ahead of time.

When treating patients who have a risk of suicide, it is important for psychologists to know enough about psychopharmacology so that they can understand the anticipated benefits of medications and the extent to which the patient is responding as intended. The psychologist should strive to develop a good working relationship and open communication with the prescriber to discuss the patient's response to the medication and any unusual mental or physical side effects the patient has experienced.

If a patient is not compliant with medication recommendations, it should be a subject of immediate concern and discussion in therapy. Some patients are reluctant to take psychotropic medications because of the unpleasant side effects. These side effects may be temporary, or there may be other medications that are tolerated better by the patient. Ongoing consultation with the prescriber can be very beneficial in such situations. Regardless, problems with medications should be addressed as part of the therapy. In the rare case it may be appropriate to terminate treatment if noncompliance with medications becomes an issue that cannot be resolved therapeutically (see more information on terminations in Chapter 10 ("Other Areas of Concern for Psychologists: Consultant or Supervisor, Diversity Issues, Conflicts in Institutional Settings, Referrals, and Termination and Abandonment").

ASSESSING PATIENTS WHO HAVE A RISK OF SUICIDE

Of course, psychologists should ask patients during the first session about present and past suicide ideation or attempts. No patient is too healthy to be asked.

We review here salient issues in the assessment and treatment of patients who have a risk of suicide. Prudent psychologists go beyond what is written here and seek quality resources to guide their assessment and treatment of such patients. Excellent resources that cover the assessment and treatment of patients with a risk of suicide include, among others *Myths About Suicide* (Joiner, 2010), the Managing Suicidal Behavior system described by Oordt et al. (2005), the *Practice Guidelines for the Assessment and Treatment of Patients With Suicidal Behavior* (American Psychiatric Association, 2003), and any of the works by Rudd, Jobes, or Joiner. We cite some of their research and ideas later in this chapter. Additional resources can be found through the Suicide Prevention Resource Center (www.sprc.org) and the American Foundation for Suicide Prevention (www.afsp.org).

No mental health professional can be expected to predict or prevent all patient suicides. Because suicide is such an infrequent event, sufficient professional and the best scientifically based predictions still contain a high number of false positives and false negatives (Rudd & Joiner, 1999). Suicide prediction is complicated by the difficulty of research in this area and the inconsistency in defining suicidal behavior and risk by different researchers. Furthermore, some patients with chronic suicidal ideation represent a subset of patients with unique treatment needs. Nonetheless, extensive literature on suicide prevention has accumulated, and we recommend that all psychologists engaged in health care familiarize themselves with that literature.

RUDD AND JOINER TAXONOMY

No completely reliable algorithm based on demographic or clinical data will be of determinative value for any individual patient so psychologists must use their best judgment, informed by the professional literature, to determine the relative risk of suicidal behaviors and to modify treatment procedures accordingly. Next we present the comprehensive system developed by Rudd and Joiner (1999), although other systems may also provide a helpful framework. Nonetheless, any assessment needs to be "thorough, extensive, and multifaceted" (Jobes, 2008, p. 406).

Rudd and Joiner (1999) have recommended classifying suicidality into a continuum of five categories (nonexistent, mild, moderate, severe, and extreme) on the basis of the evaluation of eight factors (see Table 9.A). Using the continuum of suicidality should help psychologists organize how they conceptualize suicide assessment and management. Furthermore, the fact that the psychologists used a well-recognized system will demonstrate to critics that they followed an appropriate standard of care in assessing suicidal behavior and tailoring an appropriate intervention.

All of the factors must be seen in the context of the patient's life and treatment relationship, and no simple hierarchy of factors can be used to predict suicidal risk. Any of these factors or even chance and unpredictable events (such as a job layoff) may precipitate a serious suicide attempt. Nor is the list of factors exhaustive.

Table 9.A

Continuum of Suicidality

Factor	Suicidality			
	Mild	Moderate	Severe	Extreme
Predisposition	low	moderate	high	high
Precipitants	few or none	few, handled well	multiple	multiple
Symptomatic presentation	low	moderate	high	high
Hopelessness	no	no	yes	intense
Nature of suicidal thinking	low	moderate	more intense frequent	more intense frequent longer lasting
Previous suicidal behavior	no	few	multiple low lethality	multiple serious
Impulsivity	low	low	high	high
Protective factors	present	present	few	none

Note. Tables A and B adapted with permission from "Assessment of Suicidality in Outpatient Practice," by M. D. Rudd and T. Joiner, 1999, in L. VandeCreek and T. Jackson (Eds.), *Innovations in Clinical Practice* (pp. 101–117), Sarasota, FL: Professional Resource Press. Copyright 1999 by Professional Resource Press.

The eight factors used to classify suicidality are predisposition to suicidal behaviors, precipitators or stressors, symptomatic presentation, hopelessness, nature of suicidal thinking, previous suicidal behavior, impulsivity (or self-control), and protective factors. We review each of these in the discussion that follows. As can be seen, these factors overlap to some degree.

Predisposition to suicidal behaviors is determined by looking at historical factors such as previous history of psychiatric diagnoses, history of suicidal behavior, history of being abused, and presence of family violence or very punitive parenting in the family of origin. When asking about the family of origin, it may be prudent to start with general questions (e.g., Tell me about your childhood. What were your parents like? What were your brothers and sisters like?). Then one can go into increasingly more detail about how the family handled conflicts and the presence of arguing, verbal threats, pushing, hitting, and more.

We also suggest that psychologists consider other demographic and clinical risk factors for suicide. Those who are at a higher risk of suicide are older, European American, unmarried (especially widowed or divorced), male, adolescents or young adults, or members of sexual minorities.

> A psychologist did an intake interview on a depressed older white man who was a widower, had recently been diagnosed with a serious medical condition, and hunted for recreation. Although the psychologist routinely assessed all new patients for suicide, he knew that the demographics of this individual made him a high risk for suicide. (9.1)

Precipitators or stressors refer to significant life events or daily hassles. Precipitants could include exit events from the patient's social field, such as the loss of a romantic relationship, loss of a job, involvement with the criminal justice system (e.g., being a victim of crime, being sent to jail, or being involved in a legal case), or a decline in health. Daily stressors refer to day-to-day inconveniences that in isolation are not particularly stressful but that have a cumulative impact. They could include an unpleasant work environment, chronic problems with a spouse or child, or ongoing financial problems. Military personnel or veterans who were exposed to combat are at increased risk to die from suicide. One study found that 46% of veterans who were returning to college acknowledged thoughts of suicide (Rudd, Goulding, & Bryan, 2011).

> A psychologist interviewed a woman whose husband had just left her after he announced he was having an affair and would be leaving her for another woman. The separation forced her to move to a less desirable area of town. She was temporarily sharing custody of her children and missed having them around all of the time. She felt humiliated by the actions of her husband. She had been close to her husband's family and missed the contact with her mother-in-law. The psychologist appropriately understood that one event (the separation from her husband) had multiple implications for the patient. (9.2)

Yen et al. (2005) found that negative life events in the areas of criminal or legal involvement or love and marriage were related to an increased risk of suicide for patients with Cluster B personality disorders (antisocial, borderline, narcissistic, and paranoid). Of course, the same objective life event may have different implications for different individuals. The loss of a romantic relationship for one person may involve significant loss or humiliation, but for another person it may be experienced as a welcome relief. Psychologists should look at the meaning of the event for their patients and its subjective impact on them.

The symptomatic presentation can be described using nomenclature from the latest version of the diagnostic manual of the American Psychiatric Association or the

International Classification of Diseases. Although suicidal behavior is often linked to major depression, it can occur in patients with other diagnoses as well. Kessler, Berglund, Borges, Nock, and Wang (2005) found that suicidal ideation occurred across a wide range of diagnoses. For example, a patient with a generalized anxiety disorder had almost the same likelihood of attempting suicide as a patient with major depressive disorder. In fact, the diagnoses most linked to suicidal behavior were not major depression but obsessive-compulsive disorder and substance abuse disorders (albeit with the possibility that there was a secondary diagnosis of depression or depressive features). Methodological issues in this study, such as the use of lay interviewers following a structured interview scale to determine diagnosis, raise some questions about the findings. It is possible that other diagnostic techniques may have identified a higher rate of depression among persons who attempted suicide or that a secondary diagnosis of depression could have been identified. Nonetheless, the general finding is consistent with other research in this area. In addition to the presence of a diagnosis, it may also be helpful to ascertain the presence of certain key symptoms such as anger, agitation, or a sense of urgency and the means used to reduce that agitation, such as the use of alcohol or other drugs, medication, self-mutilation, and more.

Hopelessness may be gauged, for example, by asking patients to rate themselves on a scale of 1 to 10 on how hopeless they feel (with 1 being *optimistic* and 10 being *utterly hopeless*).

The nature of suicidal thinking refers to the current frequency, intensity, and duration of suicidal thoughts, specificity of plans, availability of means, and explicitness of intent. When interviewing all patients, it may be prudent to include several depression- or suicide-related questions, for example, Have you ever wished that you were dead? Did you ever feel that life was not worth living? or Did you ever wish you could go to sleep and never wake up? Depending on the responses to these questions, it may be prudent to follow up with more detailed questions concerning suicidal ideation. The practice guidelines of the American Psychiatric Association (2003) include many other useful questions that psychologists can ask to assess suicidal risk.

Discussions of intent and means should be candid. Psychologists should not only ask about the contemplated means of attempting suicide but also about details of where the individual would get the pills, gun, poison, or other means to complete the suicide and where or when he or she intends to do it. Also, it is prudent for psychologists to ask about backup plans for suicide. The frequency, intensity, and duration of these thoughts should be considered.

Coryell and Young (2005) found that for patients with a major depressive disorder, the single best predictor of a suicide attempt was how they rated the intensity of their suicidal ideation in the last week on a 7-point scale from *absent* to *very extreme*. Patients who rated themselves above 5 on this scale were significantly more likely to attempt suicide.

Nonetheless, Busch, Fawcett, and Jacobs (2003) found that approximately three fourths of patients who died from suicide while hospitalized or shortly after being discharged had denied suicidal ideation when they were last questioned. How do these apparently contradictory findings concerning the predictability of self-reported suicidal intent influence the manner in which psychologists evaluate suicidal ideation?

First, no one clinical predictor of suicide will ever approach the sensitivity or specificity found in most medical laboratory tests (Coryell & Young, 2005). Also, some patients may have been sincere in their report that they did not have current suicidal ideation but experienced a sudden increase in suicidal ideation after the last interview. Others may have experienced a significant stressor or precipitant between the time they were asked about suicide and the time that they completed it. Still others might have had poor impulse control or might have been giving a false report of their suicidal ideation. Nonetheless, one can conclude that intent is an important predictor but other factors need to be considered as well, and intent can vary considerably even within a relatively short period of time. Furthermore, the accuracy of measuring intent can be improved by using redundant measures (see the section Redundant Systems of Protection in Assessing Suicidal Behaviors in this chapter).

Previous suicidal behavior includes the frequency and method, perceived lethality and outcome, and opportunity for rescue. Part of the reason for suicidal failures is that some patients miscalculate the lethality of their suicidal attempt. This may, in part, explain why physicians have a higher rate of successful suicides than members of the population in general (Schernhammer, 2005).

Impulsivity and self-control include an evaluation of overall impulsivity, regardless of its cause. The therapist might ask the patient about feelings of being out of control or have the patient rate his or her overall degree of control on a scale of 1 to 10. The link between alcohol and suicide may be explained, in part, by the fact that alcohol reduces inhibitions and self-control. Substance abuse or significant loss may also lead otherwise well-controlled individuals to lose self-control temporarily.

Suicidal behavior has a low but significant correlation with aggressive behavior. Consequently, patients who are suicidal should be screened for aggression. Equally, patients who are aggressive or homicidal should be screened for suicidal ideation.

Protective factors refer to social support, problem-solving skills, and active treatment. The factors that can mitigate against a suicide attempt include marriage, having dependent children, an appreciation that the suicide would cause pain to relatives or friends, facing a future event of importance such as a wedding, anniversary, high school or college reunion, holding religious convictions, having a useful social network, or possessing good problem-solving abilities. Having a strong therapeutic working relationship can also be a protective factor.

A psychologist interviewed a woman who demonstrated a very elevated risk of suicide. However, this woman also had very strong religious beliefs and stated that those beliefs forbade her from attempting to kill herself. (9.3)

Another psychologist interviewed a man who demonstrated a very elevated risk of suicide. Because of a terminal medical condition he was strongly tempted to kill himself, but he stated that such an action might have a serious negative impact on his grandchildren whom he loved dearly. He said, "I could never do that to them." (9.4)

REDUNDANT SYSTEMS OF PROTECTION IN ASSESSING SUICIDAL BEHAVIORS

As noted in Chapter 3 ("Competence") psychologists can reduce the likelihood of a serious professional error if they have a redundant system of protection. In a hospital, nurses, pharmacists, colleagues, and other medical personnel will ideally be a second "set of eyes" for the attending physician or psychologist to catch any glaring errors in the orders or prescriptions. Similarly, psychologists in outpatient practice can create a redundant system to act as a second source of data.

In outpatient settings, the sources of data include other health care professionals (such as a prescribing psychopharmacologist) and family members who can, if clinically indicated, monitor the patient and assist in treatment. We described in Chapter 3 how consultation can also provide important sources of data.

Psychologists can also use screening instruments that will act as a second source of information on a patient who has a risk of attempting suicide. These instruments do not replace clinical judgment but can be used to check the perceptions of the interviewing psychologist. Often screening instruments, such as the Scale for Suicide Ideation (A. T. Beck, Kovacs, & Weissman, 1979), the Beck Hopelessness Scale (A. T. Beck, Weissman, Lester, & Trexler, 1974), or similar scales that take about 10 minutes to administer can be used to supplement, not replace, the clinical assessment.

A psychologist interviewed a patient who claimed that his suicidal ideation was almost entirely gone and that the risk of suicide was now over. The psychologist suspected that the risk of suicide was higher than the patient acknowledged. Consequently, he had the patient complete a Beck inventory; the patient acknowledged the presence of suicidal ideation. The psychologist used this information to justify the continued emphasis on suicidal prevention. (9.5)

TREATMENT PLANNING BASED ON RISK ASSESSMENT

The treatment plan should not just focus on the diagnosis and assume that through treatment of that particular diagnosis (e.g., depression) the suicidal ideation will go away. Instead, there is a need for specific interventions to control the suicidal impulses as well as treatments designed for the diagnosis itself.

Managing and Treating Patients Who Have a Risk of Suicide (Context of Treatment)

The management and treatment of suicidal behavior can be guided by the outcome of the detailed assessment shown in Table 9.B. As a general rule, the suicidal precautions should increase as the patient moves up the suicidal risk continuum. Even at the mild level of suicide risk, however, psychologists should periodically check on the strength of the suicidal risk factors.

Table 9.B
Recommended Interventions for Patients at Risk of Suicide

Risk	Intervention
Severe or extreme	Evaluate for psychiatric hospitalization; ensure that patient is accompanied or monitored at all times
Moderate	Consider these options:
	Evaluate for psychiatric hospitalization
	Increase frequency or duration of outpatient treatment
	Involve family, friends, or support systems if clinically indicated for support or monitoring, such as through a suicide watch
	Evaluate symptoms and goals frequently
	Ensure 24/7 availability of emergency contacts
	Consider medication
	Use telephone contacts for monitoring
	Implement a safety agreement if ego-syntonic and clinically indicated
	Consult
Nonexistent or mild	Reevaluate risk if circumstances of patient deteriorate substantially

Suicide Specific Interventions for Patients With Severe or Extreme Risks

The safest treatment options include hospitalization because of the increased opportunity for continual monitoring for the patient's safety and response to medications. If hospitalization is not possible because the patient does not agree or qualify for a civil or involuntary commitment, psychologists should provide as many of the options in the moderate-risk category as possible with safety being a primary focus of treatment. For example, psychologists should remove lethal agents and keep alert to sudden changes in behavior. They can increase the frequency of sessions if possible, maximize involvement of significant others when they can help facilitate recovery, ensure that they are available for emergencies, consider between-session telephone monitoring, and develop a safety agreement if it is clinically indicated (see the section on Safety Agreements in this chapter). If the patients have access to firearms or lethal doses of medication, the psychologist should engage in means-restriction counseling, which means educating the patient or patient's family about the risks that occur when a suicidal patient has easy access to such means and working with the patient and family to develop strategies to restrict access (Bryan, Stone, & Rudd, 2011).

Suicide Specific Interventions for Patients With Moderate Risk

With moderate-risk patients psychologists should consider implementing specific safety features if clinically indicated. Next we suggest modifications in these interventions when working with patients who have serious personality disorders and a moderate risk of suicide. Nonetheless, psychologists should involve most patients as much as clinically indicated in the decisions about the suicide intervention strategies. Psychologists may, for example, ask patients if they would like to come in for an extra session this week or have the psychologist call them at home during the week or both. It is very important that psychologists fully document any interventions they make and the rationale for the interventions as well as any interventions that they considered but decided not to use along with the rationale for not using them.

> A psychologist was treating a man with strong suicidal ideation. The psychologist knew that the patient needed increased monitoring at home at least until an evaluation for medication could be arranged. He told the man, "Your wife needs to know how badly you are doing. I know she is in the waiting room and I am going to bring her into the office. Would you like me to tell her how badly you are doing or would you like to tell her yourself." (9.6)

Psychotherapy Treatment Strategies

To ensure patient safety, it is sometimes indicated to give a greater degree of emphasis on suicide-specific interventions, including individual characteristics that increase risk, such as attributional style, cognitive rigidity, and problem-solving ability. It may be helpful to address suicidogenic beliefs such as "Suicide is the only way to solve my problems" or "My sins are so great that only my death can atone for what I have done."

Generating Social Support

It may be prudent to inform the patient and the patient's family of the responsibility to protect the patient's life. For example, a psychologist might say, "If I believe that you are at a risk of killing yourself, from both a therapeutic and humane perspective, my most important treatment goal is going to be to keep you safe and alive. I therefore want to reserve the right to involve your family members in your treatment if I determine you are at a serious risk of suicide or self-harm."

When possible and appropriate, significant others should be included as part of the patient's treatment. The pros and cons of involving third parties vary from patient to patient and from time to time over the course of treatment. Psychologists need to assess whether the family can be a therapeutic ally. In outpatient treatment it is particularly important that others are available to help the patient be safe between sessions. It is also important to document when such situations are clinically contraindicated. When family is not available, psychologists should consider other sources of support including clergy, friends, and coworkers.

In some rare occasions, if it is clinically indicated, psychologists may inform third parties of the suicidal risk posed by their patients without their consent. In these situations the moral obligations of psychologists to beneficence (promoting the welfare of their patient) temporarily trump their usual respect for patient autonomy. Of course, whenever one moral principle is trumped by another, psychologists should make reasonable efforts to minimize the harm to the offended moral principle. For example, if a psychologist has a patient who presents a high risk of suicide and it is absolutely necessary to inform family members to ensure the patient's safety, the psychologist can give the patient a choice as to whether he or she can call the family with the psychologist on an extension or whether the psychologist should make the call (with the client in the room and ready to get on the phone if needed).

Medication

Do the patients hold false beliefs about medications that reduce their ability to make informed decisions about their use (Newman, 2005) such as the belief that the patient will become addicted to drugs or that medications are only for "crazy" people? Psychologists need to consider how patients from other cultures view medications and how those views can affect compliance.

Psychologists should not make taking medication a condition of treatment unless medication is necessary for effective functioning. For patients with chronic personality disorders, medication may be very helpful in some contexts and minimally helpful in others. Psychologists should not assume that the refusal to take medication is always a symptom of pathology or transference. When it doubt, psychologists consider the importance of the therapeutic relationship and do not force the medication issue unless it is clearly important.

Safety Agreements

Many psychologists use safety agreements (also called no-harm contracts or safety contracts) in which patients sign a document promising that they will not attempt suicide, or they promise to take other safety precautions. Psychologists are mistaken if they believe that these contracts or agreements have any legal value. Psychologists should only use them if they believe that they have clinical value.

These contracts are most effective when they include as many affirmative statements as possible (Newman, 2005; e.g., I recognize that I have considerable resources to battle this depression), are created collaboratively with the patient and tailored to unique life circumstances and perspectives, reflect an ongoing process that empowers patients, and encourages their involvement in the treatment plan (Rudd, Mandrusiak, & Joiner, 2006). It may be appropriate to include steps to restrict access to firearms or lethal doses of medications, identify a stimulus cue such as the feeling that the impulse of suicidality is overwhelming, and identify responsibilities and options of patients to follow when urges become strong.

From a risk reduction perspective, the only value of safety agreements is whether they facilitate the treatment process. In and of themselves, safety agreements have no legal value and certainly will not serve as a significant protection in a licensing board complaint or malpractice suit. The content of the agreement and process of getting the agreement signed should reflect underlying treatment and moral values. They should reflect the wishes of the patient (respect their autonomy), promote patient welfare (beneficence), and not be acquired through bullying or harping (nonmaleficence). If safety agreements are not done with these caveats in mind, the agreements are clinically useless and may be harmful.

Safety agreements can be clinically contraindicated if they are used only to reduce clinician anxiety, lead to reduced vigilance or a power struggle between psychologist and patient, or are perceived as a self-serving document for the benefit of the psychologist (Edwards & Sachmann, 2010). It is important to remember that we listed the advice to "always get a patient with suicidal ideation to sign a safety contract" as an example of a false risk management principle.

A psychologist was treating a patient with pervasive and long-standing relationship issues. One day the patient announced that she was revoking the safety agreement. Instead of focusing on the safety agreement the psychologist focused on the patient's current functioning and ways to decrease her dysphoria and reduce impulsivity. Given the unique characteristics of this patient, the psychologist believed it would be clinically contraindicated to push the acceptance of the safety agreement. At the end of session the patient stated that she intended to follow the safety agreement, although the psychologist was well prepared to have the patient leave without mentioning it. (9.7)

Treating Patients Who Have a Chronic Risk of Suicide and a Serious Personality Disorder

Here are some examples of troubling patient behaviors that may demonstrate a serious personality disorder or other pathology in the context of suicidality.

1. Sometimes patients discontinue medication abruptly or discontinue taking it as prescribed. Past experience may suggest that the patient will deteriorate substantially. At other times, the medication is of marginal value, and it is not worth the power struggle to get the patient back on medication.

2. The patient revokes a release of information form with the treating psychiatrist or psychopharmacologist.

3. A patient decides to discontinue the safety agreement, announcing that he or she no longer feels that it can be honored.

4. A patient announces that he or she intends to attempt suicide if a certain event occurs, such as if an ex-partner ever gets married (which may or may not be imminent), if a particular court case is lost, if he or she does not get accepted to graduate school, or if he or she fails to achieve some other personal goal.

5. A patient announces he or she will attempt suicide if the therapist ever terminates treatment. Therefore, the psychologist who might otherwise be thinking that the patient might do better elsewhere is suddenly faced with increased fear of liability if the treatment were to be terminated.

6. The patient refuses to pay for therapy or refuses to consider a referral to a more appropriate treatment modality even if it is a supplemental treatment, such as a time-limited dialectical behavior therapy (DBT) group.

A few patients have serious personality disorders characterized by chronic suicidal risk or what has been called a "suicidal career" (Maris, 1981). Usually they have serious and disruptive personality disorders (e.g., borderline). Ordinarily the treatment of patients at risk to attempt suicide requires a focus on their primary diagnosis and specific strategies designed to reduce the suicidal ideation or impulses. However, focusing on suicidal ideation or impulses may inadvertently reinforce those ideas or impulses and be clinically contraindicated.

Patients with serious personality disorders typically will not benefit from hospitalizations unless there are coexisting symptoms of serious depression or psychosis or unless they move into the areas of severe and extreme suicidality. Consequently, their treatment usually requires that the outpatient therapist tolerate a long period of chronic suicidality. In fact, the hospitalization of these patients may, at times, be clinically contraindicated.

Nonetheless, even patients with chronic risks of suicide and serious personality disorders may have acute exacerbation of their suicidal ideation or impulses and will move into the high-risk category with the same requirement for an emphasis on protection and suicide prevention. Sometimes relatively minor events can exacerbate a serious suicidal crisis, and it may take longer for the patient to return to a state of equilibrium (Rudd, 2008). Thus, there are several categories of suicidal behavior and corresponding philosophies of treatment: acute risk, chronic high risk, and chronic high risk with exacerbation (see Table 9.C).

Table 9.C
Philosophy of Treatment for Patients With Acute and Chronic Risk of Suicide

Risk	Philosophy of treatment
Acutely suicidal	Suicide focused
Chronically suicidal with personality disorders	Diagnosis focused
Chronically suicidal with personality disorders with acute exacerbation	Suicide focused

Often these patients have the diagnoses of bipolar disorder, complex posttraumatic stress disorder, or chronic mental disorder with persistent pain. They pose the most frequent psychological high-risk management problems.

Patients with serious personality disorders often have chronic thoughts of suicide and frequently mutilate themselves or have suicide gestures or attempts. About 1 in 10 will successfully complete suicide, which is a rate similar to patients with schizophrenia and major mood disorders (Paris, 2002). Most of the patients in this category are women, and some may complete suicide after multiple attempts. A comorbid diagnosis of substance abuse and major depression increases the risk of suicide.

These patients are extraordinarily hard to treat. The possibility of a suicide is often an important part of the defensive structure as the only means of escaping intractable psychic pain. Gestures are often the means of secondary gain for acting out rage. Often these patients present with a long history of numerous psychiatric hospitalizations, suicide attempts, self-mutilation, and treatment failures. However, "an excessive focus on suicide prevention with these patients can prevent therapists from doing their job" (Paris, 2002, p. 741). The treatment process becomes derailed when therapists spend too much of their time on suicidal behaviors. It may be preferable to deal with the underlying causes, such as the inability to regulate emotional states.

As described by Sanderson (2002), some mistakes are commonly made by therapists who treat such patients as shown in the example that follows.

> *They may become emotionally over involved, engaging in heroic efforts to save their patient's lives, only to pull back abruptly when they run out of ways to save the patient or the patient fails to be sufficiently grateful. Therapists may become demoralized by the patient's lack of progress and frightened, in particular, by the patient's ongoing urges to die. Or, they may get angry and punitive toward the patient, blaming the patient for not getting better more quickly. (pp. 36–37)*

It is highly recommended that therapists have training and experience in treatments specifically designed for such persons, such as DBT (Kliem, Kröger, & Kosfelder, 2010; Sanderson, 2002), which involves a balancing of acceptance of the patient's current struggles and problem-solving strategies. The same dialectic of "empathic understanding and striving for therapeutic change" (Newman, 2005, p. 77) appears in the treatment of individuals with bipolar and other serious mental disorders. Other treatments, such as transference-focused psychotherapy or schema-focused therapy, have also shown effectiveness with borderline personality disorder (Zanarini, 2009).

When psychologists doubt their ability to treat patients with chronic suicidal ideation and a serious personality disorder, they may be wise to err on the side of caution and refer these patients to a therapist with more expertise. At times, these patients will benefit more from day hospital or intensive outpatient treatments. Some kindhearted and well-meaning psychologists make the mistake of allowing their compassion and good intentions to get in the way of their better judgment.

If the decision is made to treat such patients, wise psychologists will ensure that they have regular consultation. It is important for psychologists to ensure that they have the emotional resources for this work because these situations create high stress and require enormous clinical and personal resources. Psychologists who do take such cases need to be alert to countertransference issues, feelings of personal responsibility, rage, and burnout. Often DBT is best done with consultation teams. Regular attendance is expected. "A current maxim is that therapists cannot say that they are doing DBT unless they attend a consultation team regularly" (Sanderson, 2002, p. 37).

When treating patients with a serious personality disorder, it is important to insist on adherence to the treatment plan. Psychologists should explore the failure to cooperate with treatment carefully. At times, the patient might not have understood the tasks, or the tasks were beyond the patient's ability to perform. Nonadherence issues should be addressed early. If the failure to adhere to treatment is compromising the quality of services, the psychologist may need to consider terminating the client (see Chapter 10, "Other Areas of Concern for Psychologists: Consultant or Supervisor, Diversity Issues, Conflicts in Institutional Settings, Referrals, and Termination and Abandonment").

Involving family members in treatment may be clinically indicated. The goal of involving the family is to inform them of the nature of treatment, the reasons for it, and how they can cooperate with the treatment goals and assist recovery. As discussed earlier, involving family members requires attention to other ethical and risk management issues.

RISK MANAGEMENT WITH PATIENTS WHO HAVE A RISK OF SUICIDE

Good risk management with patients at risk to attempt suicide focuses on the triad of risk management: informed consent, documentation, and consultation. Informed consent is especially important because effective treatments for suicide emphasize structure, transparency, and clear expectations for the patient to cooperate and collaborate in treatment (Jobes, 2008). As much as possible, patients should be informed of the general nature of the treatment plan, including the need of the psychologist to communicate with any prescribers, family members, or significant others (if clinically indicated). Rudd et al. (2009) recommended that the compassionate discussion with the patient include a candid acknowledgement that the suicidal thoughts may persist and that the discussion of some issues may be painful or upsetting, although pain remediation is the ultimate goal.

When creating records for patients at risk for suicide, we recommend that psychologists follow the analogy of the math teachers who give credit to students for showing the steps of their problem solving even if the final answer is not completely correct. Prudent psychologists ensure that terminology is used with precision. For example, they would not use the phrase *suicide gesture* without explaining what it means. Clinicians use that phrase differently. Some use it to describe self-harming acts with a low risk of lethality or that were done without the intent of killing oneself. Others use it to describe actions designed to communicate to others the extent of the patient's psychological distress or attempts to manipulate the behavior of others (Heilbron, Compton, Daniel, & Goldston, 2010). Also, psychologists should never raise an issue of suicidal risk without addressing it later in the notes. It would be contraindicated, both clinically and from a risk management perspective, to record that a patient had suicidal thoughts in a note, yet never address the issue in subsequent notes.

Good records are a must for both clinical and risk management reasons. Future clinicians and members of a review team or jury should be able to read the records of the treating psychologist and develop a general understanding of what was done and why, and what was not done and why. Such careful records may discourage future potential lawsuits. Or, if a lawsuit occurs, those good records will assist in the defense, may help with a positive jury verdict, or may reduce settlement costs. For example, if a psychologist decided not to hospitalize a patient, it would be prudent to detail the reasons why this decision was made.

> A psychologist was treating a man who was in the moderate range of suicide risk. Ordinarily it would have been appropriate to contact the man's family about his clinical condition and solicit their involvement, monitoring him and assisting in furthering the goals of treatment. However, there were unusual clinical features that strongly argued against this approach. Consequently, the psychologist documented why she made the decision not to inform the patient's family. Fortunately, the course of treatment was successful. If a tragedy had occurred and the conduct of the psychologist had been called into question, she could have provided sound clinical reasons why she did not solicit the family's involvement. (9.8)

This example provides another illustration of several points we have raised throughout this book. First, good risk management principles should be consistent with good patient care. It would have been poor practice (and poor risk management) to have contacted the family without considering the impact on this particular patient. Second, it illustrates that whatever general rules may apply, ultimately psychologists have to make decisions based on sound clinical judgment for the particular patient. The practice of psychology cannot be performed by rote or by following predetermined algorithms. Instead, it requires informed clinical judgment.

Finally, this example shows how documentation, if done properly at the highest level of Bloom's taxonomy, reflects careful thought as an integral part of good patient care. It is important to recall that at the lower levels of Bloom's taxonomy, psychologists would only document the minimum required by law. At the higher levels, however, their notes would demonstrate their thinking process; reflect careful considerations for the quality of care; and justify their actions on clinical, ethical, and legal grounds. This is especially important when dealing with life-endangering patients. A note in the chart "No suicide risk" is insufficient to convey the symptoms, stressors, and personal dynamics that gave rise to the concern about suicide in the first place. The failure of treatment providers to communicate clearly, such as when a patient transitions from inpatient to outpatient treatment (or vice versa), greatly increases the risk of a successful suicide (Rudd, 2008).

Psychologists should always document consultations and, when clinically indicated, discuss strategies with other involved professionals or consultants on a regular basis. If appropriate they may also consult with the patient's family or consult with managed care representatives or case managers about alternative resources. Psychologists who supervise others should make certain that their supervisees speak to them frequently about patients at risk to die from suicide.

Patients at Risk for Suicide in Institutional Settings

Institutions such as psychiatric hospitals, jails, juvenile detention facilities, or half-way houses have greater obligations to prevent suicides because they have a greater degree of control over the patients, inmates, or residents. When liability occurs in such settings, it can be for failure to diagnose suicidal ideation or impulses or failure to plan adequately for the treatment. However, liability can also occur for failure to communicate the risk (e.g., a patient tells a nurse she is suicidal, but the nurse does not tell anyone else or document the statement), failure to order adequate precautions (e.g., a patient is noted as more suicidal in the record, but the institution fails to order an increase in precautions), failure to implement orders to increase precautions (e.g., the health professional in charge of treatment orders increased precautions, but they are not implemented as ordered), or failure to reevaluate the suicidal individual at crucial time periods (e.g., before a discharge or transfer).

Documentation is essential to note what was done or not done and why.

A psychologist worked in a prison that had the philosophy that "suicide is everyone's business." Guards were instructed to report all threats of suicide immediately, whereupon a predetermined suicide assessment and prevention procedure was put into place. The facility has not had a suicide in more than 20 years. (9.9)

Postventions

The loss of a patient by suicide is a very upsetting experience for mental health professionals. Many psychologists experience great grief or even become depressed following the suicide of a patient. It can also be a severe narcissistic injury because the psychologists may begin to question themselves and their competence. The death of a patient needs to be processed. If necessary, it is safer for psychologists to do this in their own personal therapeutic relationship, which is confidential. Careful psychologists do not to engage in self-recrimination in a nonconfidential relationship. Publicly stating, "I should have seen it coming" could be used against a psychologist in the event that the case ever came before a disciplinary body. The suicide of a patient is an occupational hazard of being a psychologist. We recommend that psychologists show concern for their colleagues when they learn that one of their patients has died from suicide. Even a brief phone call or a tactful note can do much for a colleague in distress.

These experiences can be especially difficult for interns and beginning psychologists. Often they do not have the confidence that develops with years of experience and cannot place the event into perspective.

Fortunately, many institutions now consider the suicide or attempted suicide of a patient to be a sentinel event and will do a root cause analysis of what led to the suicide. Ideally, there will be no presumption that any professional made an error. The institution, though, may review its internal procedures to determine if more could have been done to prevent the suicide. If this review is done as part of the institution's peer review process, the information and findings may be confidential under the laws of the state.

Also, it may be clinically indicated to respond to an outreach from the family of the patient. In most states a family member is the legal executor, sometimes referred to as the personal representative, who has the authority to waive the confidentiality of the psychologist–patient relationship. Psychologists need to check the law in their state for the exact rules. When permitted by state law, psychologists may discuss some of the general therapeutic issues with the patient's family, share condolences, and try to give the family a sense of closure. Not only is this a humane thing to do, it also reduces the risk to psychologists of being sued if they are open, caring, and forthright with the family. At times, families have found it healing to have the psychologist attend the funeral of the loved one.

The actions of psychologists should be governed by whether or how they can benefit the family. Psychologists who are extremely distraught themselves may want to delay the meeting until they can better control their own feelings.

> Tact and therapeutic discretion are important when a patient has died from suicide. A psychologist accurately noted in his records that the patient engaged in a vitriolic diatribe against his wife in the last session. After the suicide, the widow insisted on receiving a copy of her husband's records, and under the laws of that state, she was entitled to see them. The psychologist turned over the records in his office but initiated the meeting by describing how anger is a common manifestation of depression, and the anger is usually directed against persons whom the individual loves the most. The comments of the psychologist and his detailed discussion afterward helped the widow to place the comments of her late husband into perspective. (9.10)

APPLICATION OF SUICIDAL ASSESSMENT AND TREATMENT RECOMMENDATIONS TO THE DETAILED CASE EXAMPLE

The treating psychologist would be wise to review the suicidal risk for the patient in the detailed case example in Chapter 1 ("Calculations of Risk"). Table 9.C provides an evaluation of the case on the eight factors previously identified as relevant to the assessment of suicidal risk.

At this time, the psychologist does not know enough about the patient to make an accurate assessment. Depending on the results of further inquiry, the patient may fall into the moderate or perhaps severe or extreme range of suicidality. The example presents the woman as a chronic patient and hints at a serious personality disorder. Consequently, it is not clear whether she should be receiving suicide-focused or diagnosis-focused treatment (see Table 9.D). If she falls into the severe or extreme range of suicidality, she should not be terminated at this time.

ASSESSING AND TREATING PATIENTS WHO POSE A RISK OF HARMING OTHERS

When psychologists think of violence toward others, they often think of the duty-to-warn or duty-to-protect standards that resulted from the well-known case, *Tarasoff v. Regents of the University of California et al.* (1976). However, the most common situation involving violence that psychologists can expect to encounter is that of domestic abuse, although it does not present a high risk to the psychologist from a disciplinary perspective. There is typically no duty to warn or protect in cases of domestic violence because the spouse already knows that she has been harmed or threatened (we are using the feminine pronoun to refer to the victim because the large majority of victims of domestic violence are female). Also, psychologists may encounter children who are endangered by their caregivers or other situations in which patients or others are at risk of harm.

Table 9.D

Factors Relevant to the Assessment of Suicidal Risk

Factor	Evaluation
Predisposition	Need to know about family of origin and the possibility of abuse or overly punitive parenting
Precipitants	Few or none, although termination of treatment should probably be considered one
Symptomatic presentation	High at this time; in the recent past, moderate
Hopelessness	Not reported in the case example
Nature of suicidal thinking	Need to assess in terms of frequency, intensity, and duration
Previous suicidal behavior	Some attempts, lethality not specified
Impulsivity	High during periods of stress, although there is no report of using recreational drugs
Protective factors	Few social supports, family relationships strained

Duty to Warn or Protect

From a risk management perspective, the duty to warn or protect is a low-frequency, high-impact event. Some duty-to-warn cases have been highly publicized, but they are relatively rare in occurrence. Since *Tarasoff*, many state courts or state legislatures have established some form of the duty. There is no substitute for psychologists to learn the laws in their states (see review by Benjamin, Kent, & Sirikantraporn, 2009). Most states establish a duty to warn or protect; some states specify how that duty is to be discharged; some states provide immunity to mental health professionals who make a good faith effort to notify or protect identifiable third parties; and a few states specifically do not permit a breach of confidentiality even to protect an identifiable third party who may be harmed by a patient.

In the original *Tarasoff* case a psychologist was treating a patient who made a serious threat to kill an identifiable third party. The psychologist took the threat seriously and attempted to commit the patient to a psychiatric hospital. The commitment attempt failed; the patient dropped out of treatment; and the supervisors of the psychologist forbade him from taking any more steps to protect the identified victim. Less than 3 months after the aborted commitment attempt, the ex-patient killed his intended victim.

The parents of the victim sued, and in 1974, the California Supreme Court ruled that the psychologist had a duty to warn the identified victim. The decision was followed by extensive criticism from both legal and mental health experts. The California Supreme Court then took the unusual step of rehearing its own case. In the second *Tarasoff* decision in 1976, the California Supreme Court ruled that the psychologist had a duty to protect the identified victim. According to that decision, a mental health professional may discharge the duty to protect through steps designed to diffuse the danger, such as implementing a psychiatric hospitalization, other than just notifying the intended victim.

The treatment of patients who present an imminent threat to third parties requires three steps: assessment, development of an appropriate treatment plan, and implementation of the treatment plan (Appelbaum, 1985). The assessment of danger usually means more than just having a patient utter a verbal threat of harm to an identifiable third party.

Typically, psychologists do not need to issue a warning or take protective measures simply because a patient has issued a verbal threat. Instead, the verbal warning or threat is only one of several factors (albeit a serious one) to consider when assessing the dangerousness of a patient. Other factors to consider include the context in which the threat was made, the intent, and the availability of opportunity. The likelihood of acting on threats is increased if the patient abuses alcohol or other drugs, has a background of violence, or lives in a subculture in which violence is accepted or endorsed.

It is common for patients to express an attempt to harm, or at least extreme anger at, an identifiable individual. However, in most instances, when patients express anger against a third party, the therapist can address this issue in therapy or modify the focus or frequency of therapy, and this may be a sufficient means of providing protection for the third party. Notifying a third party of potential danger is a fairly rare event. Whenever a patient makes such a threat, it is important to document the decision making concerning the threat. Even if psychologists decide not to warn or act to protect an identified victim, it is still prudent to describe their decision making in detail. Although the anger of the patient may be dissipating, it is good practice to revisit the issue of harming the third party regularly throughout therapy.

Violence assessment instruments may be used as a redundant measure. As was noted in Chapter 8 ("Psychological Assessment and Testing"), these instruments have many limitations that must be factored into their use for decision making.

Finally, it is good practice to assess for suicidal intentions whenever an individual expresses a strong intention to harm a third party. There is a significant correlation between homicidal and suicidal behaviors, especially for persons with impulse control problems.

If the determination is made that the individual does present an imminent danger of harming an identifiable third party, the second step is to develop an intervention plan that is likely to diffuse the danger. Unless mandated by state law, warning the intended victim should be only one of several possible interventions. Other interventions include a psychiatric hospitalization, a referral for medication, a shift to family therapy (to strengthen the monitoring by other family members or to reduce intrafamily conflict), a request to remove lethal weapons, increasing the frequency of therapeutic contact through increased sessions, between-sessions telephone monitoring, and more. As with other patients, it is important to focus on the therapeutic relationship. Sometimes psychologists feel so bothered by the threat of violence that it impedes their ability to form a productive working relationship.

As much as possible, involve the patient in these decisions. If patients have informed the psychologist of their impulses to harm an identifiable third person, they may still have some ambivalence about harming that individual. Psychologists should be able to harness that healthy ambivalence to motivate them to participate in actions to diffuse the danger. Often family members or friends can be part of the intervention and may act as a redundant system of protection. For example, a family member may agree to be caretaker for the guns until the situation becomes diffused.

The third step is to implement the treatment plan. Although this step may seem self-evident, it is helpful to remember that in the original *Tarasoff* decision, the treating psychologist decided to reduce the danger to the identifiable third party by hospitalizing his patient. However, the police failed to implement the involuntary hospitalization; the patient dropped out of treatment; no further attempts were made to protect the identified victim; and she was subsequently murdered.

If the decision is made to hospitalize the patient, it is essential that the admitting physician understand the severity of the patient's threat. If the decision is made to increase the frequency of outpatient contacts, it is essential that the patient keep those appointments. Failure to do so requires a reconsideration of the treatment plan (VandeCreek & Knapp, 2001). The psychologist must be fully familiar with the various state statutes regarding admission and discharge of patients in mental health facilities or psychiatric hospitals, including the requirements for voluntary and involuntary hospitalization.

These three steps are not always sequential. It is necessary to continually reevaluate the degree of dangerousness throughout the course of therapy and to modify the treatment plan as conditions change.

Informed consent is important throughout this process. Psychologists will reduce the potential sense of betrayal if they have notified their patient at the start of therapy, either directly or through the Health Insurance Portability and Accountability Act Privacy Notice, of their obligations to protect when patients present an imminent danger to harm an identifiable third party. If such a threat occurs and psychologists live in a state that has a duty to warn or protect or provides immunity if they warn an intended victim, it may be necessary for psychologists to reiterate their obligations to the patient. Also, the informed consent process involves more than just notifying the patient of the legal obligations and can also include an active effort to involve the patient in the treatment and safety planning. Of course, whenever a patient makes a halfway credible threat against an identifiable third party, it is desirable to rely on consultation and careful documentation.

Other Dangerous Situations

Psychologists can expect to encounter patients who are HIV positive or who carry hepatitis or other sexually transmitted diseases. Sometimes these patients engage in indiscriminate behavior that risks infecting others. State laws vary considerably in identifying legal obligations in these situations, and it is important for psychologists to have current knowledge of the specific requirements in their state.

Our recommendation is to think clinically in these situations even if psychologists do not have an obligation to warn or protect. Strive to understand the reasons for a patient's nondisclosure of HIV status. The patient may be dealing with fear of domestic abuse, fear of being abandoned (and having one's children abandoned by the primary wage earner as well), social isolation or stigma (Smith, Rosetto, & Peterson, 2008), or other relationship issues. Fortunately, a wealth of clinical information has emerged that can guide psychologists who are treating patients who have HIV/AIDS or other diseases (see, e.g., J. Anderson & Barret, 2001; Lyles et al., 2007).

Every state requires psychologists to report suspected child abuse. The criteria for reporting vary from state to state; again, there is no substitute for knowing the state law. Typically the statutes require that psychologists must be treating the abused child for the requirement to apply, although in some states psychologists are mandated to report if they learn of the abuse through any professional contact. The standard for reporting is set deliberately low; often a reason to suspect the abuse is sufficient to trigger the reporting requirement. The state agency, not the psychologist, must make the determination whether to investigate the abuse. The website of the United States Department of Health and Human Services contains information on the mandated child abuse reporting statutes of individual states. It can be accessed at: www.childwelfare.gov/systemwide/laws_policies/state/can.

Some states have reporting laws for elder abuse, impaired automobile drivers, treating patients who have had sexual contact with a psychotherapist, or encountering medical errors. The focus and requirements of these reporting laws vary substantially. Sometimes they are mandatory; sometimes they are discretionary. Sometimes they require the permission of the patient; sometimes they do not. Psychologists must know the exact law in their state.

Domestic Violence

Between 15% and 20% of women experience violence from a spouse or intimate partner each year (Harway & Hansen, 2004), and a smaller percentage of men also experience physical abuse. Although researchers may differ on the classifications of violent acts, there is general agreement that sometimes the injuries can be quite severe or result in death, especially for women (Ver Steegh & Dalton, 2008). Although lower income patients are more likely to come to battered women's shelters, domestic abuse occurs across income, racial, and religious groups. Many senior citizens have been abused for years without publicly acknowledging it. The frequency of female abuse against men is increasing, although the large number of victims continues to be women.

Anytime psychologists take a marital case or see one member in a marital relationship they should screen for domestic violence (Rosenbaum & Dowd, 2009) and be prepared to respond clinically when it is identified. The interview can start with general questions, for example, What do you disagree about and how do you express your disagreements? followed by more specific questions, for example, Do you ever shout, yell, feel afraid, place hands on each other? Sometimes victims will deny or minimize the consequences of domestic violence if asked directly or attribute their injuries to accidents (e.g., black eye from running into a door, sprained ankles from falling down several steps). Also, about 20% of the American population, including many women, believe that domestic violence is justified.

The treatment of domestic abuse often requires special skills and access to alternative services to ensure that the abuse is stopped and to determine if and how the relationship can be saved. Treatment may require an extensive network such as a victims support group, legal services, and housing or shelter options. Stover, Meadows, and Kaufman (2009) have reviewed treatments for interpersonal violence and note the advantages of using treatments that address comorbid issues of substance abuse and trauma when clinically indicated.

SEVEN ESSENTIAL POINTS TO REMEMBER

1. Suicide is the most prevalent mental health emergency for psychologists.

2. Psychologists should have a systematic method for assessing suicide and developing a treatment plan.

3. Patients who have a risk for suicide along with a serious personality disorder may require treatment procedures different from those for patients who have a risk for suicide and no serious personality disorder.

4. Psychologists should know the specific procedures needed to reduce the likelihood of suicidal behavior and how to integrate them into the overall treatment of the patient.

5. Psychologists should know the law in their states concerning the duty to warn or protect, how to hospitalize patients in psychiatric facilities, how to assess the potential for violence, and how to develop and implement treatment plans to reduce the likelihood that violence will occur.

6. Psychologists should know the mandated reporting laws in their states.

7. Psychologists should screen all marital couples for domestic violence.

CHAPTER 10: OTHER AREAS OF CONCERN FOR PSYCHOLOGISTS: CONSULTANT OR SUPERVISOR, DIVERSITY ISSUES, CONFLICTS IN INSTITUTIONAL SETTINGS, REFERRALS, AND TERMINATION AND ABANDONMENT

In this chapter, we review several areas of concern for psychologists, including the roles of consultants and supervisors, ways to be of assistance to persons from culturally diverse backgrounds, unique issues that arise when working in institutions, and issues surrounding termination and abandonment.

PSYCHOLOGIST AS CONSULTANT

Sometimes psychologists inaccurately use the term *supervisor* to refer to any activity when two or more psychologists talk about a case. Instead, supervision is best understood as occurring when professionals are overseeing those who cannot legally do what they are doing without oversight. When supervising others, psychologists have legal responsibility for others' actions. In consultation, the person seeking the consultation (the consultee) retains the responsibility to accept or reject whatever advice is received. Consultants have no assurance that the information provided by the consultee is accurate or comprehensive, and they have no control over the behavior of the consultee.

In Chapter 2 ("Key Elements of Risk Management") we discussed the risk management benefit of obtaining consultation as a way to determine risk by better understanding patient, contextual, and individual psychologist factors. Here, we discuss the legal risks that may arise when psychologists act as a consultant, which are very low except when the consultant spends face-to-face time with the consultee's patient.

One might argue that spouses or close friends (assuming they are mental health professionals) can be very helpful with advice if they have a good appreciation of the clinical skills and personal factors of the psychologists. They may be able to discern when the psychologists are being overly confident or hypercritical. On the other hand, spouses or close friends may be reluctant to be critical of their psychologist friends or spouses and, therefore, be of no consultative value, especially if the friends or spouses are inclined to reinforce each other's clinical idiosyncrasies. At the other extreme, impartial experts theoretically have no secondary relationship with the psychologists that would contaminate their comments. When psychologists want objective information about their techniques or a particular diagnosis, arms-length consultants are often best.

A husband and wife therapy team (who were eventually disciplined by their licensing board) typically had their patients engage in unusual practices, such as stripping naked during therapy. Although they participated in a consultation group with other mental health professionals, they never shared their "idiosyncratic" (and iatrogenic) method of doing therapy with the group. They self-validated the technique by talking only with each other. The members of the consultation group, however, had no liability. (10.1)

Psychologists who are approached for a consultation should try to specify the goals of the consultation. They should ask themselves, Do I have expertise in the area in which consultation is requested? Is the request for consultation on a specific case or for ongoing feedback? Sometimes, albeit rarely, consultants may want to see patients directly, although usually they can be of service by reviewing the clinical details, the chart, or the report with the consultee. In either case, the consultants need to obtain the necessary level of detail to give a useful opinion. Effective consultation may focus on the therapeutic process as well as case-specific facts. Consultation will help identify the pros and cons of different options or present the devil's advocate perspective, thus challenging the consultee's assumptions and requiring him or her to consider other options.

A psychologist started a consultation group for licensed practitioners who used eye movement desensitization and reprocessing. This time-limited consultation and education group met for 2 hours a week for 15 weeks. The psychologist used a format that combined lecture and case discussion. Each participant was guaranteed an equal amount of time to discuss cases. (10.2)

A key element of this group is that all of the participants are licensed mental health professionals each of whom retains the final decision-making authority and may accept or reject the recommendations of the group leader as they see fit. A prudent group leader would clarify the nature of the consulting relationship, preferably in writing, before the group began. However, if the group leader accepted unlicensed individuals into the group, did not clarify the consultative nature of the group (or referred to it as peer supervision), or allowed her name to be used on external communications about patients, the relationship would be more like supervision (see the next section). Typically consultants have little legal liability unless they meet with the patients directly.

Over the years we have all sought consultation for professional services both as practicing psychologists and as risk management consultants. Personally we have found that our most helpful consultants have been excellent listeners who helped us solve problems, challenged us with relevant questions, and of course, provided expert information if needed.

When we have acted as consultants ourselves, we have found that almost all consultees are forthright about their issues and are receptive to and appreciative of feedback. On rare occasions, a consultee appears to have desired a predetermined answer and selectively presented information to support the position he or she had already reached. In such situations, we have been surprised at the advice we supposedly gave! Consultants should be aware of this possibility and ensure that they are listening to the consultee carefully and taking enough time to understand the issues clearly. At times consultants may question their consultee about the information being provided or ask him or her to repeat the recommendation made. Sometimes consultants follow up on the consultation and document what was recommended and what the consultee supposedly did. Although consultants usually are not held legally liable for consultees' gross distortions or for opinions based on their selective reporting of facts, they nonetheless want to be as useful as possible to consultees.

PSYCHOLOGIST AS SUPERVISOR

In contrast to the role of consultant, psychologists who serve as supervisors accrue significantly more legal risks than consultants, although these risks are manageable. Supervisors are legally and ethically responsible for the work product of their supervisees who legally become the "hands and legs" of the supervisor. Effective supervisors can reduce their legal risks by prudent hiring and monitoring practices. Supervision occurs most frequently in graduate school training; in practicum and residency training programs; in postdoctoral fellowships; in the required one year of supervised practice prior to taking the licensing exam; and when the psychologist is responsible for the treatment provided by others in institutional settings, such as hospitals, schools, prisons, or mental health centers.

Selecting and Hiring Supervisees

Supervisors can reduce their liability by carefully selecting supervisees and orienting them to the practice's policies and procedures. Many thorough supervisors have a comprehensive application and interview form that requests information back to the time the individual graduated from college, and they review applicants' resumes. They ask applicants why they left previous jobs. They ask about any gaps in applicants' employment history. They check references and are cautious if the past employer will only give the dates of employment without comment or uses code words such as "he left by mutual decision" or "we had to agree to disagree on certain issues." Conscientious supervisors verify all licenses and the existence of any complaints against the potential supervisee. Some states require background checks for reports of founded child abuse and legal convictions for any providers who work with minors. Prudent supervisors will require and review those background reports.

We are aware of one agency that hired a "psychologist" only to learn several years later that he had lied about having a psychology license. The agency had to pay back more than $100,000 to insurers because the agency had inadvertently billed for the services of a person who was not properly credentialed.

Prudent supervisors check the ability of their supervisees to get along with others, to accommodate themselves to agency rules, and to contribute to the practice in terms of technical skills and personality. No one wants to hire the "walking lawsuit," or individuals who believe that they are entitled to certain unrealistic benefits, who have an exaggerated sense of their own competence, or who perceive that they are continually the victim of unfair practices.

Supervisors can ask the prospects what they want from this job or training program. Problems can be avoided if both parties clarify their expectations. Supervisors do not want to hire someone who cannot work overtime, if overtime is frequently required. Supervisors do not want to hire someone who needs two hours of personal supervision a week to get licensed if they are unable to provide such supervision.

Unfortunately, we have known of several situations in which psychologists-in-training arranged for supervision to complete their postdoctoral year for licensing, but neither they nor the supervisor read the requirements of the licensing law thoroughly. After a year of supervised experience they learned that what they had done in the last year did not meet the supervisory standards of the licensing board, and they needed to repeat the year of postdoctoral supervision.

Most conscientious supervisors develop an employment agreement that among other things requires the prospect to follow the American Psychological Association's (APA's) "Ethical Principles of Psychologists and Code of Conduct" (hereinafter referred to as the Ethics Code; APA, 2010a) and applicable state and federal laws. They specify that the failure to follow these rules could be grounds for employment termination.

Finally, good supervisors check to ensure that their professional liability policy covers them for their supervisory activities. The policy will probably not provide coverage for the supervisee unless he or she is employed by the psychologist, in which case an additional premium will be charged for the supervisee. Supervisees should be covered by a malpractice policy.

Helping Supervisees Succeed

Ultimately, the goals of the supervisor and the supervisee should be congruent. That is, both the supervisors and their supervisees should want the supervisees to excel in their work. This can be done by monitoring the work product of the supervisees and creating a work environment in which they can succeed.

Monitoring Supervisees

As supervisors, psychologists assume full responsibility for the work product of their supervisees. They should undertake supervision with the expectation that they will take full legal responsibility for the services delivered. To their credit, most psychologists tend to be democratic in nature and are reluctant to tell people, "Just do it because I told you so." They believe in the value of educating and empowering employees and trainees, treating them with respect, and encouraging independent thought. Legally, however, the supervisory relationship is a hierarchal one. As supervisors, psychologists are responsible when their supervisee makes mistakes. They are responsible when their supervisee decides to do massage therapy with the patient with a serious personality disorder, gives the patient a ride home, and gives the patient his or her private phone number. Psychologists are responsible when their intern fails to read the patient intake sheet in which the patient writes in large bold letters "HELP ME! I THINK I WILL KILL MYSELF" and fails to address suicide in the intake session, and the patient subsequently attempts suicide. Psychologists are responsible when their supervisee writes a letter to an attorney stating that the child she is treating would be better off living with the mother or father, even though she has not conducted a custody evaluation and has never seen one of the parents. Psychologists are responsible when their practicum student diagnoses every child she sees as having reactive attachment disorder, regardless of the symptom presentation.

Of course, most supervisees will not make such glaring errors of judgment, but a few will. The general rule is that supervisors are responsible for these errors, although courts may make an exception if the supervisee deliberately withheld information from the supervisor or directly violated instructions. Nonetheless, if supervisors failed to meet with their supervisees on a regular basis, failed to correct ongoing problems that had been identified, ignored supervisees' requests for help, disregarded their concerns, in other ways provided poor supervision, or did not keep good supervision notes, their legal exposure will be substantially increased.

> A practicum student was cautioned to be very careful of the boundaries she maintained with one of her patients. Against the knowledge and advice of the supervising psychologist, the practicum student developed a social relationship with this patient that soon went sour. When responding to the investigator from the licensing board, the supervisor was able to produce notes relevant to this particular patient that documented her explicit instructions to avoid any boundary crossings. (10.3)

Psychologists should take supervision seriously because of the risks that it creates. They need to let their supervisees know the standards and procedures that will be used in evaluating them. Psychologists can devise a method of assessment appropriate to the supervisee and his or her needs and level of training. When possible, good supervisors directly observe or listen to audiotapes or watch videotapes, review all reports that go to external agencies, and may even participate in cotherapy. It is mandatory to give supervisees routine and timely feedback; it is equally important to follow up on implementation of the feedback and evaluate them on the basis of their performance. Psychologists should create clear performance criteria (preferably in writing) and use objective performance measures that are applied in a timely manner. Good supervisors are not lulled into thinking that their supervisees can handle every issue that comes up.

Supervisors ensure that patients know the supervised status of their therapist (Standard 10.01c, Informed Consent to Therapy) and that they know how to contact the supervisor directly if problems arise. This means that psychologists do not permit supervisees to market their practice as if it were their own practice. Nor do psychologists permit supervisees to collect fees for themselves or otherwise act as if they were practicing independently. When patients consent to receive care from a trainee or supervisee, they do not consent to receive substandard care. If such a patient sues, the trainee or supervisee, the supervisor, the agency, and the educational institution may all be defendants.

> An enthusiastic unlicensed postdoctoral fellow had, without the knowledge of his supervisor, arranged to have some patients receive therapy privately from him at his home. On learning of this arrangement the supervisor confronted the postdoctoral fellow and noted that his employment contract required that he follow the APA Ethics Code and state law, which among other things prohibited postdoctoral fellows from practicing psychology independently. (10.4)

In recent years a divide has occurred between younger supervisees who tend to be more electronically sophisticated and their supervisors who tend to be less familiar with electronic means of communication. Examples include supervisees who texted their patients, "friended" them on Facebook, or otherwise communicated with them electronically without the knowledge of their supervisor, under the assumption that this was a normal and acceptable manner of communication. As we noted previously, it may be clinically indicated to communicate with patients, but supervisees should understand their supervisors' rules and standards for doing so.

Supervisors must ensure that their supervisees are competent to perform all of the activities assigned to them (Standard 2.05, Delegation of Work to Others). For example, supervisors should only assign neuropsychological assessments to trainees if they themselves are qualified to perform them. Supervisors should not assign patients with substance abuse to supervisees, unless they can work with these patients. A supervisee is held to the same standard of care as a licensed professional. Supervisors should intervene when their supervisees do not provide adequate care. Also, supervisors need to ensure that their supervisees are free of any contraindicated multiple relationships or conflicts of interests with patients (Standard 2.05).

> A postdoctoral fellow expressed an interest in learning more about neuropsychology, but his supervisor had limited knowledge in that area of practice. The supervisor, however, arranged for the fellow to receive additional supervision from a neuropsychologist who had the experience and skills necessary to provide the supervision. (10.5)

Ideally psychologists should have training as a supervisor, and some states now require this. No one is qualified to be a clinical supervisor merely because he or she was once supervised. Most important, supervision is not therapy, and therapy is no substitute for supervision. Developing skills as a supervisor parallels the development of other professional skills; it improves with education, self-reflection, and experience. Psychologists who are asked by a training program to supervise students but have not received any training to carry out this role should ask the training program for assistance or secure training on their own. Supervision is now considered a core competency in professional practice (Malloy, Dobbins, Ducheny, & Winfrey, 2010), although that has not always been the case.

It is prudent for psychologists to document their supervisory work. They should make notes for each patient discussed in supervision and know enough about each patient to develop and monitor a treatment plan and to intervene when necessary. Some states require supervisory notes. Good supervisory notes can protect supervisors if they or their supervisees are charged with misconduct.

Promoting the Welfare of Supervisees

The APA Ethics Code states that psychologists do not harm, exploit, or have sex with their supervisees (Standards 3.04, Avoiding Harm; 3.08, Exploitative Relationships; and 7.07, Sexual Relationships With Students and Supervisees). However, psychologists want to do more than just avoid harming their supervisees. Most supervisors actively strive to create a pleasant work environment for their employees and supervisees. Not only are such environments intrinsically desirable, they also improve morale and set a positive tone that may be reflected in the quality of patient care.

Readers may remember the discussion in Chapter 1 ("Calculations of Risk") that reported the study that obstetrical practices with good work environments tended to provide a higher quality of care. This is consistent with research in workplace productivity in general wherein a positive and supportive atmosphere is related to productivity and creativity (Amabile & Kramer, 2011). The impact of didactic lectures on ethics or well-considered formal organizational policies can be undercut if the day-by-day interactions between employees are characterized by cynicism or mistrust (Bazerman & Tenbrunsel, 2011). Readers can also think about Bloom's taxonomy on competence and how supervisors can help supervisees move to the highest level.

From a practical perspective, the legal liability of supervisors increases when supervisees are less than forthright about their dilemmas or clinical problems. Supervisors are in a unique role in which they should be both supportive and nurturing of their supervisees, particularly because they also have an evaluative function.

The nature of the supervisory relationship tends to reinforce the supervisee for "looking good" and avoiding self-disclosure of ignorance or shortcomings. The supervisor needs to facilitate a climate in which honesty and healthy self-reflection occur (Orchowski, Evangelista, & Probst, 2010). Such conduct is more likely to occur when supervisors invest themselves in the supervisory relationship, search out ways to be positive and reinforcing, and give helpful information. One way to meet the obligations of supervisors is to consider communitarian Amitai Etzioni's (1996) reformulation of the Golden Rule: "Respect and uphold society's moral order as you would have society respect and uphold your autonomy" (p. xviii). That is, the best way to promote the welfare of supervisees may be to help them promote the welfare of their patients. Good supervisors will treat supervisees with respect and also encourage them to treat their patients with the same respect (Knapp & VandeCreek, 2012b).

> A psychologist in charge of the university training clinic took his job very seriously. He was quite explicit about the high standards of conduct he expected from practicum students. Yet, he was very generous with praise when it was deserved. His feedback was useful, specific, and frequent. Despite the inherent stress of working in a university clinic, he made the work place as pleasant and relaxing as possible. (10.6)

Supervision of Nonprofessional Employees

Many of the principles applicable to professional supervisees and employees apply to nonprofessional employees as well. Care should be taken in recruiting them, defining their responsibilities, giving them feedback on their performance, and creating a pleasant work environment. It may be helpful to draft a written contract or letter of agreement. All employees need to be trained on confidentiality requirements even if the psychology practice is not a covered entity under the Health Insurance Portability and Accountability Act. The extent of the training varies according to the job responsibilities of the employee.

Many successful psychologists claim that their support personnel are a major reason for their success. They pay these individuals well, try to make working conditions pleasant, and treat them with great respect. They ensure that the staff have the resources to do their jobs well and are trained in the professional and legal aspects of their work, such as on state and federal confidentiality laws such as the Health Insurance Portability and Accountability Act. For example, good employers may need to purchase up-to-date computer equipment, provide continuing education opportunities, and have regular staff meetings. In return, they expect their employees to interact professionally with patients, show initiative, troubleshoot, and ensure the smooth and efficient running of the practice. One psychologist commented that he would rather spend his time treating patients than cleaning up billing problems.

DIVERSITY

Diversity issues are addressed throughout this book (see, e.g., Chapter 3, "Competence," and Chapter 8, "Psychological Assessment and Testing") but deserve to be emphasized again here. From a risk management perspective, the diagnosis and treatment of individuals from diverse backgrounds has not, as yet, become a major source of disciplinary actions for psychologists. Indeed the literature on therapy outcome with persons of diverse linguistic or cultural backgrounds has not yet shown that matching the cultural background of the therapist and client is a necessary condition for effective outcomes. Nonetheless, psychotherapy with culturally diverse groups is more effective when the psychologist considers the interaction of cultural background with gender, sexual orientation, disability, or other factors (Brown, 2009).

Anecdotal information is growing concerning misdiagnoses of patients because of the failure to understand their cultural background or treatment failures because the mental health professional did not make accommodations for the cultural background of the patient. Consequently, psychologists who deliver the highest quality of services ensure that they have the necessary competence to treat patients from diverse backgrounds. Even in emergencies or in situations in which otherwise competent professionals cannot be found, psychologists who treat diverse populations attempt to ensure the adequacy of their treatment through readings, study, or consultation. Among other things, this requires awareness of the unique ways that patients from diverse backgrounds can express their distress or how they may react to psychological treatment. Psychologists invite patients from diverse backgrounds to share their perspectives in a collaborative manner.

A psychologist conducted an initial interview with a young woman from India who was seriously depressed and acknowledged suicidal ideation. The psychologist knew enough about Indian culture to understand that her patient's older brother, who lived in the same city, was presumed by the family to be responsible for her welfare. With the permission of her patient, the psychologist contacted the older brother and asked him to participate as a collateral contact in therapy. (10.7)

When using interpreters, psychologists should ensure that the interpreters have a command of the non-English language appropriate for clinical or testing purposes. Psychologists also have a duty to educate them on the need for confidentiality. Psychologists should also obtain the informed consent of patients before seeing them (Standard 9.03c, Informed Consent in Assessments) and avoid using interpreters if they have a clinically contraindicated multiple relationship with the patient (Standard 2.05, Delegation of Work to Others).

A psychologist at a mental health clinic completed an intake interview with a man of Chinese descent who was born and raised in Vietnam and who spoke little English. He had an unusual Chinese dialect, and no appropriate interpreter could be found. Consequently, his adult children were used as interpreters. This was not an ideal situation, but it appeared to be the only way to deliver services. (10.8)

When conducting assessments, psychologists use assessment instruments appropriate for the population tested and, if appropriate tests are not available, note the limitations in their test interpretations (Standard 9.02b, Use of Assessments). Adaptations of psychological tests are made from a sound knowledge base. Unless done for testing linguistic ability, psychologists administer tests in the primary language of the patient or note why they did not. Interpretations made by psychologists consider the situational, personal, linguistic, and cultural differences and how they may influence the testing results (Standard 9.06, Interpreting Assessment Results; see also American Psychological Association, 2003).

> A psychologist conducted an assessment for a learning disability for an adolescent who came from a family and school environment in which street slang was primarily spoken. The adolescent's scores on the intelligence measure were lower than expected, in part because the slang words did not earn points on some of the subtests. (10.9)

An astute psychologist would point out this fact to the adolescent and ask if he could use Standard English. If the adolescent could not, the psychologist could shift to another test or indicate in the report that the scores are likely biased against the adolescent.

Psychologists should be aware that diversity issues can also apply to individuals with physical or mental disabilities, including deafness and hearing impairments. They should be familiar with the provisions of the Americans With Disabilities Act and its implications for their services. For example, psychologists should be aware of their obligation to provide reasonable accommodations for individuals with disabilities. This may mean, for example, hiring an interpreter when treating a deaf patient (Harris, n.d.-b) and learning about the culture of the deaf community, or ensuring that arrangements can be made to see a patient who needs an accessible office. (More information on the Americans With Disabilities Act can be found in Chapter 8, "Psychological Assessment and Testing.")

Furthermore, diversity issues may also apply to individuals who are lesbian, gay, transgendered, or uncertain about their sexual orientation. As with other individuals, psychologists should treat them only if they can provide the necessary services, if it is an emergency, if they are working in an underserved area, if other qualified professionals cannot be located, and if they undertake the necessary activities to acquire competence.

CONFLICTS IN INSTITUTIONAL SETTINGS

Some psychologists work in institutions that provide less than optimal services to patients or work for employers who do things that appear contrary to the APA Ethics Code or patient welfare. It is helpful to consider these examples that are based on real cases.

> A psychologist working in a prison was given a case load of hundreds of inmates, many of whom were suicidal or had serious mental disorders. There was inadequate medical backup. The psychologist was justified in his fear that one or more of the inmates would "hang up" (commit suicide) and worried about the extensive unmet needs among the prisoners. (10.10)

A psychologist working in a hospital warned that a particular patient still harbored strongly homicidal thoughts toward an identified third party. Nonetheless, the supervising psychiatrist ordered the release of this patient and instructed the staff that they were to make no effort to warn or protect the identified victims, even though the person lived in a state that had a duty-to-warn or duty-to-protect statute. The psychiatrist dismissed the concerns of the psychologist. (10.11)

A psychologist worked for a community agency that was having a difficult time meeting its budget. To draw more medical assistance funds, the director instructed staff to start seeing more patients but only for 30 minutes instead of 45 minutes, with the expectation that they could bill more per hour by billing two half-hour sessions instead of one 1-hour session. The director also instructed the staff to double-book patients. (10.12)

A psychologist working as a therapist in a student counseling center was informed by the institution that he would have to inform the institution about students who were potentially suicidal or homicidal without the student being aware of this requirement. It was the opinion of the administration that access to this information was in the best interest of the institution and the student. (10.13)

In addition to their concerns for the patients, psychologists working in these settings worried about their legal liability. Could the psychologist in the prison be held liable for the suicide of one of the prisoners? Could the psychologist in the hospital be held liable if the patient harmed the identifiable third party? Could the psychologist in the community agency be held liable for harm that comes from delivering second-rate care? Could the psychologist in the student counseling center be liable for the harmful acts of his clients or for violating their confidentiality if disclosures to the administrative staff were done without legal justification?

Again it is appropriate to consider the risk management factors (patient characteristics, context, and psychologist factors). In these situations, the issue is whether the context created by the institution, combined with the patient factors and individual psychologist factors, will lead to unacceptable risks. In each of these cases the psychologists are at an increased risk for disciplinary actions as the institutional demands increase the risk that patients or third parties will be harmed. However, psychologists who find themselves in similar situations can take steps to reduce their liability. Their obligations are to try to protect the welfare of the patients as much as possible and to bring the problems to the attention of the administrative personnel.

It is impossible to identify a certain number of steps that qualify as adequate measures in each of these examples. Much depends on the specific circumstances, the politics of the agencies, the informed consent procedure used, and the personalities of the individuals involved. Administrators are not always heartless bean counters. Often they are aware of the problems (or wish to become aware of the problems) in the delivery of services. Unfortunately, funding shortfalls or other pressures may call for compromises for what is perceived as the greater good. Generally it is better to start with the assumption that the directors are well intentioned. It is helpful for psychologists to try to understand their perspective on why these decisions were made. On the other hand, psychologists can be assertive about the impact of the decisions on the patients, on the welfare of the institution, and on them personally. Psychologists might request that the agency agree in writing to indemnify them for any harm that results from the agency's policies, which may be of some benefit to the psychologist in the event that a complaint is filed.

We recommend that psychologists be tactful and use their skills as a psychologist as much as possible to resolve these problems. If an educational approach fails to resolve the situation, they may decide to escalate the tactics, be more confrontational, or go over the head of the administrator. Even when psychologists feel the need to be more confrontational, they should avoid personalizing the issue whenever possible. It is better to focus on the policy or the action than on the character or competence of the individuals involved unless there is clear incompetence at the base of the problem that those responsible for governance of the institution need to address.

It is suggested that psychologists document the means they used to correct the situation, protect patient welfare, and bring the problems to the attention of the administrators. In the worst-case scenario in which a tragedy occurs, they will have documented that they tried to address the issue ahead of time and took reasonable steps considering the circumstances.

For example, in Case Example 10.10, the prison warden was sympathetic to the mental health needs of the inmates, made an effort to secure additional services, and was very clear that other prison staff were to cooperate with the psychologist as much as possible. In the meantime, the psychologist gave priority to prisoners who had a risk to attempt suicide until more resources could be devoted to prisoner care. The support of the warden made it possible for the psychologist, in good conscience, to continue working under these difficult circumstances until more resources could be found.

Sometimes problems can be worked out. Sometimes they cannot. It helps some early career psychologists to remember that someday they may be an administrator and have to instruct staff to do things that they do not want to do or that they believe are unethical. Consequently they may ask themselves how they would like disgruntled employees to approach them.

REFERRALS

Psychologists often give referrals to prospective patients seeking treatment or assessments when the presenting problems are outside of the psychologist's area of competence, when the patient needs someone in their insurance panel and the psychologist is not in-network, when the travel required by the patient appears too long, or for other reasons. Also, psychologists may give referrals to current patients who are terminating treatment for whatever reason and still need care.

Psychologists tell us that they often hear in risk management workshops that they should give patients or prospective patients three referrals. This is a useful rule of thumb. However, like other useful rules of thumb, its usefulness depends on the context. No law or standard in the APA Ethics Code requires that a psychologist has to give a patient or prospective patient three names, and at times it could be contraindicated to do so. The goal behind giving referrals is to provide the patient with some reasonable options for services. It makes little sense to give three names if one or more of the three names are not appropriate for the patient or it is unlikely that the patient will take advantage of them. For example, one of the names given may be located at such a distance from the patient that it is highly unlikely that the patient would take advantage of that referral. It makes little sense to include this third referral as an option, only so the psychologists can say that they gave three names.

Also, selecting a provider from in-network is often a financial requirement for patients because of their personal financial limits. Managed care companies vary in the diligence that they use in keeping the public list of panels up to date. If the psychologist has had the experience that the public list of in-network providers is padded with psychologists who have retired or dropped off the panel or who no longer take that insurance, it is not helpful to the patient or prospective patient to simply go through the list of providers and select three names with the expectation that there is a high likelihood that some or none of these referrals will pan out. Instead, it may be fairer to recommend that the patient call the managed care company directly to get an appropriate referral.

TERMINATION AND ABANDONMENT

Usually psychologists and their patients jointly decide to end treatment (D. D. Davis, 2008). Sometimes termination may occur because the therapist is moving or has a serious illness or because of another major life change that prohibits the treatment from continuing. In some instances, however, patients terminate unilaterally either by canceling the last appointment, failing to reschedule, or otherwise discontinuing appointments. At other times, however, psychologists may want to terminate therapy against the wishes of their patients. Often this occurs when the patients are not making progress in or are noncompliant with treatment. In those circumstances psychologists may worry that terminating treatment against the wishes of their patients will be abandoning them. This fear represents a misunderstanding of abandonment (Younggren, 2011). "Abandonment represents the failure of the psychologist to take the clinically indicated and ethically appropriate steps to terminate a professional relationship" (Younggren & Gottlieb, 2008, p. 500).

The APA Ethics Code provides general rules about terminating patients without their consent. Standard 10.10a, Terminating Therapy, states, "Psychologists terminate therapy when it becomes reasonably clear that the client/patient no longer needs the service, is not likely to benefit, or is being harmed by continued service." Standard 10.10c states, "Except where precluded by the actions of clients/patients or third-party payers, prior to termination psychologists provide pretermination counseling and suggest alternative service providers as appropriate." Also, any psychologist may terminate a patient if the patient or someone close to the patient threatens to harm the psychologist (Standard 10.10b).

The general risk management rule is not to terminate against the wishes of patients if they are in life-endangering crises. If therapists decide to terminate the treatment, they should give adequate notice and provide referrals for other treatment opportunities if more treatment is needed. Proper termination is a dynamic driven by many circumstances: the client's psychological condition, the client's behavior, the skills of the psychologist, the circumstances under which the service is being provided, and the agreements that have been made between the psychologist and the client.

Financial Reasons

Perhaps the psychologist wishes to terminate because the patient lacks financial resources to pay for treatment. The insurance for the patient may have been exhausted, or the patient has had a sudden decline in income through a job loss. Perhaps the patient says that he or she will no longer make payments because other expenses are a higher priority. At times, it may be obvious that patients are struggling to make necessary payments for food, mortgage, and other essentials. At other times, patients may appear insensitive to their obligations to pay and give a higher priority to other discretionary expenses (such as a costly vacation, new computers, or a wide-screen high-definition television). Except in an emergency, nothing requires psychologists to continue to treat patients who cannot or will not pay for services.

Some of these problems can be avoided by being very clear in the informed consent process at the start of therapy. Standard 10.01a, Informed Consent to Therapy, of the Ethics Code requires psychologists to inform patients about the anticipated course of therapy and fees.

Problems arise when psychologists allow patients to accumulate debts without addressing the issue forthrightly. If patients are having problems paying for services, it is better to deal with the issue early rather than allowing debts to accumulate. It is not in the interest of the psychologist, nor in the interest of the patient, for the psychologists to passively allow the patient to take advantage of their kind nature. Perhaps the patients are in denial and are avoiding looking at finances objectively or are insensitive to financial obligations to others. In either case, they are manifesting an unhealthy trait that should not be reinforced.

> A patient pleaded that he was unable to pay for services and had not paid the psychologist in months, but later the psychologist learned that the patient had insurance, submitted bills to the insurance company, collected the payments, and pocketed the money. (10.14)

Of course, it is preferable to prevent these nonpayment problems as much as possible. Anticipate financial limitations ahead of time. Psychologists should not take on patients who are unable to meet the expectations for payment. It is unfortunate but true that the risk of a complaint before a licensing board increases dramatically when a psychologist files a collection action against a former patient for an outstanding bill. The time, effort, money, and other resources rarely justify the amount of money that may be collected by filing a collection suit (see Chapter 11, "The Reluctant Business Person").

To reduce nonpayment problems, many psychologists adopt a pay-as-you-go approach and require payment at the time of service, much as many physicians and dentists do. If the patient cannot afford services, psychologists can consider other options in addition to terminating the patient, such as reducing the fee, having the patient attend sessions every other week (if clinically indicated), moving the patient to group therapy, referring the patient to a free or low-fee outpatient clinic, or some combination of these arrangements. Psychologists should make these arrangements specific; they should not just let financial problems go unaddressed.

The Ethics Code requires that psychologists discuss the termination or transfer of services early in treatment if limitations in services because of finances can be anticipated (Standard 6.04d, Fees and Financial Arrangements). It is preferable not to "skim the cream" of insurance reimbursement. That is, psychologists should be very reluctant to accept patients who are likely to need long-term therapy with the goal of using their insurance and then referring them elsewhere when the insurance reimbursement ends. The criteria for accepting patients should include the ability to be of professional benefit to them and should not be based solely on their financial status. Just as psychologists would not accept patients who have problems outside of their area of competence with the intent of referring them out, they should not accept patients for whom financial limitations will cause a potentially painful and clinically contraindicated termination.

Of course psychologists cannot always predict the length of treatment when they first accept a patient. The degree of pathology might not be obvious until the patient has been seen in treatment for several weeks or even months. Or the patient may deteriorate substantially over time as a result of unpredictable life circumstances. Nonetheless, to the best of their ability, psychologists should try to anticipate the length of treatment and the financial resources of the patient ahead of time.

Patients No Longer Benefit From or Are Harmed by Therapy

Sometimes psychologists may want to terminate treatment because it has become obvious that their ability to treat the patient effectively has been compromised. Perhaps their inability to help the patient was not obvious until they had seen the patient for several sessions, or perhaps the needs of the patient changed over time. For example, a patient may benefit from treatment of depression but then express an interest in improving parenting ability, which may or may not be an area of expertise for the treating psychologist.

At other times, therapy may reach a stalemate because of the actions or inactions of the patient or because the patient has reached a plateau in therapy. Perhaps the patient is noncompliant with treatment, is resistive to further treatment suggestions, refuses to follow through with a recommendation to consult a physician, or misses too many sessions despite repeated efforts on the psychologist's part to motivate the patient to comply. Some patients use the sessions unproductively and discuss superficial issues that are more appropriate for chitchat than therapy. Other patients may repeatedly arrive late for appointments without justification and with such frequency that the quality of therapy is compromised. Unless these behaviors are addressed and rectified, treatment will likely be unsuccessful.

Psychologists can and should terminate a patient if they are unable to provide a reasonable level of quality of care (Standard 10.10a, Terminating Therapy). The patient does not have to agree to the termination. However, it is in these situations that it is necessary for psychologists to bolster their decision with the risk management strategies: informed consent, documentation, and consultation.

Psychologists who are considering terminating such patients should clarify their reasons with the patient as soon as possible and give the patient the opportunity to provide feedback on the decision. Perhaps the therapy can be modified and become helpful for the patient. In any event, psychologists need to prepare the patient for the possibility of termination. If psychologists do decide to terminate the patient, it is important to document that they discussed the clinical reasons for the termination and involved the patient in the decision as much as was clinically indicated. When patients are terminated against their wishes, psychologists are in a situation in which one moral principle such as beneficence (the desire to promote the patient's welfare) or nonmaleficence (the desire to avoid harming the patient) temporarily trumps another moral principle (respect for patient autonomy). Whenever one moral principle is used to trump another, it is desirable to minimize the impact on the offended moral principle. In this case, that might mean making an effort to give the patient as much autonomy as clinically indicated in determining the nature of the termination. A psychologist might say, for example, As we have discussed, I will no longer be seeing you after June 1. Do you want to have any more weekly sessions with me until then?

Many psychologists will not terminate patients against their wishes unless they receive a professional consultation first. If the patient needs more treatment, but the psychologist is unable or unwilling to provide it because of lack of expertise or the patient's lack of progress, it is preferable to give the patient the option of referrals to mental health professionals or agencies that can be of help. How much more the psychologist should do becomes a clinical decision. Depending on the circumstances, some psychologists have made the appointments for some patients, attended the first session with the new therapist, or made themselves available for a limited period of time until the patients have their first session with the new therapist. For other patients such extra steps would be clinically contraindicated.

Some patients may feel intense anger at their psychologist for terminating treatment despite great efforts to explain the reasons for the termination and despite efforts to seek a transfer to more appropriate services. If further contact is clinically contraindicated, we recommend that psychologists stick to that decision. That is, they should not respond to crisis phone calls after the termination date, respond to letters urging them to resume therapeutic contact, or talk to intermediaries who will plead the case for the patient. At times, ex-patients have gone to extremes and filed complaints against their former therapists for the purpose of being able to see them (and talk to them) at the hearing. Responding to any outreach after termination may result in intermittent reinforcement of unwanted behaviors.

A patient was highly resistive to treatment, missed many appointments, called the emergency service for relatively minor complaints, discontinued medications against medical advice, stopped paying for services, and tried to argue with the therapist over innocuous comments. After repeated efforts to motivate the patient and cautions that continued noncompliance would result in termination, the psychologist eventually terminated the patient. At their last session the patient refused to leave the office, but after 2 hours was cajoled into leaving. The patient continued to call the emergency service, refused to follow up with any recommendations for referrals, and appeared at the psychologist's office unannounced and told the patients in the waiting room that this psychologist had "ruined her life." (10.15)

Appropriately, after termination the psychologist refused to return emergency phone calls and had office staff handle the ex-patient's uninvited entrance into the office. The psychologist understood that contact with the ex-patient would result in intermittent reinforcement of intrusive behavior. This psychologist knew the importance of establishing firm boundaries. Earlier in her career she knew an unfortunate colleague who, when faced with a similar situation, refunded fees to the patient in an effort to appease her. Unfortunately, the patient construed this as an admission of guilt and filed a malpractice suit.

The general rule is not to terminate or transfer patients who are in a crisis. However, the transfer of some patients who have a low level of chronic suicidality becomes a problem, especially if the termination temporarily increases suicidal ideation. The psychologist needs to balance carefully the long-term interests of the patient versus the short-term risks and recognize that in rare circumstances it may be necessary to terminate with patients who have a moderate risk of suicide. Psychologists should be reluctant to transfer a patient if the suicidal risk is severe or extreme. One psychologist reported that he continued to see a patient with a moderate risk of suicide for 3 months after informing the patient of the necessity to terminate. In this case the psychologist believed it was important for him to get a clearer baseline for the functioning of the patient and the immediacy of the risk of suicide. Also, this psychologist designated a fixed date for the termination. That firm date removed any ambiguity about the end of the relationship.

Subtle Terminations

At times, psychologists encounter patients who are ambivalent about treatment and give subtle or not so subtle indications that they intend to terminate treatment. The question arises as to how much energy the psychologist should put into persuading them to continue with treatment.

Much of the decision is context dependent. For a patient with a more transient disorder and substantial emotional and social (but not financial) resources, it would most likely be clinically indicated and sufficient to review the likely nature and course of therapy and feel confident that the patient can balance the advantages and costs of therapy without substantial harm.

On the other hand, some patients may have more serious disorders or evidence serious suicidal ideation. For these patients it may be clinically indicated and necessary to expend more effort. For example, psychologists may make a phone call to check on how patients are doing or send an encouraging reminder letter. They need to use their clinical judgment. The specific type of outreach varies from patient to patient, and for some patients, such an outreach may be interpreted as "ambulance chasing" or otherwise be clinically contraindicated.

> A psychologist was treating a seriously disturbed patient who displayed highly offensive behavior in the therapy sessions. It would have been the dream of the psychologist for her to go away and never come back, and he was aware that he might, without attempting to do so, discourage her from returning through nonverbal or other subtle responses. The psychologist was aware of this propensity on his part and did what he could to confront the problematic behaviors, address her presenting problems, and avoid creating an unpleasant therapeutic atmosphere that would encourage the patient to terminate. (10.16)

Unavoidable Terminations

Some involuntary terminations are unavoidable. Perhaps the psychologist is moving away or retiring. Or perhaps the psychologist has a physical illness that requires a reduction in workload. Perhaps a personal problem impairs the psychologist's ability to provide the necessary service (Standard 2.06b, Personal Problems and Conflicts). Other psychologists have suspended services when they started a family. Others suspend services when they are employed by a third party or when ending work as an independent contractor on a time-limited assignment.

From a clinical perspective, the unavoidable termination of a patient through retirement or the psychologist's pregnancy requires tact and sensitivity in introducing the topic to the patient and handling emotional reactions to it.

A psychologist with a chronic health condition was required to undergo surgery that necessitated a long absence from her professional obligations. She had to balance the need to give an honest explanation to her patients about why she was withdrawing professional services temporarily (and would be back on only a limited basis afterward) with the need to protect her privacy. She was also concerned that in the small town where she lived, some patients might hear about her surgery from other persons in town. Consequently, she mailed a general letter to all of her current patients at the same time, briefly noting the changes in her professional service caused by her health condition and stating that they could discuss the issue in more detail at their next therapy session. (10.17)

This type of termination involves little risk of disciplinary actions, assuming that the patient has been informed in a reasonable period of time and the psychologist has made reasonable efforts to facilitate the transfer of services (Standard 3.12, Interruption of Psychological Services).

Psychologists who are employed by or are participating in a contract relationship with a third party should "make reasonable efforts to provide for orderly and appropriate resolution of responsibility for client/patient care in the event that the employment or contractual relationship ends, with paramount consideration given to the welfare of the client/patient" (Standard 10.09, Interruption of Therapy).

We recommend that psychologists seriously consider terminating a patient immediately when the patient or a close friend or relative of a patient threatens to harm the psychologist. Threats against psychologists should not be dismissed lightly. A 1990 study found that 40% of psychologists had reported being assaulted at least once in their careers. Although most of these assaults occurred in psychiatric hospitals, 14% reported being assaulted in their private practices (Guy, Brown, & Poelstra, 1990). As noted previously, terminating threatening patients is permitted according to Standard 10.10b (Terminating Therapy) of the APA Ethics Code. This is a good standard for several reasons. First, the personal safety of the psychologist is inherently very important. Second, it is unlikely that they can do effective therapy if the patient or a family member is intimidating them. Finally, it is not productive for the patient to be in a relationship characterized by mistrust and fear. The obligations of psychologists to their patients are not unlimited, and patients bear some responsibility for the consequences of their behavior (Hjelt 2011).

Other Uncovered Absences

It can be considered abandonment when psychologists are unable to respond to patients' crises because of lack of an adequate on-call system or lack of adequate coverage when they are on vacation or because they are otherwise unavailable and fail to ensure that the patients understand the coverage arrangements. There are no absolute standards for coverage after hours or when psychologists are on vacation. The exact nature of their after-hours or vacation coverage may vary according to the needs of the caseload. However, psychologists should not take patients with certain serious diagnoses who are likely to need emergency services without making adequate provisions to be available to them.

> One psychologist saw clients primarily for career counseling or personal coaching, although she sometimes had patients with somewhat more serious mental health needs. Given her caseload, the likelihood of after-hours emergencies was quite low. (10.18)

> Another psychologist had a heavy case load and often was unable to schedule patients for 2 or 3 weeks after their last appointment. His reduced availability for routine appointments greatly increased the likelihood that patients would use the after-hours emergency services. Both for risk management and clinical care reasons, this psychologist sought ways to reduce his case load. (10.19)

Of course, psychologists should arrange for coverage when they are out of town or otherwise unavailable. The nature of the substitute coverage should be explained to patients at the beginning of treatment as part of the informed consent process. Psychologists may wish to reiterate their procedures for coverage to their patients before they leave town.

> A patient became outraged when she called the answering service of her therapist and received a return phone call from another therapist who was covering for him. The patient filed a complaint with the licensing board alleging a breach of confidentiality. Fortunately, the treating psychologist could produce an informed consent document signed by the patient informing her that the psychologist shared after-hours coverage with several other psychologists when she went out of town. Although the psychologist was exonerated from any wrongdoing, the whole episode might have been avoided if the psychologist had reminded the patient of this policy. (10.20)

APPLICATION OF RISK MANAGEMENT PROCEDURES TO THE DETAILED CASE EXAMPLE

The clinical situation described in the detailed case example presented in Chapter 1 ("Calculations of Risk") illustrates some of the important considerations when deciding to terminate patients against their will.

As noted in Chapter 9 ("Assessing and Treating Patients Who Are Potentially Suicidal or Dangerous to Others"), it is not clear if this patient is in the moderate or severe range of suicidal risk. Because this patient may present a high risk, Dr. Doe should get more information and seek consultation before concluding that he should terminate the patient. The focus of the consultation should be on the suicidal risk of the patient, whether Dr. Doe can be of benefit to this patient, whether the service is iatrogenic, and what options could be available for this patient.

The individual psychologist factors might not be adequate to address the patient's needs. She would benefit from, among other things, a more supportive family involvement, a relationship with a more skilled psychopharmacologist (preferably a psychiatrist or a prescribing psychologist), and a supplemental dialectical behavior therapy group. Furthermore, the Dr. Doe may feel emotionally strained by her demands on his time and frustrated by the patient's failure to adhere to the treatment protocol.

The consultation could involve one of several questions. Should I terminate this patient? Can I get a sense of refreshment so that I can continue with this patient? And if so, What can I do differently from a therapeutic perspective to mobilize her to adhere more conscientiously to the treatment recommendations?

If Dr. Doe decides to terminate, he should document that he discussed the termination with his patient and gave her reasons why he decided to terminate. The documentation should be detailed and include clinical reasons why treatment is no longer in her best interest. Dr. Doe's treatment notes provide an opportunity to present his reasoning including the pros and cons of continuing treatment. He should be certain to give her referral information for further treatment. If permitted by the patient and clinically indicated, Dr. Doe could communicate to the parents why the decision was made to terminate treatment.

Dr. Doe should be prepared to receive substantial hostility from the patient if he decides to terminate against the patient's wishes. After the termination date, Dr. Doe should be prepared for a barrage of phone calls, emails, and other communications. If he responds to these advances, he may reinforce the patient and encourage her to make further attempts to contact him.

SEVEN ESSENTIAL POINTS TO REMEMBER

1. A consulting relationship is between legal equals.

2. Except in narrow circumstances, supervisors are legally responsible for the actions of their supervisees.

3. Supervisors can greatly reduce legal risks by carefully selecting and monitoring their supervisees.

4. Psychologists who are insensitive to the unique needs of diverse populations risk providing a substandard quality of care.

5. Psychologists may terminate patients if they do not pay for services or are not benefiting from services. Psychologists should not terminate patients who are in a crisis.

6. Psychologists are to work hard to ensure that they and their patients agree on the need to terminate. If they must terminate a patient, they thoroughly explain the reasons to their patients, document the discussion, and if the patient needs more treatment, provide referrals.

7. Psychologists address problems with employers with tact and sensitivity and are prepared to be assertive if the employer is showing disregard for public welfare or safety.

CHAPTER 11: THE RELUCTANT BUSINESS PERSON

Many psychologists are reluctant business persons. They entered the field to deliver health care services and were not adequately trained to deal with the business aspects of practice such as advertising, collecting and paying bills, following up on insurance claims, or pursuing unpaid debts, not to mention developing a business plan. Nonetheless, a psychological practice is a business, and the manner in which psychologists conduct their businesses can have a substantial impact on the quality of their careers. On one hand, tasteful advertising and clear and efficient billing practices create an air of efficiency and professionalism and can give patients a favorable impression. On the other, fee disputes can spill over into the clinical area, and dissatisfaction with clinical services can be reflected in nonpayment of fees. Misunderstandings or disagreements about fees often precipitate charges of professional misconduct from disgruntled patients. Although it is not illegal to run an inefficient or disorganized business, ensuing distractions may prevent psychologists from attending to their professional responsibilities.

MARKETING SERVICES

Often patients develop their first impressions of their psychologists from their marketing, a general term that includes all activities by which psychologists let others know about their services. Marketing includes word-of-mouth, professional business cards, advertising in yellow pages, magazines, websites, and more. Although psychologists want their advertising to attract patients, it is important to advertise carefully so that accurate information is conveyed tastefully. Of course, psychologists must avoid false, deceptive, or misleading advertising. They also should avoid the use of vanity credentials (see Chapter 3, "Competence"), report their areas of proficiency and expertise accurately, and include only those degrees that are from regionally accredited universities or that were the basis on which they became licensed.

> A psychologist developed an extensive practice in sport psychology. It appeared to be a natural extension of her earlier career as a health education teacher. Her advertisement represented her credentials as "M. Brown, PsyD, licensed psychologist; PhD in physical education." Thus potential clients would more clearly understand her training and credentials. (11.1)

It is increasingly common for psychologists to have professional websites. Often these sites contain articles on a particular topic designed to attract interested persons to the psychologists' website. These articles, called *advertorials*, are part advertisements and part public education. Great effort should be put into advertorials to ensure that they are accurate, up-to-date, and helpful.

> A psychologist with a specialty in anxiety disorders had a well-developed website that included links to the Anxiety Disorders Association of America and other specialty organizations. He included several reviews he had written on contemporary books on the treatment of anxiety disorders and other brief but useful articles. Among other things, he gave a fair and balanced review of the relative roles of the nonpharmacological and pharmacological options for treatment. (11.2)

Some psychologists have developed interactive websites or developed professionally related platforms through Twitter or Facebook that include the opportunity for members of the public to "follow" or "friend" them. Psychologists should ensure that active patients understand what "follow" and "friend" mean in these contexts in light of their overall policy on boundaries and social media (see detailed discussion in Chapter 4, "Multiple Relationships and Boundaries"). In addition, it is important to periodically check any links to see if they are functioning and that their content is generally helpful. Most viewers will assume that psychologists have placed links on the website because they believe that they have some value.

Many companies have developed websites that will allow consumers to rate services, including those of health care providers. The usefulness of these ratings with health care professionals is questionable. For example, one company rated Dr. So-and-So as the "top psychologist in Pittsburgh." We have no reason to doubt that Dr. So-and-So does a very good job, but the designation was based on only three client reviews. In another city, a psychiatrist was rated the "top psychiatrist" on the basis of 20 reviews. No other psychiatrist on that website had more than one or two reviews, leading us to assume that the "top psychiatrist" had selectively asked satisfied patients to rate her, and this made us wonder if the "top psychiatrist" was really that good at all. Asking clients to post positive comments on a website is professionally risky and should be done carefully and thoughtfully because it could be construed as soliciting a testimonial and would therefore be in violation of Standard 5.05 (Testimonials) of the American Psychological Association's (APA's) "Ethical Principles of Psychologists and Code of Conduct" (hereinafter known as the Ethics Code; APA, 2010a).

At times, a disturbed patient will post a highly offensive and unwarranted review. Given that most psychologists will only have one or two reviews at all, these postings stand out and have the potential to deter potential patients. The company hosting the website will be unlikely to remove a posting only because it gave the psychologist a negative rating; however, some will remove reviews if they fail to meet reasonable standards of decorum or if the conduct on the part of the rater appears to be part of an attempt to purposefully damage the professional through distortion, exaggeration, and misstatement.

Marketing services can include speaking engagements as well. For example, one psychologist gave a series of lectures on autism at a local bookstore. Another psychologist gave a grand rounds lecture at the local hospital on the psychological aspects of infertility. Another psychologist spoke to local churches on the psychological aspects of international and interracial adoptions.

> A psychologist who had been a well-known local athlete acquired a doctorate in psychology and then returned to practice in the town where he attended undergraduate school. He lectured on the problems associated with head trauma in sports and developed a head trauma protocol for student athletes. Several high schools adopted his protocol when a high school athlete died after returning to practice prematurely from a head injury. (11.3)

Although psychologists should not minimize the social value of their work, they need to be appropriately humble. We do not have the knowledge or skills to help everyone, but we have considerable knowledge and skills that can substantially improve the lives of our patients. In public presentations psychologists should feel free to put their best foot forward. They can do that by ensuring that the information given is accurate and up-to-date. Psychologists should never be afraid to say "I don't know," and they should not be flustered by questions or rude behavior.

> Once while giving a presentation, a psychologist was interrupted by a member of the audience who claimed that psychologists were people who were not good enough to get into medical school; psychology was a pseudoscience; and chemists and physicists were the real scientists. In this case, the psychologist responded tactfully and patiently to these comments. After the presentation the commentator said privately "I was just testing you." (11.4)

Many psychologists make contacts and get referrals through their local or state psychological association. They serve on committees and volunteer for any kind of work that needs to be done. In addition to contributing to the profession and probably learning some things of value, these psychologists make many professional contacts through their professional associations (Wunsch, 2005).

LOOK AT THE WHOLE PRACTICE

Psychologists can ensure the overall quality of their work experience by carefully attending to the details of their practices. For example, many psychologists take special steps to incorporate art and decor into their offices. They may select wall paintings that are especially meaningful for them. One psychologist had a stunning painting given to him by a family member who survived cancer. It reminded him of the human determination to thrive despite adversity. Another psychologist decorated her office beautifully and always had classical music playing in the office. Details such as the availability of parking, lighting of the street outside of the office, cleanliness of rest rooms, comfort of the furniture, tidiness of the waiting area, and sound control within the office area can influence overall patient satisfaction with services.

Billing and Bill Collection

Billing issues should be considered from the very first contact with prospective patients. It is prudent to establish the patient's ability to pay before services begin. Psychologists should not accept patients into their practices who cannot pay for services unless they are willing to accept them at a reduced rate consistent with their ability to pay. Psychologists can minimize patient dissatisfaction in this area by clearly explaining policies on fees ahead of time. It is desirable to inform patients of the fee, what services are billed, when payment is due, the policy on the use of credit cards, insurance coverage issues, and other aspects of billing. The prudent psychologist will give patients a written policy that covers all of these issues when they begin therapy (see The Trust's sample Psychologist–Patient Agreement at www.apait.org).

Explaining the billing procedures and expectations regarding payment clearly helps patients to make an informed decision about whether they can afford to pursue treatment. It is important to remember that true informed consent means more than having a patient sign an informed consent form. Psychologists should try to ensure that their patients clearly understand their financial obligations and the psychologist's relevant billing practices. Although the patient's signature may ensure the right to pursue collection of disputed fees, the failure of patients to pay their bills creates an area of contention that may impede the quality of the treatment relationship. Also, from a risk management perspective, the psychologist now has a disgruntled patient who may file a formal complaint.

The office practices of psychologists vary considerably with regard to insurance payments. Some psychologists bill the insurance company themselves; others only accept payment directly from patients; and many psychologists contract directly with insurers or managed care companies. Unless specified otherwise in a contract between the psychologist and an insurer or a managed care company, it is important to remember that the professional relationship exists between the psychologist and the patient, not between the psychologist and the insurance company. Regardless of payment arrangements, the services provided will be judged according to the accepted ethical standards and practice guidelines governing the profession. The standards that apply to the treatment of paying patients apply equally to pro bono or volunteer services.

Psychologists vary on how they handle insurance billing for couples. The relevant questions are: Who is the identified patient? Does this individual have a disorder covered by the insurance policy? Is the treatment directed toward relieving this disorder? If the answers to these questions are yes, a chart can be opened on that patient and the insurance company can be billed. Of course, the spouse may attend the sessions as a collateral contact. What is very is important to remember here is that most insurance companies do not pay for marital enrichment or couples therapy designed only to improve the nature of the marital relationship. If a patient lacks a diagnosis from the most recent manual for mental disorders, most insurers will not pay for the services (Younggren & Harris, 2011).

> A psychologist accepted a young man into treatment for his anxiety that was, among other things, creating strains in his marriage. His wife attended several sessions as a collateral contact. The psychologist billed the insurance company for treating the man. (11.5)

In the preceding example, the psychologist was acting appropriately. The patient had a diagnosis; the treatment was directed toward alleviating the symptoms of the diagnosis; and the wife attended therapy to assist in the treatment of her husband.

> A psychologist accepted into treatment both members of a couple who were having marital problems. Although the wife was in substantial distress, the husband was not. The psychologist saw them together and directed therapy at alleviating the distress of the wife, with the husband acting in a supportive role. The psychologist billed several sessions under the wife's name and then several sessions under the husband's name. He gave the husband the diagnosis of adjustment disorder, even though it could not be justified on the basis of the clinical presentation. (11.6)

In this example, the psychologist's procedures were problematic. In contrast to the first psychologist, the second psychologist gave a diagnosis that was not warranted, could not be justified by the treatment notes, and did not guide treatment.

The practice of deliberately giving unwarranted diagnoses or otherwise misrepresenting services is an example of insurance fraud, which is the systematic misrepresentation of billing information for personal gain (Kalb, 1999). Of course, all psychologists should try to bill as accurately as possible, but even the most honest health care providers may sometimes make a billing error or misunderstand an ambiguous billing procedure. A mistake in billing can be corrected by contacting the payer (or the insurer) and offering to correct the error. On the other hand, those psychologists who routinely misrepresent information to insurance companies could be charged with fraud. In the preceding example, the actions of the second psychologist could be interpreted as fraud.

Psychologists may waive copayments only on a case-by-case basis if permitted by the insurer and state or federal law. Some psychologists actually have established sliding fee scales. Although we appreciate the attempt on the part of some to make services affordable to persons who otherwise cannot afford services, such arrangements may create problems. Health care providers frequently lose sight of the fact that the co-pay reflects the belief by the insurance company that the patient should share in the cost of their healthcare. In addition, it is hard to be entirely fair in establishing sliding scales. Patients may learn that others are paying less for services than they are; there is the potential that some patients may abuse the sliding fee scale; and psychologists need to ensure that the sliding scale does not put them in violation of the insurance contracts they signed. Some psychologists have stopped using sliding scales but will waive a portion of the fee on a case-by-case basis as needed. We are aware of instances in which the misuse of sliding scales has resulted in charges of insurance fraud.

Some psychologists barter if it is not exploitative or clinically contraindicated. For a few patients bartering may be justified if it is the only way that they can afford treatment. One suggestion is to barter only when the value of bartered objects is agreed on in advance. Bartering for services creates a greater possibility of misunderstanding or ill feelings and, depending on where the services take place, may involve a boundary violation.

> A psychologist allowed a patient to pay off part of his debt by providing lawn care to her office building. The patient dutifully spent three hours mowing the lawn, but he did not trim the grass along the sidewalk nor did he sweep the grass clippings off the sidewalk. The psychologist felt she was getting second-rate service. When she confronted her patient on the quality of his service, he was indignant, noting that the $40 she credited toward his debt was far below average payment for equivalent services. Both parties believed they had been shortchanged in the deal. (11.7)

Wise psychologists avoid allowing a patient's bills to accumulate. When patients are unable to pay, psychologists should immediately address the problem and make special payment arrangements. For example, the patient can use credit cards or can take out a loan to make payments. Many patients go into debt for something they perceive as valuable, such as a new television set, and the same rules should apply to therapy if they perceive it as valuable. It is unwise clinically and from a business perspective for psychologists to let unpaid bills accumulate without addressing the issues directly with patients. In some cases, "forgotten" or unpaid co-pays or statements can reflect treatment resistance. In rare cases, some patients have a sense of entitlement and will take advantage of well-meaning and compassionate psychologists. These situations all impact the quality of the relationship between the psychologist and patient and can influence the effectiveness of treatment.

> Whenever he did psychological testing, a psychologist always ensured that the patients paid for the entire testing ahead of time. His experience suggested that parents or patients may sometimes complete the testing and then refuse to pay, especially if they are not totally satisfied with the results. He also was aware of the ambiguity in Health Insurance Portability and Accountability Act (HIPAA) wherein it could be interpreted to mean that patients have a right to the written test report once it is completed whether they have paid or not because it is part of the protected health information HIPAA. (11.8)

> Another psychologist took an imprint of the patient's credit card with the intention of billing for any services that were unpaid at the end of the month. Although this is not inherently unethical, it would be preferable to have the patients pay at the time of each service. (11.9)

As long as psychologists have informed their patients ahead of time, they may charge them for any professional services provided. Although we do not recommend "nickel-and-diming" patients for brief phone calls, brief notes to other professionals, or other de minimis services, we do recommend that psychologists inform patients of the cost of performing professional services of substance, such as a detailed consultation with an attorney or a detailed letter that takes considerable time to produce.

As noted in Chapter 10 ("Other Areas of Concern for Psychologists: Consultant or Supervisor, Diversity Issues, Conflicts in Institutional Settings, Referrals, and Termination and Abandonment"), psychologists may terminate patients because they have not paid for services. Psychologists can minimize the problems associated with nonpayment by being clear about their billing procedures and payment expectations ahead of time, and addressing nonpayment issues as soon as they arise. If nonpayment is an issue, psychologists ascertain why patients have not paid for service, and if appropriate, psychologists may negotiate a payment plan, discuss other payment arrangements or review other options. It is crucial to remember that absent a crisis, psychologists have no obligation to provide services for a patient who is unwilling or unable to pay for services. Psychologists who terminate patients for nonpayment of services should refer them for any needed services.

We recommend that psychologists use bill collection agencies or small claims courts with great discretion or not at all. They should never use a small claims court or collection agency "on principle" or to "teach the patient a lesson." The use of small claims courts or collection agencies is a billing and risk management decision and any sense of betrayal or anger should not be a factor in this decision. Some patients fail to pay their bills because they are unconcerned with their obligations to others. They may have had no intention of making payment in the first place and have no intention of doing so now. Going to small claims court or using collection agencies to collect outstanding balances can precipitate an allegation of misconduct, especially if the patients thought the services they received were unsatisfactory or unhelpful. In addition, a legal judgment from a small claims court does not insure payment for the services and the psychologist who secured the judgment could be forced to take other time-consuming legal actions to secure the funds they are due. All of this can absorb a significant amount of the psychologist's time.

It is desirable for psychologists to select and use collection agencies carefully because these companies are acting on behalf of the psychologist who is ultimately responsible for their actions. If they are abusive or unprofessional, it will reflect poorly on the psychologist. If psychologists use a collection agency, they should provide no more information than necessary (e.g., amount owed) to protect the patient's right to privacy (Standard 4.04, Minimizing Intrusions on Privacy). Psychologists should alert patients before turning over the account for collection and give them an opportunity to make payment arrangements. Interestingly, not one of the previous issues applies to those psychologists who collect their fees at the time they render a service.

Dealing With Insurance Companies and Managed Care Organizations

Absent a contract specifying otherwise, we recommend that psychologists ensure that their patients know that they, not the insurance company, are ultimately responsible for payment of services. Psychologists operating under a managed care organization's contract need to be scrupulous about recording and following the billing procedures of the insurer. They must fully understand the specific provisions of each managed care organization's contract that they have entered and be able to interpret the requirements of each contract to patients covered under that contract.

The passage of mental health parity legislation has eliminated session limits for many patients. Nonetheless, psychologists still need to clarify session limits with some patients, and it is good to do so as early in the treatment as possible. In doing so, psychologists will be heading off allegations of abandonment (abandonment is discussed in detail in Chapter 10, "Other Areas of Concern for Psychologists: Consultant or Supervisor, Diversity Issues, Conflicts in Institutional Settings, Referrals, and Termination and Abandonment"). It is important for psychologists to discuss with their patients the treatment options that will be available should more care be needed than the contract will provide. Options may include referral to a low-cost center and shifting to fee-for-service payment at full or reduced rates (Acuff et al., 1999). Psychologists should read their contracts carefully to determine if these contracts permit the shifting of patients into private fee arrangements for covered or noncovered services.

The risk management features we discussed in Chapter 2 ("Key Elements of Risk Management") have relevance for this topic. Informed consent is important for informing patients about fees because it reduces the likelihood of a sense of betrayal. Also, documentation is important because it provides evidence that the patient agreed to the billing and fee arrangements.

Running a Professional Office

Psychologists vary in the business arrangements of their practices. Some operate sole proprietorships, whereas others work in groups, have professional corporations, are in partnerships, or are in other business arrangements. Psychologists should consult with professionals before deciding which business arrangement is best for them.

It is common for psychologists to share office arrangements or services with other mental health professionals in a way that gives an appearance of a group practice. There may be a central reception or waiting area, shared secretarial services, a common phone number or letterhead, shared advertising in the yellow pages or local newspapers, or otherwise an impression that they are in a professional group. Such arrangements can be convenient because they reduce overhead for each practitioner involved.

However, such loosely organized groups have special risk management implications. If one partner is sued, the other parties may be implicated in the suit on the basis of their public appearance as members of a group practice even though there is no formal arrangement or agreement for a group practice. Psychologists can take measures to limit such impressions by using a disclaimer, indicating the separateness of the professionals in the Privacy Notice, or by posting public notices of nonaffiliation in their office and elsewhere. On its website, The Trust provides language that psychologists involved with loosely organized groups can use to describe their services to clients ("Minimizing Vicarious Liability Exposure," n.d.; this can be downloaded at www.apait.org). Psychologists can also check with their attorneys for advice regarding the risk involved with loosely associated group practices. Finally, they can check with their malpractice carriers about their coverage if they are named as a defendant when allegations are made against a colleague. Most malpractice carriers will provide coverage for this risk for a modest premium.

When Employees or Partners Leave

One major source of ill feelings may be the departure of psychologists or other therapists from a practice. Employees who leave group practices often want to take their patients and patient records with them. Although it is not a major source of professional liability complaints for psychologists, it often leads to ill feelings that could have been avoided if this possibility had been anticipated and discussed ahead of time. It is best to develop a written agreement at the outset that clarifies the parameters of leaving the practice. The terms of the agreement should give the highest priority to the welfare of the patients.

Some employers have restrictive covenants that prohibit employees from practicing within a certain mile radius or for a certain period of time after leaving the practice. For example, a restrictive covenant might prohibit a former employee from practicing within 5 miles of the group practice for 1 year after leaving. Some courts have overturned these types of agreements because they are too restrictive. It is also problematic for patients if such covenants are enforced because the restrictions reduce the choices of the patients who may want to continue with the departing employee.

SEVEN ESSENTIAL POINTS TO REMEMBER

1. Invest time and effort in ensuring that all psychologists and staff act in a professional manner.

2. Be tasteful and accurate in marketing services. Claiming too much expertise in too many areas of practice diminishes credibility.

3. Informed consent and documentation are very important in reducing patient dissatisfaction about fees or billing policies.

4. Do not let debts accumulate.

5. Waive copayments cautiously and only in a manner consistent with the law and insurance contracts.

6. Use small claims courts or collection agencies judiciously.

7. Clarify group practice and/or employment agreements ahead of time.

CHAPTER 12: CLOSING A PRACTICE AND RETIREMENT

Retirement from practice or leaving psychology to pursue a different line of work is an issue that eventually all psychologists must address. Retirement can come about in many ways, such as a systematically planned cessation of practice; death or disability; an externally imposed change in lifestyle; a decision to change careers; or a necessary relocation, to name a few. Like taxes, retirement is inevitable, and it is highly advisable for all psychologists to have a plan to address the numerous issues they will face when they retire.

The purpose of this chapter is to identify the major issues involved when closing a practice or retiring and to provide some guidance on managing risk during this phase of life. Much of the following advice and many of the examples we use apply to psychologists who provide psychotherapeutic or counseling services. One must keep in mind, however, that, in addition to psychologists who provide direct health care services, retirement will impact all psychologists, including those who are primarily engaged in teaching, research, industrial organizational consultation, or evaluative or forensic services. Psychologists in these various areas of practice will face unique challenges when they retire.

WHEN IS RETIREMENT, RETIREMENT?

One of the wonderful things about the profession of psychology is that it has no mandatory retirement age. For psychologists who love their work and can continue to provide services competently, age may not be a determinant in the retirement equation. Psychologists in good health can continue to practice psychology long after they close their full time practices. Part-time teaching, consultation, supervision, and *pro bono* work opportunities are readily available for retired psychologists, especially those well-known in their community. It is a wise person who remains active during retirement years. It was in this spirit that former American Psychological Association (APA) President Dr. Diane Halpern (2004) strongly advised psychologists to engage in volunteer work during retirement. Of importance, however, is that psychologists who follow this advice remember that they are still providing psychological services. Therefore, the liabilities and risks associated with providing health care services, teaching, consultation, supervision, testing, and a myriad of other activities, whether for a fee or pro bono, *remain the same* as during preretirement years.

Many psychologists retire from practice and then provide voluntary or pro bono services to organizations or agencies. This can take many forms to include consulting, seeing the occasional patient, teaching, or supervising staff. Some believe they are retired when they stop providing psychotherapeutic services even though they continue to provide other psychological services pro bono. In a sense they have retired from their major area of practice, but from a risk management perspective, they are still providing professional services and can be held liable for mistakes or bad outcomes.

For many psychologists retirement is viewed more as a transition to a different level or kind of work than a termination of all professional activities. Many psychologists who retire continue their same line of work, although at a lower frequency. Others take part-time jobs in related fields or volunteer their services. A survey of APA members showed that 64% of psychologists who planned to retire expected to continue working part-time as psychologists (Chamberlin, 2004).

The Good Samaritan aspects of these commendable contributions should not cloud the risk management concerns. The same issues concerning risk management apply here as in other professional services. In such situations it is important for psychologists to restrict their services to their areas of competence and keep up-to-date with the literature. Unfortunately, some patients, including perhaps not-so-well-meaning and litigious patients, may seek disciplinary actions against psychologists for what they perceive as incompetence or misconduct, even though these psychologists are volunteering or working for nonprofit organizations for a token salary. Even if psychologists provide a reduced level of professional services, whether for a small fee or pro bono, they should maintain their professional liability insurance to protect them from any risks associated with those services during the period of part-time work.

Well-meaning leaders of charitable organizations may entice psychologists into providing or supervising clinical services. No doubt, many psychologists make valuable contributions through such services, and our comments should not be construed as trying to discourage psychologists from contributing to worthwhile organizations or maintaining a connection with the profession they practiced for many years. However, these services can be more meaningful for psychologists who conscientiously apply the risk management principles we have discussed in this book.

Psychologists who are considering providing limited services should clarify exactly what is being asked of them. Will they serve as a supervisor (in which case they assume full clinical responsibility for services) or a consultant (in which case they provide input that the agency can choose to accept or reject as it sees fit)? Although functioning in the role of a consultant may reduce exposure for damages, it does not eliminate the possibility that a suit could be filed. Psychologists should ensure that they are competent to provide the services required and insist on certain patient protections and risk management standards. The agency or organization may be willing to pay the cost for their professional liability insurance. Often insurers offer reduced premiums for psychologists who work part-time.

A retired psychologist was approached by the chair of the Board of Directors of a local HIV/AIDS clinic to become a supervisor of counseling services. Over time the paraprofessional counselors working at the clinic had evolved their own independent and idiosyncratic styles of intervention and strongly opposed the decision to appoint a supervisor. There was a possibility that the paraprofessional counselors might sabotage the efforts to retain the services of the supervising psychologist at the clinic. It was apparent to the psychologist that the chair of the board had not thought through the implications of the decision to seek these special services. Did he want to rein in the volunteers or was he looking for a figurehead consultant to add prestige to the clinic or was he hoping the consultant would "take the heat" for some difficult decisions that needed to be made? (12.1)

The psychologist met with the volunteer paraprofessional counselors and demonstrated that she was going to be respectful of their perspectives. The psychologist was able to gain the trust of the volunteer paraprofessionals, and they soon modified their strong stand against working with the psychologist. The psychologist also consulted with the chair of the board and helped him to clarify his expectations of her role.

RETIREMENT PLANNING

How psychologists should go about closing or significantly reducing a practice depends on a variety of factors, including the nature of the practice, whether they are closing the practice temporarily (such as for parental or sick leave) or permanently, and whether they have a solo practice or work with others in a group practice or an agency setting. Sometimes the transition will be planned, welcomed, and expected. However, psychologists also need to think about the difficult issues that their death or disability may create,[1] considering their own needs as well as those of their patients, office partners, and other affected persons.

The APA's "Ethical Principles of Psychologists and Code of Conduct" (hereinafter referred to as the Ethics Code; APA, 2010a) requires that "unless otherwise covered by contract, psychologists make reasonable efforts to plan for facilitating services in the event that psychological services are interrupted by factors such as the psychologist's illness, death, unavailability, relocation, or retirement" (Standard 3.12, Interruption of Psychological Services) and that they "make plans in advance to facilitate the appropriate transfer and to protect the confidentiality of records" (Standard 6.02c, Maintenance, Dissemination, and Disposal of Confidential Records of Professional and Scientific Work).

Psychologists who are planning to leave practice need to decide when to close the office, when to stop taking new referrals, when and how to tell patients that they

---

[1] From "Some (Relatively) Simple Risk Management Strategies," by E. Harris, 2004, Spring/Summer, *MassPsych: The Journal of the Massachusetts Psychological Association, 48*, pp. 27–28. Reprinted with permission of the author.

are retiring or leaving practice, when to take down web pages, and when to notify referral sources. They will also need to decide to whom they will be referring current patients who will need on-going treatment after they retire, and how they will handle contractual obligations such as office leases, bank accounts, billing services, managed care organization contracts, and phone answering services. In addition, they need to be aware of the ethical and statutory requirements for keeping records after they leave practice; proper procedures for forwarding patient records, if requested; protocols for responding to inquiries from patients after they retire; and other practice matters.

These decisions need to be informed by any specific state laws concerning retirement. Psychologists also should contact their state board of psychology to determine if it has specific regulations or policies concerning closing practices. Some states require psychologists to publish ads in the paper. If this is required, then psychologists should also specify this in the instructions to whoever will manage the dissolution of their practices in the event of their death.

Clinical Issues

Psychologists may wish to set a firm date for closing their practices well in advance and to announce this to patients and other interested parties well ahead of time. Ideally, at some predetermined time, they would simply not take on any new cases and allow for the gradual attrition of current patients. The therapy for some patients will have to be interrupted at the point of retirement, and the psychologist will need to refer them for additional care. Some patients, especially those with chronic needs, may react with anger, loss, or a sense of abandonment on learning of their psychologist's retirement and could need more time to process the change. It is important for psychologists to identify those patients who might react in this way and give them ample notice of retirement so they have the additional time to work through these issues.

In small communities where information travels quickly by word of mouth, psychologists may wish to inform all of their patients about their plan to close their practices at the same time. One way to guarantee consistency of information is to send all current and recently terminated patients a letter announcing the closing of the practice assuming that the psychologist obtained the clients' permission to send letters to their homes.

Psychologists need to use their discretion in deciding which former patients to notify. Some former patients will appreciate knowing the decision, and it may help them avoid inconvenience and emotional upset if they feel they need additional services and always thought that their psychologist would be available. In addition, some former patients may wish to have copies of their records sent to another provider.

How much information should psychologists give to patients concerning the reason for their leaving practice? Psychologists may decide to leave practice for reasons that may not be entirely voluntary and may be prompted by growing health concerns, family obligations, new opportunities, or other occurrences outside of their control. Patients vary in the extent to which they need to know or can handle this type of information. These are individual clinical decisions that need special consideration.

Psychologists should be certain that they have informed managed care companies of their plans to make sure that they are operating within their contractual obligations. They also should notify referral sources. If they sell their practices to another provider or wish to recommend other providers to former patients, a letter can provide the necessary information. Some states (e.g., New York) require a written authorization from the patient before records may be turned over to a purchaser or successor practitioner. Psychologists who are selling their practices would be prudent to work closely with an attorney familiar with the laws and regulations regarding confidentiality, record keeping and record transfer in their states, and any new interpretations of the requirements of the Health Insurance Portability and Accountability Act Privacy Rule.

Part of the planning for psychologists may involve the development of a referral list for current and former patients. In some cases, it may be desirable to speak with the new therapist personally. Psychologists need to obtain patient consent for providing copies of their records or information to new therapists. They should retain the originals of all patient records for the period of time legally required by state law or the APA (2007) "Record Keeping Guidelines" if their state does not have a law on record retention. As noted in the section titled The Slippery Slope of Practice During Retirement, from a risk management position, it is preferable that psychologists make professional referrals while they are still covered by a malpractice insurance policy rather than after they have terminated it.

Psychologists may consider placing their licenses on inactive status. Many psychologists desire to maintain their licenses on full active status to provide flexibility should they decide to provide services in the future or to maintain a professional identity. Psychologists who terminate their licenses and continue to practice psychology may be subject to an investigation and possibly a fine from the licensing board for practicing without a license. In addition, if psychologists terminate their licenses and continue to practice but maintain their professional liability insurance, any claim brought against them may not be covered by their insurance because professional liability policies generally do not cover the unlawful practice of psychology.

Of course, psychologists need to consider the possibility that they will want to return to professional practice and the cost of reactivating the license. For example, they should learn the mandatory continuing education requirements, if any, for reactivating their licenses.

Business and Practical Issues

Psychologists also need to attend to business issues. They should close unnecessary bank accounts and review and, as appropriate, terminate leases, office agreements, contracts with billing agencies and answering services, agreements for marketing and advertising, ads or columns in local newspapers, or other contracts with business associates. If possible, psychologists should settle unpaid accounts before they formally close their practices.

Special Issues With Psychological Assessment and Forensic Practices

Special considerations apply for psychologists who primarily provide forensic or evaluative services (such as neuropsychological evaluations; child custody evaluations; evaluations of individuals who have been injured in an accident; testing for worker's compensation and social security cases; testing for school placement; or evaluations for hiring, promotion, and retention in employment settings). These services are generally characterized by short-term contact with clients to provide important information for businesses, schools, or regulatory and legal systems.

Although the services are performed short-term, the psychologist may be called to testify some time well into the future. Psychologists who perform these evaluative services are frequently called on to testify in court regarding the results of their evaluations. In addition, their former clients may request that their records be sent to lawyers, regulatory agencies, schools, courts, or other providers of psychological services. These requests may continue well beyond the time of retirement. However, psychological services that are provided after the professional liability insurance is terminated will not be covered, and exactly what constitutes a new psychological service could be a matter of debate.

Psychologists who provide evaluative services have several options to reduce their risk when they close their practices. One is to continue to carry professional liability insurance until all cases have been completed and there are no future expectations for providing additional services. Another somewhat more drastic option would be for psychologists to terminate all activity at a certain time and turn over all records to another practitioner who agrees to respond to any request for information from the files. Under this scenario psychologists would be placed in the position with the least chance of providing future services. The risk, however, of being compelled to testify in some future legal action still remains, and this could easily be interpreted as the practice of psychology.

INSURANCE

Psychologists who are semiretired should maintain their professional liability insurance during their retirement years if they plan to provide any psychological services, even if for reduced or no fees on a very part-time basis. Although this advice, on first glance, could appear to favor the interests of the insurance industry, the value of this recommendation will be instantly clear if a malpractice suit or licensing board complaint is filed against a psychologist after leaving practice. Whether successful or not, malpractice suits against uninsured psychologists could potentially wipe out their entire retirement savings portfolio. In the final analysis, it is a business decision where cost is weighed against the risk of a negative outcome. Psychologists who provide pro bono services for an agency or clinic might want to negotiate with the clinic to pay the cost of the insurance.

THE SLIPPERY SLOPE OF PRACTICE DURING RETIREMENT

Psychologists should be prepared to receive inquiries from former patients and third-party sources for several years after they retire. This may mean responding to requests for records or even a subpoena for testimony on a case evaluated several years before.

> Three years after a forensic psychologist retired, an attorney contacted her, requesting her test results and records on one of the psychologist's former clients. The attorney suggested that the psychologist's records and testimony might be needed for a personal injury case in which her records might have had some relevance. The attorney provided a signed authorization and wanted to use the materials in a case. The psychologist sent the unaltered records in response to an appropriately signed release and informed the attorney of the charges for her services if called to testify. The psychologist was aware that testifying in court about the examination would constitute new professional services. The activities factored in the psychologist's realization that she needed to reactivate her professional liability insurance. (12.2)

Retired psychologists who receive a request for records after they have cancelled a professional liability policy should not respond by reevaluating the data or offering a summary rather than the record itself. Reevaluating the data for the current request or writing the summary would be considered a new professional act that may not be a covered event. In contrast, the post retirement release of records, which were developed and maintained during active practice when the policy was in force, is an extension of the past practice.

If psychologists must testify at a hearing or deposition pursuant to a subpoena or court order, it is very important that they only refer to the historical record and not offer any new professional opinions. Testifying in court or at a deposition in any role other than that of a percipient or fact witness, once again may constitute a new professional service and any lawsuit or licensing board complaint resulting from that activity may not be covered by a terminated professional liability policy. These are complicated and tricky situations. Therefore, it would be prudent to consult with legal counsel before responding to a court order or subpoena.

Psychologists should be careful when former patients contact them concerning a referral. They should keep in mind that although while relatively rare, one of the reasons psychologists are sued is for *improper referral*. If former patients request information on where they should go for services, the psychologist can refer the patients back to their family physicians, the managed care company if one is involved, another provider who has agreed to assist in the referral process, or a local or state psychological association that may have a referral service. Psychologists who are not up-to-date with the developments in their local psychological communities run the risk of giving a less-than-optimal (or even bad) referral. Although the likelihood is remote, a psychologist who highly recommends a specific referral source that then delivers negligent services could be named as a defendant in a malpractice suit alleging an improper referral.

As noted in Chapter 4 ("Multiple Relationships and Boundaries"), psychologists should be prudent about giving psychological advice, even in social situations. This advice is applicable both pre and post retirement. Engaging in this type of activity after retirement is potentially more problematic, especially if the professional liability insurance has been cancelled. Well-meaning professionals, thinking they were being polite or helpful while at a social function, have been criticized (and sometimes sued) for giving professional advice. The key is whether a professional relationship has been established when giving advice in a nonprofessional setting such as a social event. A plaintiff's attorney will argue strongly that the recipient of the advice thought it was a professional service; that is, in the eye of the beholder it was a professional request and a professional service. Needless to say, this can be dangerous territory.

SUDDEN CLOSURE DUE TO DEATH OR DISABILITY

All people are at risk for sudden death or disability. In fact, at most ages, incapacity due to disability is far more likely than death. It is best to prepare for any unforeseen traumatic event while healthy. Many psychologists have written instructions and have designated specific persons to manage the dissolution of their practices on their death (this is sometimes referred to as a *professional will*). Ideally, the individuals named will be another psychologist or attorney with experience in such matters, although often other mental health professionals can handle the responsibilities adequately. Very specific instructions should include important practice information such as the location of the appointment book and office keys, computer passwords, banking institutions and bank accounts, and other business details (Ragusea, 2002). These instructions could also include how to contact current patients and how their records are to be handled, maintained, or disposed of and which insurers or referral sources should be contacted. Psychologists should be certain that the instructions are in compliance with statutory requirements, such as whether to announce the retirement in the paper (if the state so requires). Although it is unlikely that an estate would be sued because records are missing, it can happen. Psychologists who lack preparation may place an unusually difficult burden on their families or partners at a time when they already have enough emotional and practical issues to consider.

SUMMARY

One might ask, Why spend so much time on a chapter on retirement or leaving practice? There are several reasons. First, this topic is rarely discussed in the literature, especially from a risk management perspective. Second, the available data indicate that many psychologists are nearing retirement age. And third, specific issues related to retirement and closing a practice and insurance need to be understood to ensure that psychologists are protected from potentially devastating malpractice claims after they have closed their practice.

As noted previously, most psychologists want to continue to practice, at least part-time, for many years after their "official" retirement. The risks involved in providing professional services are not removed, however, at the time of the official closing of a practice. Semiretired psychologists need to consider risk management issues, including the potential for an ongoing decrease in their psychologist factors if their energy decreases or if they fail to keep up to date with advances in the profession. Equally important, however, when psychologists drop their professional liability insurance is the fact that the consequences of a disciplinary action become so high that every professional act involves significant risk. Therefore, psychologists who keep working, whether as volunteers, as practitioners with reduced hours, or in any way subject to liability for providing psychological services, should maintain their professional liability insurance.

SEVEN POINTS TO REMEMBER

1. Psychologists planning to retire or close their practices need to have a comprehensive plan and think through their decisions.

2. Psychologists planning to retire or close their practices need to anticipate such issues as informing their patients and referral sources, maintaining or destroying business and clinical records, and deciding whether to keep their licenses active.

3. State laws vary on what is required of psychologists who retire or discontinue practicing, and psychologists should check to make sure their plans are consistent with any prevailing legal requirements.

4. Retired psychologists who do any kind of professional work should keep their professional liability insurance.

5. Forensic practices or practices involving assessments may require additional planning before closing a practice.

6. Psychologists should prepare for their sudden death or disability by creating a specific and detailed professional will.

7. Psychologists who are semiretired (and working or volunteering part-time) are held to the same standards of professional conduct as psychologists who are working full-time.

CHAPTER 13: PROFESSIONAL LIABILITY INSURANCE

At first glance it might appear that a chapter on professional liability insurance will present nothing that could improve patient outcomes, reduce anxiety, or increase psychologists' level of competence in delivering professional services. Also, some psychologists who provide a high level of service in a dedicated and conscientious manner may believe that they will never need to use their professional liability insurance and, therefore, that the information in this chapter would be of little importance to them.

Of course most psychologists, fortunately, will never need to refer to the fine details of their insurance policies. Research shows that unethical practice is directly correlated with the likelihood of having a complaint filed. The correlation, however, is not as high as some may suspect, and we know many psychologists who were the subject of a complaint, even though they did nothing wrong (and often did outstanding work and acted in an exemplary manner). They just happened to encounter a particularly angry or pathological patient who had some ulterior motive in filing a licensing board complaint or a malpractice suit. In those situations, the seeming minutiae often found in professional liability policies take on significant importance. We hope the information in this chapter will help psychologists become informed purchasers of professional liability insurance.

Furthermore, we believe that the information in this chapter can help psychologists provide a higher level of service. We believe that psychologists who have confidence in their carrier and take advantage of the risk reduction services of that carrier, may improve the quality of services that they provide.

For example, one patient threatened a licensing board complaint because the psychologist refused to falsify a report. The patient, who was applying to enter a branch of the military, wanted the psychologist to alter his diagnosis and destroy any notes that had a reference to a previous psychiatric hospitalization. In another situation, the husband of a patient threatened to file a complaint against a psychologist if his wife (who had just started treatment with the psychologist) left him. In a third situation, a parent threatened a complaint against a psychologist who failed to alter the IQ score of her child in order for the child to qualify for a gifted program. The child's score was not close to the criterion to qualify her for the gifted program, even though, as it later came out, the parent had acquired a copy of the Wechsler scales and had coached the child prior to the assessment.

In each of these cases, the psychologists continued to act with integrity and refused to violate the standards of the profession. Their worry was greatly reduced because they knew that their professional liability policy included coverage for licensing board complaints. In addition, they had the opportunity to seek consultation with a risk management expert even before a complaint was filed. It is hard to put a price on that peace of mind.

The goal of this chapter is to review some basic information and address some common questions about professional liability insurance. In writing this chapter we have tried to present essential information without burdening the reader with the more technical issues or details. Nonetheless readers should review the Professional Liability Insurance Purchasing Checklist (see Table 13.A) before make purchasing decisions.

WHY PURCHASE PROFESSIONAL LIABILITY INSURANCE?

Psychologists purchase professional liability insurance to protect themselves from the financial consequences of a loss, such as losses associated with allegations of professional misconduct either before a licensing board or a claim of malpractice. The cost of a malpractice claim could be so high that it could easily wipe out the savings of a psychologist. Even the cost of defending a frivolous claim can exceed what most psychologists have in savings. The cost of defending against a licensing board complaint, even if it is frivolous, could also run into tens of thousands of dollars. Consequently, we recommend that psychologists never practice without professional liability coverage.

Many psychologists employed in agencies or institutional settings do not have their own professional liability coverage and rely on the agency to cover any claims against them. Often this is sufficient; however, agencies will not defend psychologists for activities outside of their employment contract. Most commonly this involves services provided outside the agency setting (e.g., teaching or a part-time private practice), but it could also include clinical practice outside of what the agency considers the psychologist's or agency's scope of practice to be. Psychologists who are covered by an agency policy should find out whether it would cover the costs of defending a complaint filed with a licensure board.

Table 13.A
Professional Liability Insurance Purchasing Checklist

1. Do you want occurrence or claims-made coverage?

2. If you purchase claims-made coverage, do you understand the importance of Extended Reporting Period (tail) coverage if you should end your policy or do you understand ways to ensure continuous coverage in the event that you change policies?

3. Does the policy include licensing board coverage?

4. Does the policy have unusual clauses such as exclusions from certain work locations, coverage for defense of sexual misconduct claims, and more?

5. Does the carrier offer discounts for continuing education or part-time practice?

6. Does the insurer offer quality risk management services such as that provided by The Trust?

QUALITY OF COVERAGE

The typical professional liability insurance policy includes coverage for malpractice claims for professional services by the psychologist. It is our opinion, however, that adequate coverage should include coverage for licensing board complaints. From the standpoint of the psychologist, this coverage makes sense because it protects against the most common threat to professional psychologists. In addition, because the findings of a licensing board may be used as evidence in a malpractice suit, it is wise to have an excellent defense against a board complaint from the very beginning.

It is unknown how many psychologists will have to respond to a licensing board complaint because many states do not publish data on the number of complaints that fail to pass the initial screening of becoming a formal complaint. Nonetheless, licensing board complaints against psychologists can be high-impact events. Even if the complaint is frivolous or is dismissed, it can be stressful and time consuming, and the psychologist may have to spend thousands of dollars on attorney fees and dozens of hours preparing for the defense.

Emotionally, the process can be upsetting (Montgomery, Cupit, & Wimberly, 1999; Schoenfeld, Hatch, & Gonzalez, 2001). We have known psychologists who had many sleepless nights, lost weight, or became clinically depressed following a licensing board complaint (even a frivolous one). It can be a major emotional wound for a psychologist to be accused of unethical conduct. On the other hand, a good attorney experienced in defending psychologists before state licensing boards can greatly reduce stress, help the psychologist put the complaint into perspective, and increase the likelihood that a frivolous suit will be dismissed quickly.

For malpractice coverage, the devil is often in the details. That is, the wording of the contract spells out the scope of coverage, and an inexpensive policy may reflect very limited protection of the insured. For example, the insurer may not cover psychologists who work in prisons; work with victims of trauma; perform custody evaluations; or use techniques to recover memories. The insurer may not provide adequate defense for charges of sexual misconduct and may have deductibles psychologists have to pay. Further, the insurer may allow legal costs (which can be quite substantial) to erode policy limits leaving psychologists with little coverage left to pay the damages portion of a judgment or settlement. In addition, policies may only cover the defense of claims filed by the psychologist's patient (not third-party complaints, such as might occur if a patient injured a third party). When combined, these limits or exclusions can result in substantially less protection than the psychologist expected.

Most policies exclude coverage for certain events, such as claims against the psychologist for the unlicensed practice of medicine; dishonest, criminal, fraudulent, or intentional acts; and business relationships with current or former clients. Also, most policies have specific limitations for sexual misconduct claims, but the nature of these limitations is especially important. Some carriers will not defend any sexual misconduct claims. Not all sexual misconduct claims are valid, however. Sometimes psychologists acting honorably are falsely accused of sexual misconduct. Fortunately, the best policies will defend a psychologist accused of sexual misconduct (but will not pay damages or only pay a limited amount of damages).

The coverage problem arises when a frivolous claim for sexual misconduct is filed against the psychologist. A policy that excludes all coverage, including a legal defense, would not be helpful. It is also important to know whether a policy that caps damages will provide multiple defenses for multiple claims against the practitioner.

The Trust and some other professional liability insurers offer consultative services for their members even before a complaint is filed. Two of the authors (JNY and EAH) of this book are heavily involved in consultation for The Trust. The availability of these services greatly improves the quality of the work life of psychologists. Often these consultations are fairly routine in that the psychologist has a general idea of what to do and is simply seeking information or feels a need to double-check a decision.

At other times these consultations involve situations with a high degree of risk and uncertainty, and the psychologist needs to act quickly while in a state of understandable emotional turmoil. In addition to consultation services, The Trust offers special risk management workshops, independent study courses, and other risk management materials to help practitioners keep away from avoidable complaints or allegations of misconduct.

OTHER ISSUES RELATED TO PROFESSIONAL LIABILITY COVERAGE

Insurance can be complex and it is not the purpose of this chapter to review all of the nuances and subtleties of coverage. We do, however, want to consider other questions that commonly arise in discussions of professional liability insurance, such as how the cost of premiums are determined, the difference between occurrence and claims-made policies, out-of-court settlements, how much coverage to purchase, and special issues with insurance for group practices.

Cost of Coverage

The cost of professional liability insurance for psychologists varies according to several factors, such as the state in which the policy is held, the nature of the insurance market, whether the psychologist purchases an occurrence or a claims-made policy (this difference will be described in more detail in the section titled Occurrence or Claims-Made Coverage), and the quality and extent of the coverage offered. These factors will be described in the sections that follow.

For a variety of reasons, in part reflecting idiosyncratic legal rules and traditions concerning professional liability, psychologists and other health care professionals in some states have greater exposure to licensing board and malpractice complaints than do psychologists in other states, and therefore, the frequency and amount of malpractice awards and other costs of insurance businesses vary by state. These cost differences are reflected in premium differences by state and exist so that psychologists in low risk states do not end up subsidizing psychologists who practice in high risk states.

Also, premiums for professional liability coverage may vary according to whether the market is "soft" or "hard." In a soft market, the competition for premium dollars is intense and insurance companies increase their cash flow by offering new lines of coverage or by lowering premiums on existing products to lure customers away from another company. In this scenario, competition may work to the advantage of the insured: Prices are stable or may be reduced, and policy features and enhancements may be improved. However, carriers who significantly lower premium rates to gain market share risk not having adequate reserves in the event of multiple and expensive claims.

Insurance premiums run in cycles and hard markets follow soft markets. In a hard market, the competition for premium dollars is less intense and insurance companies attempt to control costs by adding new exclusions to policies or dropping certain lines of coverage. Periodically some carriers have even discontinued their professional liability program for psychologists. Other carriers offer professional liability policies only in a limited number of states.

Occurrence or Claims-Made Coverage

Malpractice policies are offered in two forms: occurrence or claims-made. Occurrence coverage is usually more expensive than claims-made coverage, but it is generally easier to understand and administer. Claims-made coverage costs less, especially in early years, but the coverage issues are more complicated.

An occurrence policy covers any alleged misconduct that occurred during the policy period. The claim can be reported anytime regardless of whether the policy is in force at the time of the report. Therefore, an occurrence policy covers a psychologist in perpetuity for any covered incident that occurred while the policy was in force, regardless of when the claim is filed. Psychologists who purchase occurrence coverage should be certain that they are dealing with a carrier with significant financial resources to withstand the changes in the insurance marketplace. This is important because if a carrier becomes insolvent, there may not be sufficient assets to respond to a claim filed in the future.

The premiums collected for any year for an occurrence policy must be adequate to cover all potential claims that occur during that policy year regardless of when the claims are filed against the insured in the future. Therefore, the premiums for an occurrence policy are substantially higher than the premiums for a claims-made policy, especially when compared with the premiums for a claims-made policy during the first years of coverage. A special feature of the occurrence coverage is that a practitioner may drop an occurrence policy at any time (e.g., as a result of retirement, a job change, a change in carriers, or a change to a claims-made policy) without fear that a suit filed in the future for alleged malpractice that occurred when the policy was in force would not be covered. Under an occurrence policy, claims are covered according to the terms and conditions of the policy in force at the time the alleged incident occurred.

In contrast, a claims-made policy covers any alleged misconduct that occurred during the policy period if the claim is reported during the time the policy is in force. Put differently, for a claim to be covered under a claims-made policy, the insured must have been covered under the same policy both when the covered incident occurred and when the claim is filed later. All claims-made policies have a retro date, or the date the policy was first issued. The policy will not cover any claims alleging malpractice that occurred prior to the retro date.

Premiums for the first year of a claims-made policy cover claims that were filed during the first year. Premiums for the second year cover any claims from both the first and second year that are filed in the second year. Premiums for the third year cover three years of potential claims, and so on thereafter, thus potentially compounding risk. Therefore, premiums for claims-made policies are lower during the first years of coverage and increase as the policy continues in force. Each additional year of coverage represents a new step rate in the premium for a claims-made policy. When the policy "matures" (typically sometime between the fifth and eighth years), the premium costs level off and begin to mimic those under an occurrence policy.

Psychologists who drop a claims-made policy (e.g., as a result of retirement, a job change, a change to a different carrier, or a change to a different type of coverage) should purchase an Extended Reporting Period endorsement (or ERP, often referred to as "tail" coverage) to extend the period into the future for reporting claims beyond the policy termination date, and verify that their preferred carrier offers an unlimited ERP. Under The Trust's Professional Liability Program, tail coverage costs 175% of the last year's premium for unlimited extended reporting period coverage. The money saved during the policy's first years will generally exceed the cost of the tail coverage. If psychologists drop a claims-made policy, they should purchase the tail coverage, or if purchasing a new policy, they should purchase other insurance policies with the same retro date as the terminated policy to ensure continuous coverage. Psychologists who wish to change from claims-made coverage to occurrence coverage will need to purchase the tail coverage on the claims-made policy to close out coverage under the terminated policy and pay the current premium for the occurrence policy. Psychologists who wish to keep claims-made coverage but change insurance carriers need to talk to their potential new carrier about details necessary to ensure continuity of coverage.

Out-of-Court Settlements

Most cases against psychologists (that are not dismissed or won outright by the psychologist) are settled prior to going to trial. Often psychologists feel offended that the insurer is willing to settle a complaint if they did nothing wrong and the suit appears frivolous to them. Experienced insurers can predict with relative certainty how a particular claim will resolve, and they take strong measures to discourage frivolous claims. Nonetheless, settlement often is the preferred option for several reasons: Juries are unpredictable, particularly when a case involves extremes such as suicide or serious injury, and often the settlement is for less money than it would cost to defend the case. Also, settlements avoid prolonged litigation, including depositions, a public hearing, and court testimony. In addition, a settlement resolves a very painful situation for the practitioner, one that is frequently associated with loss of income due to a harsh verdict or the time involved in this type of litigation. The settlement of a frivolous case generally does not have a significant negative impact on the psychologist's practice. That said, it is important to know that large settlements, however, may evidence serious misconduct and may have significant consequences. Psychologists should discuss with their attorney the details of the settlement and any professional impact that could result from such a settlement. For example, psychologists are often required to report such actions to insurance panels as part of their credentialing process, and the wording of the settlement may be important.

How Much Coverage to Have

The limits of liability in a professional liability policy are listed as a dollar amount for each incident and an aggregate dollar amount available during the policy period. Today most practitioners purchase $1million/$3million in coverage, meaning the policy will pay a maximum of $1 million for a single incident and up to $3 million in losses for the year the policy was in force.

Special Issues With Group Insurance

In group practices the risk of exposure to litigation becomes more complicated because a suit resulting from the negligence of one member of the group may well name all members as defendants as well as the corporation or partnership. Therefore, a single incident of alleged malpractice may result in suits against each of the practitioners in the group. Even when psychologists share office space and other office services without creating a legal entity, patients may sue all members of the informal group. It is wise to discuss with the insurance carrier how best to insure each type of group.

In the final analysis, professional liability insurance should provide the comfort psychologists need to engage in their profession without excess worry and sleepless nights. Psychologists with questions regarding their professional liability coverage or other important insurance products can contact The Trust at 1-800-477-1200 or view the website, www.apait.org.

SEVEN ESSENTIAL POINTS TO REMEMBER

1. No psychologist should practice without professional liability insurance.

2. An agency's malpractice insurance policy is unlikely to cover activities outside of the regular job responsibilities of the psychologist and may not cover board complaints.

3. Low cost insurance policies often have limits on coverage which could make a big difference in the event a claim is filed.

4. The best professional liability policies cover complaints before licensing boards.

5. Occurrence policies differ from claims-made policies.

6. All policies have some limits to coverage.

7. Take advantage of risk management programs that the insurer may offer.

AFTERWORD

The goals of this book are to help psychologists to decrease the likelihood that they will be the subject of a disciplinary complaint and, at the same time, increase the likelihood that they will deliver high-quality services. In striving for those goals, we rejected a fear-based, formulaic, one-size-fits-all approach to ethics and risk management. Of course, all psychologists must follow certain rules. However, many situations and clinical conundrums cannot be easily resolved by a strict obedience to a finite set of rules. Therefore, psychologists should inform their decisions by situational or contextual factors, patient or client characteristics, and an accurate understanding of their own resources. Although psychologists should always retain a realistic understanding of potential problems that may lead to disciplinary actions, they should not let excessive or unrealistic fear inhibit them from delivering ethically and professionally sound services.

Psychologists belong to a great tradition of healers. They can be proud of their services and how they have benefited individual patients and society as a whole. We hope that this book will further that tradition.

REFERENCES

Ackerman, M. J., & Pritzl, T. B. (2011). Child custody evaluation practices: A 20-year follow-up. *Family Court Review, 49*, 618–628.

Acuff, C., Bennett, B., Bricklin, P., Canter, M., Knapp, S., Moldawsky, S., & Phelps, R. (1999). Considerations for ethical practice in managed care. *Professional Psychology: Research and Practice, 30*, 563–575.

AFCC. (2006). *Model standards of practice for child custody evaluation.* Madison, WI: Author.

AFCC Task Force on Court-Involved Therapy. (2011). Guidelines for court-involved therapy. *Family Court Review, 49*, 564–581.

Aguilera, A., & Muñoz, R. F. (2011). Text messaging as an adjunct to CBT in low-income populations: A usability and feasibility pilot study. *Professional Psychology: Research and Practice, 42*, 472–478.

Alexander, G. C., Humensky, J., Guerrero, C., Park, H., & Loewenstein, G. (2010). Brief report: Physician narcissism, ego threats, and confidence in the face of uncertainty. *Journal of Applied Social Psychology, 40*, 947–955.

Amabile, T., & Kramer, S. (2011). *The progress principle: Using small wins to ignite joy, engagement, and creativity at work.* Boston, MA: Harvard Business Review Press.

American Educational Research Association, American Psychological Association, & National Council on Measurement in Education. (1999). *The standards for educational and psychological testing.* Washington, DC: American Educational Research Association.

American Psychiatric Association. (2003). Practice guidelines for the assessment and treatment of patients with suicidal behaviors. *American Journal of Psychiatry, 160* (Suppl. 11).

American Psychoanalytic Association. (1995). *Practice Bulletin 2: Charting psychoanalysis.* Retrieved from www.apsa.org/About_APsaA/Practice_Bulletins/Charting_Psychoanalysis.aspx

American Psychological Association. (1992). Ethical principles of psychologists and code of conduct. *American Psychologist, 47*, 1597–1611.

American Psychological Association. (2003). Guidelines on multicultural education, training, research, practice, and organizational change for psychologists. *American Psychologist, 58*, 377–402.

American Psychological Association. (2006). *Advancing colleague assistance in professional psychology.* Retrieved from www.apa.org/practice/resources/assistance/monograph.pdf

American Psychological Association. (2007). Record keeping guidelines. *American Psychologist, 62*, 993–1004.

American Psychological Association. (2010a). *Ethical principles of psychologists and code of conduct (2002, Amended June 1, 2010).* Retrieved from www.apa.org/ethics/code/index.aspx?item=3

American Psychological Association. (2010b). Guidelines for child custody evaluations in family law proceedings. *American Psychologist, 65*, 863–867.

American Psychological Association. (2011b). Practice guidelines regarding psychologists' involvement in pharmacological issues. *American Psychologist, 66,* 835–849.

American Psychological Association. (2012a). Guidelines for the assessment of and intervention with persons with disabilities. *American Psychologist, 67,* 43–62.

American Psychological Association. (2012b). Guidelines for the evaluation of dementia and age-related cognitive change. *American Psychologist, 67,* 1–9.

American Psychological Association. (2012c). Guidelines for psychological practice with lesbian, gay, and bisexual clients. *American Psychologist, 67,* 10–42.

American Psychological Association. (2012d). Guidelines for the practice of parenting coordination. *American Psychologist, 67,* 63–71.

American Psychological Association. (2013a). Guidelines for psychological evaluations in child protection matters. *American Psychologist, 68,* 20–31.

American Psychological Association. (2013b). Specialty guidelines for forensic psychology. *American Psychologist, 68,* 7-19.

American Psychological Association, Ethics Committee. (1996). Report of the Ethics Committee, 1995. *American Psychologist, 51,* 1279–1286.

American Psychological Association, Ethics Committee. (2007). Report of the Ethics Committee, 2006. *American Psychologist, 62,* 504–511.

American Psychological Association, Ethics Committee. (2008). Report of the Ethics Committee, 2007. *American Psychologist, 63,* 452–459.

American Psychological Association, Ethics Committee. (2009). Report of the Ethics Committee, 2008. *American Psychologist, 64,* 464–473.

American Psychological Association, Ethics Committee. (2010). Report of the Ethics Committee, 2009. *American Psychologist, 65,* 483–492.

American Psychological Association, Ethics Committee. (2011). Report of the Ethics Committee, 2010. *American Psychologist, 66,* 393–403.

American Psychological Association, Ethics Committee. (2012). Report of the Ethics Committee, 2011. *American Psychologist, 67,* 398–408.

American Psychological Association, Task Force on Appropriate Therapeutic Responses to Sexual Orientation. (2009). *Report of the Task Force on Appropriate Therapeutic Response to Sexual Orientation.* Retrieved from www.apa.org/pi/lgbt/resources/therapeutic-response.pdf

Americans With Disabilities Act of 1990, 42 U.S.C.A. §12101 *et seq.* (West 1993). Available from www.ada.gov/pubs/ada.htm

Anderson, J., & Barret, B. (2001). *Ethics in HIV-related psychotherapy: Clinical decision making in complex cases.* Washington, DC: American Psychological Association.

Anderson, S. K., Williams, P., & Kramer, A. L. (2012). Life and executive coaching: Some ethical issues for consideration. In S. Knapp, M. C. Gottlieb, M. M. Handelsman, & L. VandeCreek (Eds.). *APA handbook on ethics in psychology,* (Vol. 2, pp. 169–181). Washington, DC: American Psychological Association.

Appelbaum, P. S. (1985). Tarasoff and the clinician: Problems in fulfilling the duty to protect. *American Journal of Psychiatry, 142*, 425–429.

Association of State and Provincial Psychology Boards. (2005). ASPPB *code of conduct*. Retrieved from www.asppb.net/i4a/pages/index.cfm?pageid=3353

Baker, D. C., & Bufka, L. F. (2011). Preparing for the telehealth world: Navigating legal, regulatory, reimbursement, and ethical issues in an electronic age. *Professional Psychology: Research and Practice, 42*, 405–411.

Bauchowitz, A. U., Gonder-Frederick, L. A., Olbrisch, M.-E., Azarbad, L., Ryee, M-Y., Woodson, M., Schirmer, B. (2005). Psychosocial evaluation of bariatric surgery candidates: A survey of present practice. *Psychosomatic Medicine, 67*, 825–832.

Baumeister, R. F., & Tierney, J. (2011). *Willpower: Rediscovering the greatest human strength*. New York, NY: Penguin.

Bazerman, M. H., & Tenbrunsel, A. E. (2011). *Blind spots*. Princeton, NJ: Princeton University Press.

Beahrs, J., & Guthiel, T. (2001). Informed consent in psychotherapy. *American Journal of Psychiatry, 158*, 4–10.

Beauchamp, T., & Childress, J. (2009). *Principles of biomedical ethics* (6th ed.). New York, NY: Oxford University Press.

Beauregard, E., & Mieczkowski, T. (2009). Testing the predictive utility of the STATIC-99: A Bayes analysis. *Legal and Criminological Psychology, 14*, 187–200.

Beck, A. T., Kovacs, M., & Weissman, A. (1979). Assessment of suicidal ideation: The Scale for Suicidal Ideation. *Journal of Consulting and Clinical Psychology, 47*, 343–352.

Beck, A. T., Weissman, A., Lester, D., & Trexler, L. (1974). The measurement of pessimism: The Hopelessness Scale. *Journal of Consulting and Clinical Psychology, 42*, 861–865.

Beck, R. S., Daughtridge, R., & Sloane, P. D. (2002). Physician–patient communication in the primary care office: A systematic review. *Journal of the American Board of Family Practice, 15*, 25–38.

Beckman, H. B., Markakis, K. M., Suchman, A. L., & Frankel, R. M. (1994). The doctor–patient relationship and malpractice. Lessons from plaintiff depositions. *Archives of Internal Medicine, 154*, 1365–1370.

Belar, C. D., Brown, R. A., Hersch, L., Hornyak, L. E., Rozensky, R. H., Sheridan, E. P., . . . Reed, G. (2001). Self-assessment in clinical health psychology: A model for ethical expansion of practice. *Professional Psychology: Research and Practice, 32*, 135–141.

Bellet, P., & Maloney, M. J. (1991). The importance of empathy as an interviewing skill in medicine. *JAMA, 266*, 1831–1832.

Bender, E. (2005, May 20). Cost of malpractice suits requires more than money. *Psychiatric News, 40*, 25.

Benjamin, G. A. H., Kent, L., & Sirikantraporn, S. (2009). Duty-to-protect statutes, cases, and procedures for positive practice. In J. L. Werth, E. R. Welfel, & G. A. H. Benjamin (Eds.). *The duty to protect: Ethical, legal, and professional responsibilities of mental health professionals* (pp. 9–28). Washington, DC: American Psychological Association.

Bloom, B. (Ed.). (1956). *Taxonomy of educational objectives: The classification of educational goals.* New York, NY: Longman, Green.

Boccaccini, M. T., Murrie, D. C., Caperton, J. D., & Hawes, S. W. (2009). Field validity of the STATIC-99 and MnSOST-R among sex offenders evaluated for civil commitment as sexually violent predators. *Psychology, Public Policy, and Law, 15,* 278–314.

Borkovec, T., Echemendia, R., Ragusea, S., & Ruiz, M. (2001). The Pennsylvania Practice Research Network and future possibilities for clinically meaningful and scientifically rigorous psychotherapy effectiveness research. *Clinical Psychology: Science and Practice, 8,* 155–167.

Bow, J. N., Gottlieb, M. C., Gould-Saltman, D., & Hendershot, L. (2011). Partners in the process: How attorneys prepare their clients for custody evaluation and litigation. *Family Court Review, 49,* 750–759.

Bow, J. N., Gottlieb, M. C., Siegel, J. C., & Noble, G. S. (2010). Licensing board complaints in child custody practice. *Journal of Forensic Psychology Practice, 10,* 403–418.

Bow, J. N., Gould, J. W., & Flens, J. R. (2009). Examining parental alienation in child custody cases: A survey of mental health and legal professionals. *The American Journal of Family Therapy, 37,* 127–145.

Bow, J. N., & Martindale, D. A. (2009). Developing and managing a child custody practice. *Journal of Forensic Psychology Practice, 9,* 127–137.

Braaten, E., & Handelsman, M. (1997). Client preferences for informed consent information. *Ethics & Behavior, 7,* 311–328.

Brenes, G. A., Ingram, C. W., & Danhauer, S. C. (2011). Benefits and challenges of conducting psychotherapy by telephone. *Professional Psychology: Research and Practice, 42,* 543–549.

Brenner, E. (2003). Consumer-focused psychological assessment. *Professional Psychology: Research and Practice, 34,* 240–247.

Bricklin, P. (2001). Being ethical: More than obeying the law and avoiding harm. *Journal of Personality Assessment, 77,* 195–202.

Bricklin, P., Bennett, B., & Carroll, W. (2003). *Understanding licensing board disciplinary procedures.* Retrieved from www.apait.org/apait/applications/Disciplinary_Complaint.pdf

Brown, L. S. (2000). Feminist ethical considerations in forensic practice. In M. Brabeck (Ed.), *Practicing feminist ethics in psychology* (pp. 75–100). Washington, DC: American Psychological Association.

Brown, L. S. (2009). Cultural competence: A new way of thinking about integration in therapy. *Journal of Psychotherapy Integration, 19,* 340–353.

Bryan, C. J., Stone, S. L., & Rudd, M. D. (2011). A practical, evidence-based approach for means-restriction counseling with suicidal patients. *Professional Psychology: Research and Practice, 42,* 339–346.

Burstin, H. R., Johnson, W. G., Lipsitz, S. R., & Brennan, T. A. (1993). Do the poor sue more? A case-control study of malpractice claims and socioeconomic status. *JAMA, 270,* 1697–1701.

Busch, K., Fawcett, J., & Jacobs, D. (2003). Clinical correlates of inpatient suicide. *Journal of Clinical Psychiatry, 64*, 14–19

Butcher, J. N. (Ed.). (2009). *Oxford handbook of personality assessment.* New York, NY: Oxford University Press.

Campanelli, R. (2005). Letter to Harcourt Publishing. Cited in Pearson Assessment and Information, Legal Policies, Retrieved from www.pearsonassessments.com/haiweb/Cultures/en-US/Site/general/LegalPolicies.htm

Caudill, O. B., & Pope, K. (1995). *Law and mental health professionals: California.* Washington, DC: American Psychological Association.

Chamberlin, J. (2004, November). No desire to fully retire. *Monitor on Psychology, 35*(10), 82–83.

Chamberlin, J. (2007, March). Too much information. *GradPsych. 5*(2), 14–16.

Chemtob, C., Bauer, G., Hamada, R., Pelowski, S., & Muraoka, M. (1989). Patient suicide: Occupational hazard for psychologists and psychiatrists. *Professional Psychology: Research and Practice, 20*, 294–300.

Choudhry, N., Fletcher, R., & Soumerai, S. (2005). The relationship between clinical experience and quality of health care. *Annals of Internal Medicine, 142*, 260–273.

Clayton, S., & Bongar, B. (1994). The use of consultation in psychological practice: Ethical, legal, and clinical considerations. *Ethics & Behavior, 4*, 43–57.

Coryell, W., & Young, E. (2005). Clinical predictors of suicide in primary major depressive disorder. *Journal of Clinical Psychiatry, 66*, 412–417.

Coster, J., & Schwebel, M. (1997). Well-functioning in professional psychologists. *Professional Psychology: Research and Practice, 28*, 5–13.

Cullari, S. (2009, June). Analysis of board of psychology disciplinary actions: 1990–2007. *Pennsylvania State Board of Psychology Newsletter*, 1–2.

Daubert v. Merrell Dow Pharmaceuticals, 509 U.S. 579 (1993).

Davis, D. A., Mazmanian, P. E., Fordis, M., Van Harrison, R., Thorpe, K. E., & Perrier, L. (2006). Accuracy of physician self-assessment compared with observed measures of competence: A systematic review. *JAMA, 296*, 1094–1102.

Davis, D. D. (2008). *Terminating therapy: A professional guide to ending therapy on a positive note.* Hoboken, NJ: Wiley.

DeMatteo, D., Batastini, A., Foster, E., & Hunt, E. (2010). Individualizing risk assessment: Balancing idiographic and nomothetic data. *Journal of Forensic Psychology Practice, 10*, 360–371.

DeMatteo, D., Marcyzk, G., Krauss, D. A., & Burl, J. (2009). Educational and training models in forensic psychology, *Training and Education in Professional Psychology, 3*, 184–191.

DeMers, S. T., & Schaffer, J. B. (2012). The regulation of professional psychology. In S. Knapp, M. C. Gottlieb, M. M. Handelsman, & L. VandeCreek, (Eds.). *APA handbook on ethics in psychology* (Vol 1., pp. 453–482). Washington, DC: American Psychological Association.

Dewey, L. M., & Gottlieb, M. C. (2011). Ethical guidelines for providing court-ordered outpatient psychotherapy to juvenile offenders. *Journal of Forensic Psychology Practice, 11*, 1–20.

Dlugos, R., & Friedlander, M. (2001). Passionately committed psychotherapists: A qualitative study of their experiences. *Professional Psychology: Research and Practice, 32*, 298–304.

Edwards, S. J., & Sachmann, M. D. (2010). No-suicide contracts, no-suicide agreements, and no-suicide assurances: A study of their nature, utilization, perceived effectiveness, and potential to cause harm. *The Journal of Crisis Intervention and Suicide Prevention, 31*, 290–302.

Effective Listening Tops List of Skills Psychiatrists Need. (2000, August 4). *Psychiatric News, 35*, 8.

Ellis, E. M. (2010). Should participation in a child custody evaluation compel the release of psychotherapy records? *Journal of Child Custody, 7*, 138–154.

Elman, N., Illfelder-Kaye, J., & Robiner, W. (2005). Professional development: Training for professionalism as a foundation for competent practice in psychology. *Professional Psychology: Research and Practice, 36*, 367–375.

Epley, N., & Dunning, D. (2006). The mixed blessing of self-knowledge in behavioral prediction: Enhanced discrimination, but exacerbated bias. *Personality and Social Psychology Bulletin, 32*, 641–655.

Epstein, R., & Hundert, E. (2002). Defining and assessing professional competence. *JAMA, 287*, 226–235.

Etzioni, A. (1996). *The new golden rule: Community and morality in a democratic society.* New York, NY: Basic Books.

Everson, M., & Sandoval, J. M. (2011). Forensic sexual abuse evaluations: Assessing subjectivity and bias in professional judgments. *Child Abuse and Neglect, 35*, 287–298.

Finn, S. E. (2011). Journeys through the valley of death: Multimethod psychological assessment and personality transformation in long-term psychotherapy. *Journal of Personality Assessment, 93*, 123–141.

Fischer, C. (2004). Individualized assessment moderates the impact of HIPAA Privacy Rules. *Journal of Personality Assessment, 82*, 35–38.

Fisher, C. (2002). Respecting and protecting mentally impaired persons in medical research. *Ethics & Behavior, 12*, 280–283.

Fredrickson, B. (2009). *Positivity: Groundbreaking research reveals how to enhance the hidden strength of positive emotions, overcome negativity, and thrive.* New York, NY: Crown Archetype.

Gabbard, G. O., Kassaw, K. A., & Perez-Garcia, G. (2011). Professional boundaries in the era of the Internet. *Academic Psychiatry, 35*, 168–174.

Gigerenzer, G. (2002). *Calculated risks: How to know when numbers deceive you.* New York, NY: Simon & Shuster.

Ginsburg, G., Albano, A. M., Findling, R., Kratochvil, C., & Walkup, J. (2005). Integrating cognitive behavior therapy and pharmacotherapy in the treatment of adolescent depression.

Cognitive and Behavioral Practice, 12, 252–262.

Glassgold, J. M., & Knapp, S. (2008). Ethical issues in screening clergy or candidates for religious professions for denominations that exclude homosexual clergy. *Professional Psychology: Research and Practice, 39,* 346–352.

Gottlieb, M. C., & Coleman, A. (2012). Ethical challenges in forensic psychology practice. In S. Knapp, M. C. Gottlieb, M. M. Handelsman, & L. VandeCreek, (Eds). *APA handbook on ethics in psychology,* (Vol 2., pp. 91–123). Washington, DC: American Psychological Association. Gottlieb, M. C., & Younggren, J. N. (2009). Is there a slippery slope? Considerations regarding multiple relationships and risk management. *Professional Psychology: Research and Practice, 40,* 564–571.

Greenberg, L. R., Gould, J., Gould-Saltman, D. J., & Stahl, P. (2003). Is the child's therapist part of the problem? What judges, attorneys, and mental health professionals need to know about court-related treatment for children. *Family Law Quarterly, 37,* 241–271.

Greenberg, L. R., Gould-Saltman, D., & Gottlieb, M. C. (2008). Playing in their sandbox: Professional obligations of mental health professionals in custody cases. *Journal of Child Custody, 5,* 192– 216.

Greenberg, S., Caro, C. M., & Smith, I. L. (2010). *Study of the practice of licensed psychologists in the United States and Canada.* Atlanta, GA: Association of State and Provincial Psychology Boards.

Greenberg, S. A., & Shuman, D. W. (2007). When worlds collide: Therapeutic and forensic roles. *Professional Psychology: Research and Practice, 38,* 129–132.

Griner, D., & Smith, T. B. (2006). Culturally adapted mental health interventions: A meta-analytic review. *Psychotherapy: Theory, Research, Practice and Training, 43,* 531–548.

Gulec, H., Moessner, M., Mezei, A., Kohls, E., Túry, F., & Bauer, S. (2011). Internet-based maintenance treatment for patients with eating disorders. *Professional Psychology: Research and Practice, 42,* 479–486.

Guthiel, T., & Gabbard, G. (1998). Misuses and misunderstandings of boundary theory in clinical and regulatory settings. *American Journal of Psychiatry, 155,* 409–414.

Guy, J. D., Brown, C. K., & Poelstra, P. L. (1990). Who gets attacked? A national survey of patient violence directed at psychologists in clinical practice. *Professional Psychology: Research and Practice, 21,* 493–495.

Halpern, D. (2000, May). Hi yo' silver psychologists. *Monitor on Psychology, 35*(5), 5.

Handelsman, M. (1997). Colorado State Grievance Board sanctions. Cited in M. Handelsman. (2001). Learning to become ethical. In S. Walfish & A. K. Hess (Eds.), *Succeeding in graduate school: The career path for psychology students* (pp. 189–202). Mahwah, NJ: Erlbaum.

Handelsman, M. M., Knapp, S., & Gottlieb, M. C. (2009). Positive ethics: Themes and variations. In C. R. Snyder & S. J. Lopez (Eds.), *Oxford handbook of positive psychology* (2nd ed., pp. 105–113). New York, NY: Oxford University Press.

Harris, E. (n.d.-a). Coaching: A new frontier—some questions and answers. Retrieved from www.apait.org/apait/resources/articles/coaching.pdf

Harris, E. (n.d.-b) The use of interpreters when treating deaf clients. Retrieved from www. apait.org/apait/resources/articles/ADADeafInterpreters.pdf

Harris, E. (2003, Winter). Resolving some areas of continuing confusion. *MassPsych: The Journal of the Massachusetts Psychological Association, 47*, 18–22, 29.

Harris, E. (2004, Spring/Summer). Some (relatively) simple risk management strategies. *MassPsych: The Journal of the Massachusetts Psychological Association, 48*, 27–28, 32.

Harris, E., & Younggren, J. N. (2011). Risk management in the digital world. *Professional Psychology: Research and Practice, 42*, 412–418.

Harway, M., & Hansen, M. (2004). S*pouse abuse: Assessing and treating battered women, batters, and their children* (2nd ed.). Sarasota, FL: Professional Resource Press.

Hays, P. A. (2009). Integrating evidence-based practice, cognitive-behavior therapy, and multicultural therapy: Ten steps for culturally competent practice. *Professional Psychology: Research and Practice, 40*, 354–360.

Health Insurance Portability and Accountability Act of 1996, Pub. L. No. 104-191 Stat. 1936 (1996). Retrieved from www.cms.gov/Regulations-and-Guidance/HIPAA-Administrative-Simplification/HIPAAGenInfo/downloads/hipaalaw.pdf

Heilbron, N., Compton, J. S., Daniel, S. S., & Goldston, D. B. (2010). The problematic label of suicide gesture: Alternatives for clinical research and practice. *Professional Psychology: Research and Practice, 41*, 221–227.

Hickson, G. B., & Entman, S. S. (2008). Physician practice behavior and litigation risks: Evidence and opportunity. *Clinical Obstetrics and Gynecology, 51*, 668–699.

Hjelt, S. (2011). Psychotherapy termination: Duty is a two-way street. *Professional Psychology: Research & Practice, 42*, 167–168.

Holloway, J. D. (2005, January). HIPAA: Safeguarding information. *Monitor on Psychology, 36*(1), 44.

Jacobson, J., Mulick, J., & Schwartz, A. (1995). A history of facilitated communications. *American Psychologist, 50*, 750–765.

Jaffee v. Redmond, 135 L. Ed. 2d 337 (1996).

Jobes, D. A. (2008). Clinical work with suicidal patients: Emerging ethical issues and professional challenges. *Professional Psychology: Research and Practice, 39*, 405–409.

Johnston, J. R., & Goldman, J. R. (2010). Outcomes of family counseling intervention with children who resist visitation: An addendum to Friedlander and Walters. *Family Court Review, 48*, 112–115.

Joiner, T. (2010). *Myths about suicide.* Cambridge, MA: Harvard University Press.

Kalb, P. (1999). Health care fraud and abuse. *JAMA, 282*, 1163–1168.

Karraker v. Rent-a-Center, 395 F. 3rd 786 (7th Cir. 2005).

Kaslow, F. W., Patterson, T., & Gottlieb, M. (2011). Ethical dilemmas in psychologists accessing Internet data: Is it justified? *Professional Psychology: Research and Practice, 42*, 105–112.

Kessler, R., Berglund, P., Borges, G., Nock, M., & Wang, P. (2005). Trends in suicide ideation, plans, gestures, and attempts in the United States, 1990–1992 to 2001–2003. *JAMA, 293,* 2487–2495.

Kessler, R., Borges, G., & Walters, E. (1999). Prevalence of and risk factors for lifetime suicide attempts in the National Comorbidity Survey. *Archives of General Psychiatry, 56,* 617–626.

Kilmo, G., Daum, W., Brinker, M., McGruire, E., & Elliott, M. (2000). Orthopaedic medical malpractice: An attorney's perspective. *American Journal of Orthopaedics, 29,* 93–97.

Kirkland, K., Kirkland, K. L., & Reaves, R. (2004). On the professional use of disciplinary data. *Professional Psychology: Research and Practice, 35,* 179–184.

Kleespies, P., & Dettmer, E. (2000). The stress of patient emergencies for the clinician: Incidence, impact, and means of coping. *Journal of Clinical Psychology, 56,* 1353–1369.

Kliem, S., Kröger, C., & Kosfelder, J. (2010). Dialetical behavior therapy for borderline personality disorder: A meta-analysis using mixed effects modeling. *Journal of Consulting and Clinical Psychology, 78,* 936–951.

Knapp, S. (2003, August). Could the Titanic disaster have been avoided? Or promoting patient welfare through a systems approach. *The Pennsylvania Psychologist, 63,* 4, 18, 36.

Knapp, S. (2004, November). Well-being and professional development among psychologists. *The Pennsylvania Psychologist, 64,* 13, 17.

Knapp, S., & Baturin, R. (2003, March). Child custody and custody-related evaluations and interventions: What every psychologist should know. *The Pennsylvania Psychologist, 63,* 3–4.

Knapp, S., & Gavazzi, J. (2012, April). Can checklists help reduce treatment failures? *The Pennsylvania Psychologist, 72,* 8–9.

Knapp, S., & Keller, P. (2004, March). What enhances the professional skills of psychologists? *The Pennsylvania Psychologist, 64,* 11.

Knapp, S., & Lemoncelli, J. (2005), Treating children in high-conflict families. *The Pennsylvania Psychologist, 65,* 4.

Knapp, S., & Slattery, J. (2004). Professional boundaries in non-traditional settings. *Professional Psychology: Research and Practice, 34,* 553–558.

Knapp, S., Tepper, A., & Baturin, R. (2003, August). Practical considerations when responding to subpoenas and court orders. *The Pennsylvania Psychologist, 63,* 5, 16.

Knapp, S., & VandeCreek, L. (1987). *Privileged communications in the mental health professions.* New York, NY: Van Nostrand Reinhold.

Knapp, S., & VandeCreek, L. (2004). A principle-based analysis of the American Psychological Association's ethics code. *Psychotherapy: Theory, Research, Practice, Training, 41,* 247–254.

Knapp, S., & VandeCreek, L. (2012a). Disciplinary actions by a state board of psychology: Do gender and association membership matter. In G. Neimeyer & J. Taylor (Eds.). *Continuing Professional Development and Lifelong Learning: Issues, Impacts and Outcomes* (pp. 155–158). Hauppauge, NY: NOVA Science Publishers.

Knapp, S., & VandeCreek, L. (2012b). *Practical ethics for psychologists: A positive approach* (Rev. ed.). Washington, DC: American Psychological Association.

Kohn, L. T., Corrigan, J. M., & Donaldson, M. S. (2000). *To err is human: Building a safer health system.* Washington, DC: National Academies Press.

Krishnamurthy, R., VandeCreek, L., Kaslow, N., Tazeau, Y., Miville, M., Kerns, R., . . . Benton, S. (2004). Achieving competence in psychological assessment: Directions for education and training. *Journal of Clinical Psychology, 60,* 725–739.

Lambert, M. J., & Shimokawa, K. (2011). Collecting client feedback. *Psychotherapy: Theory, Research, Practice, Training, 48,* 72–79.

Lasser, J., & Goldlieb, M. (2004). Treating patients distressed regarding their sexual orientation: Clinical and ethical alternatives. *Professional Psychology: Research and Practice, 35,* 194–200.

Lazarus, A. A. (1989). *Practice of multimodal therapy: Systematic, comprehensive, and effective psychotherapy.* Baltimore, MD: Johns Hopkins University Press.

Lees-Haley, P., & Courtney, J. (2000). Disclosure of tests and raw test data to the courts: A need for reform. *Neuropsychology Review, 10,* 169–174.

Lehavot, K., Barnett, J. E., & Powers, D. (2010). Psychotherapy, professional relationships, and ethical considerations in the MySpace generation. *Professional Psychology: Research and Practice, 41,* 160–166.

LeMont, D., Moorehead, M. K., Parish, M. S., Reto, C. S., & Ritz, S. J. (2004). *Suggestions for the pre-surgical psychological assessment of bariatric surgery candidates.* American Society for Metabolic and Bariatric Surgery. Retrieved from www.asmbs.org/2012/06/pre-surgical-psychological-assessment.

Levinson, W., Roter, D., Mullooly, J., Dull, V., & Frankel, R. (1997). Physician–patient communication: The relationship with malpractice claims among primary care physicians and surgeons. *JAMA, 277,* 553– 559.

Loewenstein, G. (2005). Hot–cold empathy gaps and medical decision making. *Health Psychology, 24*(4, Suppl.), S49–S56.

Luxton, D. D., McCann, R. A., Bush, N. E., Mishkind, M. C., & Reger, G. M. (2011). mHealth for mental health: Integrating smartphone technology in behavioral healthcare. *Professional Psychology: Research and Practice, 42,* 505–512.

Lyles, C. M., Kay, L. S., Crepaz, N., Herbst, J. H., Passin, W. F., Kim, A. S., . . . Mullins, M. (2007). Best-evidence interventions: Findings from a systematic review of HIV behavioral interventions for US populations at high risk, 2000–2004. *American Journal of Public Health, 97,* 133–143.

Lyons, H. Z., Bieschke, K. J., Dendy, A. K., Worthington, R. L., & Georgemiller, R. (2010). Psychologists' competence to treat lesbian, gay, and bisexual clients: State of the field and strategies for improvement. *Professional Psychology: Research and Practice, 41,* 424–434.

Mahoney, M. (1997). Psychotherapists' personal problems and self-care patterns. *Professional Psychology: Research and Practice, 28,* 14–16.

Malloy, K. A., Dobbins, J. E., Ducheny, K., & Winfrey, L. L. (2010). The management and supervision competency: Current and future directions. In M. B. Kenkel & R. L. Peterson (Eds.). *Competency-based education for professional psychology* (pp. 161–178). Washington, DC: American Psychological Association.

Malony, H. N. (2000). The psychological evaluation of religious professionals. *Professional Psychology: Research and Practice, 31*, 521–525.

Mansouri, M., & Lockyer, J. (2007). A meta-analysis of continuing education effectiveness. *Journal of Continuing Education of Health Professionals, 27*, 6–15.

Mapes, B., & Knapp, S. (2005, December). Ethical and professional issues in assessing sexual offenders. The *Pennsylvania Psychologist, 64*, 3–4.

Marinopoulos, S. S., Dorman, T., Ratanawongsa, N., Wilson, L. M., Ashar, B. H., Magaziner, J. L., . . . Bass, E. B. (2007, January). *Effectiveness of continuing medical education* (AHRQ Pub. No. 07-E006). Rockville, MD: Agency for Healthcare Research and Quality.

Maris, R. (1981). *Pathways to suicide: A survey of self-destructive behaviors.* Baltimore, MD: Johns Hopkins University Press.

Minimizing vicarious liability exposure for loosely organized groups and certain MSO arrangements. (n.d.) Retrieved from www.apait.org/apait/resources/riskmanagement/mso.aspx

Mlodinov, L. (2008). *The drunkard's walk: How randomness rules our lives.* New York, NY: Pantheon Books.

Mokros, A., Stadtland, C., Osterheider, M., & Nedopil, N. (2010). Assessment of risk for violent recidivism through multivariate Bayesian classification. *Psychology, Public Policy, and Law, 16*, 418–450.

Monahan, J. (1981). *The clinical prediction of violent behavior.* Washington, DC: Government Printing Office.

Monahan, J., & Steadman, H. (1996). Violent storms and violent people: How meteorology can inform risk communication in mental health law. *American Psychologist, 51*, 931–938.

Montgomery, L., Cupit, B., & Wimberly, T. (1999). Complaints, malpractice, and risk management: Professional issues and personal experiences. *Professional Psychology: Research and Practice, 30*, 402–410.

Moreland, K., Eyde, L., Robertson, G., Primoff, E., & Most, R. (1995). Assessment of test user qualifications: A research-based measurement procedure. *American Psychologist, 50*, 14–23.

Neimeyer, G. J., Taylor, J. M., & Philip, D. (2010). Continuing education in psychology: Patterns of participation and perceived outcomes among mandated and nonmandated psychologists. *Professional Psychology: Theory and Research, 41*, 435–441.

Newman, C. (2005). Reducing the risk of suicide in patients with bipolar disorders: Interventions and safeguards. *Cognitive and Behavioral Practice, 12*, 76–88.

Norcross, J. C., Koocher, G. P., Fala, N. C., & Wexler, H. K. (2010). What does not work: Expert consensus on discredited treatments in addictions. *Journal of Addiction Medicine, 4*, 174–180.

Norcross, J. C., Koocher, G. P., & Garofalo, A. (2006). Discredited psychological treatments and tests: A Delphic poll. *Professional Psychology: Research and Practice, 37*, 515–522.

Norcross, J. C., & Wampold, B. E. (2011). Evidence-based therapy relationships: Research conclusions and clinical practice. *Psychotherapy: Theory, Research, Practice, Training, 48*, 98–102.

Norko, M., & Baranoski, M. (2005). The state of contemporary risk assessment research. *Canadian Journal of Psychiatry, 50*, 18–26.

Orchowski, L., Evangelista, N. M., & Probst, D. R. (2010). Enhancing supervisee reflectivity in clinical supervision: A case study illustration. *Psychotherapy: Theory, Research, Practice, Training, 47*, 51–67.

Oordt, M. S., Jobes, D. A., Rudd, M. D., Fonseca, V. P., Runyan, C. N., Stea, J. B., . . . Talcott, G. W. (2005). Development of a clinical guide to enhance care for suicidal patients. *Professional Psychology: Research and Practice, 36*, 208–218.

Otto, R., & Heilbrun, K. (2002). The practice of forensic psychology: A look toward the future in light of the past. *American Psychologist, 57*, 5–18.

Pachankis, J., & Goldfried, M. (2004). Clinical issues in working with lesbian, gay, and bisexual clients. *Psychotherapy: Theory, Research, Practice, Training, 41*, 227–246.

Paris, J. (2002). Chronic suicidality among patients with borderline personality disorder. *Psychiatric Services, 53*, 738–742.

Peteet, J. (2004). *Doing the right thing: An approach to moral issues in mental health treatment.* Washington, DC: American Psychiatric Publishing.

Pomerantz, A., & Grice, J. (2001). Ethical beliefs of mental health professionals and undergraduates regarding therapist practices. *Journal of Clinical Psychology, 57*, 737–748.

Pope, K., & Brown, L. (1996). *Recovered memories of abuse: Assessment, therapy, forensics.* Washington, DC: American Psychological Association.

Pope, K. S., & Tabachnick, B. G. (1993). Therapists' anger, hate, fear and sexual feelings: National survey of therapists' responses, client characteristics, critical events, formal complaints and training. *Professional Psychology: Research and Practice, 24*, 142–152.

Pope, K., & Vasquez, M. (2005). *How to survive and thrive as a therapist: Information, ideas, and resources for psychologists in practice.* Washington, DC: American Psychological Association.

Ragusea, S. (2002). A professional living will for psychologists and other mental health professionals. In L. VandeCreek & T. Jackson (Eds.), *Innovations in clinical practice: A sourcebook* (Vol. 20, pp. 301–305). Sarasota, FL: Professional Resource Press.

Rogerson, M. D., Gottlieb, M. C., Handelsman, M. M., Knapp, S., & Younggren, J. (2011). Nonrational processes in ethical decision making. *American Psychologist, 66*, 614–623.

Rosenbaum, A., & Dowd, L. S. (2009). Risk assessment and the duty to protect in cases involving intimate partner violence. In J. L. Werth, Jr., E. R. Welfel, & G. A. H. Benjamin (Eds.). *The duty to protect: Ethical, legal and professional considerations for mental health professionals* (pp. 79–94). Washington, DC: American Psychological Association.

Rucker, A., Hite, B., & Hathaway, W. (2005, August 18). *Preliminary practice guidelines for interventions addressing religious/spiritual issues*. Poster session presented at the meeting of the American Psychological Association, Washington, DC.

Rudd, M. D. (2008). The fluid nature of suicide risk: Implications for clinical practice. *Professional Psychology: Research and Practice, 39,* 409–410.

Rudd, M. D., Cukrowicz, K. C., & Bryan, C. J. (2008). Core competencies in suicide risk assessment and management: Implications for supervision. *Training and Education in Professional Psychology, 2,* 219–228.

Rudd, M. D., Goulding, J., & Bryan, C. J. (2011). Student veterans: A national survey exploring psychological symptoms and suicidal risk. *Professional Psychology: Research and Practice, 42,* 354–360.

Rudd, M. D., & Joiner, T. (1999). Assessment of suicidality in outpatient practice. In L. VandeCreek & T. Jackson (Eds.), *Innovations in clinical practice: A sourcebook* (Vol. 17, pp. 101–117). Sarasota, FL: Professional Resource Press.

Rudd, M. D., Joiner, T., Brown, G. K., Cukrowicz, K., Jobes, D. A., Silverman, M., & Cordero, L. (2009). Informed consent with suicidal patients: Rethinking issues in (and out of) treatment. *Psychotherapy: Theory, Research, Practice, Training, 46,* 459–468.

Rudd, M. D., Joiner, T., & Rajab, M. H. (1996). Relationships among suicide ideators, attempters, and multiple attempters in a young-adult sample. *Journal of Abnormal Psychology, 105,* 541–550.

Rudd, M. D., Mandrusiak, M., & Joiner, T. E. (2006). The case against no-suicide contracts: The commitment to treatment statement as a practice alternative. *Journal of Clinical Psychology: In Session, 62,* 243–251.

Rummell, C. M., & Joyce, N. R. (2010). "So wat do u want 2 wrk on 2day?": Ethical implications of online counseling. *Ethics & Behavior, 20,* 482–496.

Salinsky, J. (2009). *A very short introduction to Balint groups*. Retrieved from www.balint.co.uk/about/introduction.

Sanderson, C. (2002). Dialectical behavior therapy: A synthesis of acceptance and change in the treatment of borderline personality disorder. In L. VandeCreek & T. Jackson (Eds.), *Innovations in clinical practice: A sourcebook* (Vol. 20, pp. 23–39). Sarasota, FL: Professional Resource Press.

Sawyer, A. M., & Borduin, C. M. (2011). Effects of multisystemic therapy through midlife: A 21.9-year follow-up to a randomized clinical trial with serious and violent juvenile offenders. *Journal of Consulting and Clinical Psychology, 79,* 643–652.

Schernhammer, E. (2005). Taking their own lives—the high rate of physician suicide. *New England Journal of Medicine, 352,* 2473–2476.

Schneider, M. S., Brown, L. S., & Glassgold, J. M. (2002). Implementing the resolution on appropriate therapeutic responses to sexual orientation: A guide for the perplexed. *Professional Psychology: Research and Practice, 33,* 265–276.

Schoenfeld, L., Hatch, J., & Gonzalez, J. (2001). Responses of psychologists to complaints filed against them with a state licensing board. *Professional Psychology: Research and Practice, 32*, 491–495.

Simon, R. (1992). *Clinical psychiatry and the law* (Rev. ed.). Washington, DC: American Psychiatric Press.

Simon, R. (2000). Taking the "sue" out of suicide: A forensic psychiatrist's perspective. *Psychiatric Annals, 30*, 399–407.

Smith, R., Rosetto, K., & Peterson, B. L. (2008). A meta-analysis of disclosure of one's HIV-positive status, stigma, and social support. *AIDS Care, 20*, 1266–1275.

Sonne, J. L. (2012). Sexualized relationships. In S. Knapp, M. C. Gottlieb, M. M. Handelsman, & L. VandeCreek (Eds.), *APA handbook of ethics in psychology* (Vol. 1, pp. 295–310). Washington, DC: American Psychological Association.

Sternberg, R. (2003, March). Responsibility: One of the other three Rs. *Monitor on Psychology, 33*(3), 5.

Stewart, R. E., & Chambless, D. L. (2008). Treatment failures in private practice: How do psychologists proceed? *Professional Psychology: Research and Practice, 39*, 176–181.

Stover, C. S., Meadows, A. L., & Kaufman, J. (2009). Interventions for intimate partner violence: Review and implications for evidence-based practice. *Professional Psychology: Research and Practice, 40*, 223–233.

Stuart, R. (2004). Twelve practical suggestions for achieving multicultural competence. *Professional Psychology: Research and Practice, 35*, 3–9.

Studdert, D., Mello, M., Sage, W., DesRoches, C., Peugh, J., Zapert, K., & Brennan, T. (2005). Defensive medicine among high-risk specialist physicians in a volatile malpractice environment. *JAMA, 293*, 2609–2617.

Sullivan, M. J., Ward, P. A., & Deutsch, R. N. (2010). Overcoming Barriers Family Camp: A program for high-conflict divorced families where a child is resisting contact with a parent. *Family Court Review, 48*, 116–135.

Tamblyn, R., Abrahamowicz, M., Dauphinee, D., Wenghofer, E., Jacques, A., Klass, D., ... Hanley, J. A. (2007). Physician scores on a national clinical skills examination as predictors of complaints to medical regulatory authorities. *JAMA, 298*, 993–1001.

Tamura, L. J. (2012). Emotional competence and well-being. In S. Knapp, M. C. Gottlieb, M. M. Handelsman, & L. VandeCreek (Eds.), *APA handbook of ethics in psychology* (Vol. 1, pp. 175–215). Washington, DC: American Psychological Association.

Tarasoff v. Regents of the University of California et al., 551 P. 2d 334 (Cal. S. Ct. 1976).

Tesler, P. H., & Thompson, R. (2006). *Collaborative divorce.* New York, NY: HarperCollins.

Tryon, G. S., & Winograd, G. (2011). Goal consensus and collaboration. *Psychotherapy: Theory, Research, Practice, Training, 48*, 50–57.

Tunick, R. A., Mednick, L., & Conroy, C. (2011). A snapshot of child psychologists' social media activity: Professional and ethical practice implications and recommendations. *Professional Psychology: Research and Practice, 42*, 440–447.

Turner, S., DeMers, S., Fox, H. R., & Reed, G. (2001). APA's guidelines for test user qualifications: An executive summary. *American Psychologist, 56,* 1099–1113.

U.S. Equal Employment Opportunity Commission & U.S. Department of Justice, Civil Rights Division. (2002, May). *Americans With Disabilities Act: Questions and answers.* Washington, DC: Author.

Valenstein, E. (1986). *Great and desperate cures: The rise and decline of psychosurgery and other radical treatments for mental illness.* New York, NY: Basic Books.

VandeCreek, L., & Knapp, S. (2001). *Tarasoff and beyond: Legal and clinical considerations in the treatment of life-endangering patients* (3rd ed.). Sarasota, FL: Professional Resources Press.

Van Horne, B. A. (2004). Psychology licensing board disciplinary actions: The realities. *Professional Psychology: Research and Practice, 35,* 170–178.

Ver Steegh, N., & Dalton, C. (2008). Report from the Wingspread Conference on Domestic Violence and Family Courts. *Family Court Review, 46,* 454–475.

Wadden, T. A., & Sarwer, D. B. (2006). Behavioral assessment of candidates for bariatric surgery: A patient oriented approach. *Obesity, 14,* 53S–62S.

Wade, S. L., Oberjohn, K., Conaway, K., Osinska, P., & Bangert, L. (2011). Live coaching of parenting skills using the Internet: Implications for clinical practice. *Professional Psychology: Research and Practice, 42,* 487–493.

Walfish, S., Vance, D., & Fabricatore, A. N. (2007). Psychological evaluation of bariatric surgery applicants: Procedures and reasons for delay or denial of surgery. *Obesity Surgery, 17,* 1578–1583.

Warshak, R. A. (2010). Family bridges: Using insights from social science to reconnect parents and alienated children. *Family Court Review, 48,* 48–80.

Wilkinson, T., Wade, W. B., & Knock, D. (2009). A blueprint to assess professionalism: Results of a systematic survey. *Academic Medicine, 84,* 551–558.

Woody, R. H. (1997). *Legally safe mental health practice: Psycholegal questions and answers.* Madison, CT: Psychosocial Press.

Woody, R. H. (2011). Letters of protection: Ethical and legal financial considerations for forensic psychologists (revised). *Journal of Forensic Psychology Practice, 11,* 361–367.

Wunsch, M. (2005). Guidelines for employment and practice building. In L. VandeCreek & T. Jackson (Eds.), *Innovations in clinical practice: Focus on adults* (pp. 135– 152). Sarasota, FL: Professional Resource Press.

Yen, S., Pagano, M. E., Shea, M. T., Grilo, C. M., Gunderson, J. G., Skodol, A. E., . . . Zanarini, M. (2005). Recent life events preceding suicide attempts in a personality disorder sample: Findings from the collaborative longitudinal personality disorders study. *Journal of Consulting and Clinical Psychology, 73,* 99–105.

Younggren, J. N. (2007). Competence as a process of self-appraisal. *Professional Psychology: Research and Practice, 38,* 515–516.

Younggren, J. N. (2011, January/February). Too many rules. *National Psychologist, 20,* 10.

Younggren, J. N., & Gottlieb, M. C. (2004). Managing risk when contemplating multiple relationships. *Professional Psychology: Research and Practice, 35*, 255–260.

Younggren, J. N., & Gottlieb, M. C. (2008). Termination and abandonment: History, risk and risk management. *Professional Psychology: Research and Practice, 39*, 498–504.

Younggren, J. N., & Harris, E. A. (2008). Can you keep a secret? Confidentiality in psychotherapy. *Journal of Clinical Psychology: In Session, 64*, 589–600.

Younggren, J. N., & Harris, E. (2011). *Risk management: When marital therapy is.* Retrieved from www.nationalpsychologist.com/2011/02/risk-management-when-marital-therapy-is/101214.html.

Zanarini, M. C. (2009). Psychotherapy of borderline personality disorder. Acta *Psychiatrica Scandinavica, 120*, 373–377.

Zimmerman, M., Francione-Witt, C., Chelminski, I., Young, D., Boerescu, D., Attiullah, N., . . . Harrington, D.T. (2007). Presurgical psychiatric evaluations of candidates for bariatric surgery, Part 1: Reliability and reasons for and frequency of exclusion. *Journal of Clinical Psychiatry, 68*, 1557–1562.

Zur, O. (2007). *Boundaries in psychotherapy: Ethical and clinical explorations.* Washington, DC: American Psychological Association.

Index

A

M

Mahoney, M., 15, 258
Maintaining Test Security (APA Ethics Code), 133
Maintenance, Dissemination, and Disposal of Confidential Records of Professional and Scientific Work (APA Ethics Code), 46, 231
Malloy, K. A., 203, 259
Malony, H. N., 167, 259
Malpractice 13, 16, 18–22, 24, 28, 30, 46, 119, 171, 182, 200, 213, 227, 233–234, 236, 251, 252, 257–259, 262. *See also* **Professional Liability Insurance**
  actions, 18
  actions leading to complaints, 21
  contributory negligence, 18
  courts, 16
  discovery rule, 18
  duty, 18
  four D's, 18
  frequency of types of complaints, 21
  informed consent reducing risk, 19
  interpersonal skills and risk of, 19
  patient factors and, 19
  reasonable standards of care, 19
  relationship factors, 19
  retired psychologists, 229, 235, 238
  statute of limitations, 18
  suicide and, 21
  volunteer psychologists, 237
Managed care, 14, 20, 27, 107, 110, 122, 126–127, 187, 209, 222, 226, 232–233, 235, 249
Mandatory reporting laws, 116
Mansouri, M., 68, 259
Mapes, B., 4, 163, 259
Marinopoulos, S. S., 68, 259
Maris, R., 183, 259
Marital therapy, 57, 85–86, 107, 264
Marketing services, 219
Martin, J., 1, 286
Math teacher model of documentation, 45
Medical errors, 69, 116, 193
Medicare audits, 130
Medications 27–28, 40, 44, 69, 75–77, 172, 180–182, 213
  American Psychological Association's *Practice Guidelines Regarding Psychologists' Involvement in Pharmacological Issues*, 250
  knowledge of, 181

life-endangering behavior and, 9, 58, 187, 210, 263
Mental illness, pre-employment screening and, 166
Minimizing Intrusions on Privacy (APA Ethics Code), 225
Minnesota Multiphasic Personality inventory (MMPI), 160
Misconduct accusations 22, 24, 46, 58, 103, 105, 106
  child custody cases and, 21
  communications with patients, 23
  handling, 89
Mistakes, admitting, 6, 7, 14, 23, 66, 69, 184, 201, 229
Mlodinov, L., 164, 259
MMPI. *See* **Minnesota Multiphasic Personality Inventory**
Mokros, A., 164, 259
Monahan, J., 165, 259
Monitoring patients with suicidal risks, 179–180, 186, 191
Moral principles 31–34, 40, 59, 100
  and Bloom's taxonomy, 32
  conflicting, 32–34
Moreland, K., 159, 259
MOST CARE model and consultations, 57
Multiple relationships 81–82. *See also* **Boundaries**
  APA Ethics Code, 81–82, 89
  boundaries and, 82–91
  concurrent, 81, 85
  consecutive, 81, 85
  defined, 81
  documentation and, 88
  gifts, 83–84
  high-risk patients, 86
  informed consent and, 88
  interpreters and, 205
  previous therapy and, 85
  risk management applications and, 88
  self-disclosure, 83–84
  small communities and, 83, 87
  touching, 83–84
  unavoidable, 82
  "you first" rule, 82

N

Narcissistic Personality Disorder, 12
National Practitioner Data Bank, 16
Neimeyer, G. J., 68, 257, 259
Newman, C., 181–182, 185, 259

ABOUT THE AUTHORS

Samuel Knapp, Ed.D., ABPP

Dr. Knapp has been the director of professional affairs for the Pennsylvania Psychological Association since 1987. He also teaches ethics in the doctoral program in clinical psychology at the Philadelphia College of Osteopathic Medicine and in the graduate program in counseling psychology at Lehigh University. Dr. Knapp served as a member of the Task Force responsible for rewriting the 2002 APA Ethics Code. He has written an ethics text book, *Practical ethics: A positive approach*, with Leon VandeCreek now in its second edition, and was editor-in-chief of the *APA Handbook on Ethics in Psychology*. He received the first award for ethics education from the APA Ethics Committee.

Jeffrey N. Younggren, Ph.D., ABPP

Dr. Younggren is a clinical and forensic psychologist who practices in Rolling Hills Estates California, a clinical professor at the University of California, Los Angeles School of Medicine, and a Risk Management Consultant for The Trust. Dr. Younggren is a Fellow of the American Psychological Association, and has served as a member and chair of the Ethics Committee of the California Psychological Association and the American Psychological Association. Dr. Younggren also served on the Committee on Accreditation of the American Psychological Association for six years and is a past President of Division 42 (Division of Independent Practice). Finally, Dr. Younggren was one of the committee members who drafted the current *Specialty Guidelines for Forensic Psychology*.

Leon VandeCreek, Ph.D., ABPP

Dr. VandeCreek is retired as a professor at the School of Professional Psychology at Wright State University where he taught psychological assessment and ethics. He has written an ethics text book, *Practical ethics: A positive approach* (with Samuel Knapp) now in its second edition and was an associate editor of the *APA Handbook on Ethics in Psychology*. His professional interests include risk management, professional liability, and licensing.

Eric Harris, J.D., Ed.D.

Dr. Harris is a Risk Management Consultant for The Trust. He is also the legal counsel to the Massachusetts Psychological Association and is a faculty member at the Massachusetts School of Professional Psychology. He also served two terms on the APA Committee for the Advancement of Professional Practice (CAPP) and two terms on the APA Committee on Legal Issues. Dr. Harris has written, consulted, and lectured extensively on risk management, legal issues, and managed care.

Jana N. Martin, Ph.D.

Dr. Martin had extensive experience as a clinical psychologist before becoming Chief Executive Officer of The Trust in 2010. She is a past President of the California and Los Angeles County (LACPA) Psychological Associations and Division 42 (Division of Independent Practice), served on the LACPA Ethics Committee, was active in APA's Public Education Campaign, and served on the APA Committee for the Advancement of Professional Practice (CAPP) among other activities. Dr. Martin received an APA Presidential Citation for exemplary work as a modern day practitioner and public education efforts in August, 2004. She served as a Trustee of The Trust from 2006 to 2010.